COLLECTED WHEEL PUBLICATIONS

VOLUME 16

NUMBERS 231 – 247

BPS Pariyatti Editions

BPS Pariyatti Editions
An imprint of Pariyatti Publishing
www.pariyatti.org

© Buddhist Publication Society, 2008

All rights reserved. No part of this book may be used or reproduced in any manner whatsoever without the written permission of BPS Pariyatti Editions, except in the case of brief quotations embodied in critical articles and reviews.

Copies of this book for sale in the Americas only. Although this is an American edition, we have left any British spelling of words unchanged.

First BPS Pariyatti Edition, 2025
ISBN: 978-1-68172-184-2 (Print)
ISBN: 978-1-68172-185-9 (PDF)
ISBN: 978-1-68172-186-6 (ePub)
ISBN: 978-1-68172-187-3 (Mobi)
LCCN: 2018940050

Contents

WH 231 The Essentials of Buddha-Dhamma in Meditative Practice
Sayagyi Thray Sithu U Ba Khin 1

WH 232 & 233 The Value of Buddhism for the Modern World
Dr. Howard L. Parsons 15

WH 234 & 236 The Miracle of Being Awake
Thich Nhat Hanh 51

WH 237 The Psychology of Emotions in Buddhist Perspective
Dr. Padmasiri de Silva 109

WH 238 & 240 Aṅguttara Nikāya
Nyanaponika Thera and *Bhikkhu Bodhi* 137

WH 241 & 242 The Worn-out Skin
Nyanaponika Thera 189

WH 243 & 244 Forest Meditations
Bhikkhu Khantipālo 237

WH 245 & 247 The Noble Eightfold Path and its Factors Explained
The Venerable Ledi Sayādaw 283

Key to Abbreviations

A	Aṅguttara Nikāya	Paṭis	Paṭisambhidamagga
Ap	Apadāna	Peṭ	Peṭakopadesa
Bv	Buddhavaṃsa	S	Saṃyutta Nikāya
Cp	Cariyāpiṭaka	Sn	Suttanipāta
D	Dīgha Nikāya	Th	Theragāthā
Dhp	Dhammapada	Thī	Therīgāthā
Dhs	Dhammasaṅgaṇī	Ud	Udāna
It	Itivuttaka	Vibh	Vibhaṅga
Ja	Jātaka verses and commentary	Vin	Vinaya-piṭaka
Khp	Khuddakapāṭha	Vism	Visuddhimagga
M	Majjhima Nikāya	Vism-mhṭ	Visuddhimagga Sub-commentary
Mil	Milindapañha	Vv	Vimānavatthu
Nett	Nettipakaraṇa	Nidd	Niddesa

The above is the abbreviation scheme of the Pali Text Society (PTS) as given in the *Dictionary of Pali* by Margaret Cone.

The commentaries, *aṭṭhakathā*, are abbreviated by using a hyphen and an "a" ("-a") following the abbreviation of the text, e.g., *Dīgha Nikāya Aṭṭhakathā* = D-a. Likewise the sub-commentaries are abbreviated by a "ṭ" ("-ṭ") following the abbreviation of the text.

The sutta reference abbreviation system for the four Nikāyas, as is used in Bhikkhu Bodhi's translations is:

AN	Aṅguttara Nikāya	DN	Dīgha Nikāya
MN	Majjhima Nikāya	Sn	Saṃyutta Nikāya
J	Jātaka story	Mv	Mahāvagga (Vinaya Piṭaka)
Cv	Cullavagga (Vinaya Piṭaka)	SVibh	Suttavibhaṅga (Vinaya Piṭaka)

The Essentials of Buddha-Dhamma in Meditative Practice

by
Sayagyi Thray Sithu U Ba Khin

With an Essay on U Ba Khin by
Eric Lerner

WHEEL PUBLICATION NO. 231

Copyright © Kandy; Buddhist Publication Society, (1976, 1981)

The Essentials of Buddha-Dhamma in Meditative Practice

Anicca, dukkha, anattā—impermanence, suffering and egolessness—are the three essential characteristics of things in the Teaching of the Buddha. If you know anicca correctly, you will know dukkha as its corollary and anattā as ultimate truth. It takes time to understand the three together.

Impermanence (*anicca*) is, of course, the essential fact which must be first experienced and understood by practice. Mere book-knowledge of the Buddha-Dhamma will not be enough for the correct understanding of anicca because the experiential aspect will be missing. It is only through experiential understanding of the nature of anicca as an ever-changing process within you that you can understand anicca in the way the Buddha would like you to understand it. As in the days of the Buddha, so too now, this understanding of anicca can be developed by persons who have no book-knowledge whatsoever of Buddhism.

To understand impermanence (*anicca*) one must follow strictly and diligently the Eightfold Noble Path, which is divided into the three groups of *sīla, samādhi* and *paññā*—Morality, Concentration and Wisdom. Sīla, or virtuous living, is the basis for samādhi, control of the mind, leading to one-pointedness. It is only when samādhi is good that one can develop paññā. Therefore, sīla and samādhi are the prerequisites for paññā. By paññā is meant the understanding of anicca, dukkha and anattā through the practice of *vipassanā*, i.e., insight meditation.

Whether a Buddha has arisen or not, the practice of sīla and samādhi may be present in the human world. They are, in fact, the common denominators of all religious faiths. They are not, however, sufficient means for the goal of Buddhism—the complete end of suffering. In his search for the end of suffering, Prince Siddhattha, the future Buddha, found this out and worked his way through to find the path which would lead to the end of suffering. After solid work for six years, he found the way out, became completely enlightened, and *then* taught men and gods to follow the Path which would lead them to the end of suffering.

In this connection we should understand that each action—whether by deed, word or thought—leaves behind an active force called *saṅkhāra* (or *kamma* in popular terminology), which goes to the credit or debit account of the individual, according to whether the action is good or bad. There is, therefore, an accumulation of saṅkhāra (or kamma) with everyone, which functions as the supply-source of energy to sustain life, which is inevitably followed by suffering and death. It is by the development of the power inherent in the understanding of anicca, dukkha and anattā, that one is able to rid oneself of the saṅkhāra accumulated in one's own personal account. This process begins with the correct understanding of anicca, while further accumulations of fresh actions and the reduction of the supply of energy to sustain life are taking place simultaneously, from moment to moment and from day to day. It is, therefore, a matter of a whole lifetime or more to get rid of all one's saṅkhāra. He who has rid himself of all saṅkhāra comes to the end of suffering, for then no saṅkhāra remains to give the necessary energy to sustain him in any form of life. On the termination of their lives the perfected saints, i.e., the Buddhas and *arahants*, pass into *parinibbāna*, reaching the end of suffering. For us today who take to vipassanā meditation, it would suffice if we can understand anicca well enough to reach the first stage of an ariya (a Noble person), that is, a sotāpanna or stream-enterer, who will not take more than seven lives to come to the end of suffering.

The fact of anicca, which opens the door to the understanding of dukkha and anattā and eventually to the end of suffering, can be encountered in its full significance only through the Teachings of a Buddha, for so long as that Teaching relating to the Eightfold Noble Path and the Thirty-Seven Factors of Enlightenment (*bodhipakkhiyā dhammā*) remains intact and available to the aspirant.

For progress in vipassana meditation, a student must keep knowing anicca as continuously as possible. The Buddha's advice to monks is that they should try to maintain the awareness of anicca, dukkha or anattā in all postures, whether sitting, standing, walking or lying down. Continuous awareness of anicca and so of dukkha and anattā, is the secret of success. The last words of the Buddha just before he breathed his last and passed away into Mahā-parinibbāna were: "Decay (or anicca) is inherent in all component things. Work out your own salvation with diligence." This is in fact the essence of all his teachings during the forty-five years of his ministry. If you will keep up the awareness of the anicca that is inherent in all component things, you are sure to reach the goal in the course of time.

As you develop in the understanding of anicca, your insight into "What is true of nature" will become greater and greater, so much so that eventually you will have no doubt whatsoever of the three characteristics of anicca, dukkha and anattā. It is then only that you will be in a position to go ahead for the goal in view. Now that you know anicca as the first essential factor, you would try to understand what anicca is with real clarity as extensively as possible so as not to get confused in the course of practice or discussion.

The real meaning of anicca is that impermanence or decay is the inherent nature of everything that exists in the Universe—whether animate or inanimate. The Buddha taught his disciples that everything that exists at the material level is composed of *kalāpas*. Kalāpas are material units very much smaller than atoms, which die out immediately after they come into being. Each kalāpa is a mass formed of the eight basic constituents of matter, the solid, liquid, calorific and oscillatory, together with color, smell, taste, and nutriment. The first four are called primary qualities, and are predominant in a kalāpa. The other four are subsidiaries, dependent upon and springing from the former. A kalāpa is the minutest particle in the physical plane—still beyond the range of science today. It is only when the eight basic material constituents unite together that the kalāpa is formed. In other words, the momentary collocation of these eight basic elements of behavior makes a man just for that moment, which in Buddhism is known as a kalāpa. The life span of a kalāpa is termed a moment, and a trillion such moments are said to elapse during the wink of a man's eye. These kalāpas are all in a state of perpetual change or flux. To a developed student in vipassanā meditation they can be felt as a stream of energy.

The human body is not, as it may appear, a solid stable entity, but a continuum of matter (*rūpa*) coexisting with mentality (*nāma*). To know that our very body is tiny kalāpas all in a state of change is to know the true nature of change or decay. This change or decay (*anicca*) occasioned by the continual breakdown and replacement of kalāpas, all in a state of combustion, must necessarily be identified as dukkha, the truth of suffering. It is only when you experience impermanence (*anicca*) as suffering (*dukkha*) that you come to the realization of the truth of suffering, the first of the Four Noble Truths basic to the doctrine of the Buddha. Why? Because when you realize the subtle nature of dukkha from which you cannot escape for a moment, you become truly afraid of, disgusted with, and disinclined towards your very existence as mentality-materiality (*nāmarūpa*), and look for a way of escape to a state beyond dukkha, and so to *Nibbāna*, the end of suffering. What that end of suffering is like, you will be able to taste, even as a human being, when you reach the level of sotāpanna, a stream-enterer, and develop well enough by practice to attain to the unconditioned state of Nibbāna, the peace within. But even in terms of everyday ordinary life, no sooner than you are able to keep up the awareness of anicca in practice will you know for yourself that a change is taking place in you for the better, both physically and mentally.

Before entering upon the practice of vipassanā meditation, that is, after samādhi has been developed to a proper level, a student should acquaint himself with the theoretical knowledge of material and mental properties, i.e., of rūpa and nāma. For in vipassanā meditation one contemplates not only the changing nature of matter, but also the changing nature of mentality, of the thought-elements of attention directed towards the process of change going on within matter. At times attention will be focused on the impermanence of the material side of existence, i.e., upon anicca in regard to rūpa, and at other times on the impermanence of the thought-elements or mental side, i.e., upon anicca in regard to nāma. When one is contemplating the impermanence of matter, one realizes also that the thought-elements simultaneous with that awareness are also in a state of transition or change. In this case one will be knowing anicca in regard to both rūpa and nāma together.

All I have said so far relates to the understanding of anicca through bodily feelings of the process of change of rūpa or matter, and also of thought-elements depending upon such changing processes. You should know that anicca can also be understood

through other types of feeling as well. Anicca can be contemplated through feeling:
1. by contact of visible form with the sense organ of the eye;
2. by contact of sound with the sense organ of the ear;
3. by contact of smell with the sense organ of the nose;
4. by contact of taste with the sense organ of the tongue;
5. by contact of touch with the sense organ of the body;
6. by contact of mental objects with the sense organ of the mind.

Once can thus develop the understanding of anicca through any of six sense organs. In practice, however, we have found that of all the types of feeling, the feeling by contact of touch with the component parts of the body in a process of change covers the widest area for introspective meditation. Not only that, the feelings by contact of touch (by way of friction, radiation and vibration of the kalāpas within) with the component parts of the body is more evident than other types of feeling and therefore a beginner in vipassanā meditation can come to the understanding of anicca more easily through bodily feelings of the change of rūpa or matter. This is the main reason why we have chosen bodily feeling as a medium for quick understanding of anicca. It is open to anyone to try other means, but my suggestion is that one should be well established in the understanding of anicca through bodily feeling before any attempt is made through other types of feeling.

There are ten levels of knowledge in vipassanā, namely:

1. *Sammasana*: theoretical appreciation of anicca, dukkha and anattā by close observation and analysis;
2. *Udayabbaya*: knowledge of the arising and dissolution of rūpa and nāma by direct observation;
3. *Bhaṅga*: knowledge of the rapidly changing nature of rūpa and nāma as a swift current or stream of energy; in particular, clear awareness of the phase of dissolution;
4. *Bhaya*: knowledge that this very existence is dreadful;
5. *Ādīnava*: knowledge that this very existence is full of evils;
6. *Nibbidā*: knowledge that this very existence is disgusting;
7. *Muñcitukamyatā*: knowledge of the urgent need and wish to escape from this very existence;

8. *Paṭisaṅkhā*: knowledge that the time has come to work for full realization of deliverance, with anicca as the base;
9. *Saṅkhārupekkhā*: knowledge that the stage is now set to get detached from all conditioned phenomena (*saṅkhāra*) and to break away from egocentricity;
10. *Anuloma*: knowledge that would accelerate the attempt to reach the goal.

These are the levels of attainment which one goes through during the course of vipassanā meditation; in the case of those who reach the goal in a short time they can be known only in retrospect. Along with one's progress in understanding anicca, one may reach these levels of attainment, subject, however, to adjustments or help at certain levels by a competent teacher. One should avoid looking forward to such attainments in anticipation, as this will distract from the continuity of awareness of anicca, which alone can and will give the desired reward.

Let me now deal with vipassanā meditation from the point of view of a householder in everyday life and explain the benefit one can derive from it—here and now—in this very lifetime.

The initial object of vipassanā meditation is to activate the experience of anicca in oneself and to eventually reach a state of inner and outer calmness and balance. This is achieved when one becomes engrossed in the feeling of anicca within. The world is now facing serious problems which threaten all mankind. It is just the right time for everyone to take to vipassanā meditation and learn how to find a deep pool of quiet in the midst of all that is happening today. Anicca is inside of everybody. It is within reach of everybody. Just a look into oneself and there it is—anicca to be experienced. When one can feel anicca, when one can experience anicca, and when one can become engrossed in anicca, one can at will cut oneself off from the world of ideation outside. Anicca is, for the householder, the gem of life which he will treasure to create a reservoir of calm and balanced energy for his own well-being and for the welfare of the society.

The experience of anicca, when properly developed, strikes at the root of one's physical and mental ills and removes gradually whatever is bad in him, i.e., the causes of such physical and mental ills. This experience is not reserved for men who have renounced the world for the homeless life. It is for the householder as well. In spite of drawbacks which make a householder restless in these days, a competent teacher or guide can help a student to get the experience of anicca activated in a comparatively short time. Once he has got it activated, all that is necessary is for him to try and preserve it; but he must make it a point, as soon as time or opportunity presents itself for further progress, to work for the stage of *bhaṅgañāna*— the third level of knowledge in vipassanā. If he reaches this level, there will be little or no problem because he should then be able to experience anicca without much ado and almost automatically. In this case anicca will become his base, to which all his physical and mental activities return as soon as the domestic needs of daily life for such activities are over. However, there is likely to be some difficulty for one who has not reached the stage of *bhaṅga*. It will be just like a tug-of-war for him between anicca within, and physical and mental activities outside. So it would be wise for him to follow the motto of work while you work, play while you play. There is no need for him to be activating the experience of anicca all the time. It should suffice if this could be confined to a regular period, or periods, set apart in the day or night for the purpose. During this time, at least, an attempt must be made to keep the attention focused inside the body, with awareness devoted exclusively to anicca; that is to say, his awareness of anicca should go on from moment to moment so continuously as not to allow for the interpolation of any discursive or distracting thoughts which are definitely detrimental to progress. In case this is not possible, he will have to go back to respiration-mindfulness, because samādhi is the key to the contemplation of anicca. To get good samādhi, sīla (morality) has to be perfect, since samādhi is build upon sīla. For a good experience of anicca, samādhi must be good. If samādhi is excellent, awareness of anicca will also become excellent. There is no special technique for activating the experience of anicca other than the use of the mind, adjusted to a perfect state of balance, and attention projected upon the object of meditation. In vipassanā the object of meditation is anicca, and therefore in the case of those used to focusing their attention on bodily feelings, they can feel anicca directly. In experiencing anicca in relation to the body, it should first be in the area where one can easily get his attention engrossed, changing the area of attention from place to place, from head to feet and from feet to head, at times probing into the interior. At this stage, it must clearly be understood that no attention is to be paid to the anatomy of the body, but to the formations of matter—the kalāpas—and the nature of their constant change.

If these instructions are observed, there will surely be progress, but the progress depends also on *pāramī* (i.e. on one's dispositions for certain spiritual qualities) and the devotion of the individual to the work of meditation. If he attains high levels of knowledge, his power to understand the three characteristics of anicca, dukkha and anattā will increase and he will accordingly come nearer and nearer the goal of the ariya or noble saint, which every householder should keep in view.

This is the age of science. Man of today has no Utopia. He will not accept anything unless the results are good, concrete, vivid, personal, and here-and-now. When the Buddha was alive, He said to the Kālāmas:

> "Now look, you Kālāmas. Be not misled by report or tradition or hearsay. Be not misled by proficiency in the scriptural collections, or by reasoning or logic or reflection on and approval of some theory, or because some view conforms to one's inclinations, or out of respect for the prestige of a teacher. But when you know for yourselves: these things are unwholesome, these things are blameworthy, these things are censured by the wise, these things when practised and observed, conduce to loss and sorrow—then you reject them. But if at any time you know for yourselves: these things are wholesome, these things are blameless, these things are praised by the intelligent; these things, when practised and observed, conduce to welfare and happiness, then, Kālāmas, do ye, having practised them, abide."

The time-clock of vipassanā has now struck—that is, for the revival of Buddha-Dhamma vipassanā in practice. We have no doubt whatsoever that definite results would accrue to those who would with an open mind sincerely undergo a course of training under a competent teacher—I mean results which will be accepted as good, concrete, vivid, personal, here-and-now, results which will keep them in good stead and in a state of well-being and happiness for the rest of their lives.

May all beings be happy and may peace prevail in the world.

U Ba Khin: An Appreciation

by Eric Lerner

Over the centuries Theravāda Buddhist teachings have been preserved by and large in a monastic tradition. The requisite for the 'true practice' has been the renunciation of worldly existence for a life behind walls or in the forest. Householders were left with the observances of morality, almsgiving, and worship to accrue merit for future lives when they could actually embark on the formal path to liberation. As the sūtras themselves reveal, however, this was not the case at all when the Buddha was alive and preaching. Vast numbers of householders received the teaching and the practice as well, and attained high levels of spiritual development.

In the past few decades in the Theravada Buddhist countries there has been a general revival of interest in insight meditation among the robed Saṅgha, and with it a spreading of the practice outside the monastery walls. This has in a sense revivified the whole outlook toward meditation, practicalizing it, in a way, by focusing on two important aspects. First, how can a man who does not have his entire life to devote to silence and contemplation approach meditation? And second, what role can the meditative discipline play in worldly life?

These problems were dealt with in great detail and with remarkable strength of imagination by one of the most important meditation masters of modern day Burma, Thray Sithu U Ba Khin. He was well known within his country as an important Government servant, for many years the Accountant General of the Union of Burma as well as the chairman of a number of important boards and commissions. At one time he held four such posts simultaneously, was the father of six children and found the time to teach meditation at the International Meditation Center in Rangoon, which was established under his guidance in the early 1950s.

The unique characteristics of his spiritual teaching stem from his situation as a lay meditation master in an orthodox Buddhist country. It was not appropriate for him to instruct monks, so all of his practice was geared specifically to lay people. He developed a powerfully direct approach to vipassanā meditation that could be undertaken in a short period of intensive practice and continued as part of householding life. His method has been of great importance in the transmission of the Dhamma to the West, because in his twenty-five years at the Center he instructed scores of foreign visitors who needed no closer acquaintance with Buddhism *per se* to quickly grasp this practice of insight. Since U Ba Khin's demise in 1971, several of his commissioned disciples have carried on his work, both within and outside of Burma. Hundreds of Westerners have received the instruction from S.N. Goenka in India, Robert Hover and Ruth Denison in America, and John Coleman in England. In addition, several of U Ba Khin's closest disciples still teach at the Center in Rangoon.

What is the goal of Insight Meditation? And does it differ in any way for the man whose whole life is devoted to its practice and the man who earns a living and supports others? In the broadest sense there is no difference. The end of suffering is the goal. The experience of Nibbānic Peace within, as U Ba Khin referred to it, is the aim of the practice; but also the end of suffering each moment; harmony among beings, the end of internal tension, the manifestation of loving-kindness, the ability to perform one's daily tasks free from anger, greed and anxiety. For the lay person and the monk it is the same. The way to proceed, however, differs, at least at the outset.

U Ba Khin understood that unlike the monk, his students faced severe limitations of time to devote to their practice. Furthermore, they had to function in a completely uncontrolled environment generally hostile to proper moral conduct and good concentration, the requisites for insight. Thus he gave them a method that could withstand that pressure. In the short span of ten days, most of his pupils could experience at least a glimpse of the reality within and continue expanding their awareness with two hours daily of formal meditation after they left the Center.

This technique has three distinctive qualities to it. First is its emphasis on the development of sufficient one-pointed concentration. Concerning this, U Ba Khin wrote:

> *Samādhi* (concentration) is a way of training the mind to become tranquil, pure and strong and therefore forms the essence of religious life ... It is, in fact, the greatest common

denominator of all religions. Unless one can get the mind freed from the impurities and develop it to a state of purity, he can hardly identify himself with Brahmā or God. Although different methods are used by people of different religions, the goal for the development of mind is the same, viz. a perfect state of physical and mental calm. The student at the Center is helped to develop the power of concentration to one-pointedness, by encouraging him to focus his attention to a spot on the upper lip at the base of the nose, synchronizing the inward and outward motion of respiration with the silent awareness of in-breath and out-breath ... In the Ānāpānasati meditation technique (i.e. that of respiration mindfulness), which is followed at the Center, one great advantage is that the respiration is not only natural, but also available at all times for the purpose of anchoring one's attention to it, to the exclusion of all other thoughts. With a determined effort to narrow down the range of thought waves, firstly, to the area around the nose with respiration mindfulness and gradually, with the wave length of respiration becoming shorter, to a spot on the upper lip with just the warmth of the breath, there is no reason why a good student of meditation should not be able to secure the one-pointedness of mind in a few days of training.

The Real Values of True Buddhist Meditation, pp. 5–6.

The reason for the necessity of good concentration, he felt, was that with only a limited period of time available, one's mind had to have a degree of penetrating power to really experience the inner reality on more than a conceptual level. He departed from the most traditional monastic view that concentration had to be developed to very high states requiring great time and isolation. But neither did he agree with the approach that began with little specific concentration training. He was interested in a sufficient level for the work of real insight.

The second quality of his teaching was its focus on the characteristic of *anicca*, impermanence. The Buddha described reality as having three marks, or characteristics: impermanence, unsatisfactoriness, and the absence of a real "I" or self. In the practice of mindfulness, observance of just what is, focusing the attention of these true marks of reality breaks down false view and weakens attachment. U Ba Khin taught that the most direct access to understanding the process of life was through awareness of impermanence, *anicca*. He felt that *anicca* is the most apparent and readily comprehensible of the three marks and that its understanding leads naturally to the others. So the observance of change, or the alteration of all phenomena at increasingly subtler levels, was the real object of his vipassanā technique.

The method itself was the systematic awareness of physical sensation in the body. As the Satipaṭṭhāna Sutta of the Buddha makes clear, the process of life is identical in every aspect of the mind-body continuum. Choose whichever you like and observe it closely enough and all of reality unfolds. U Ba Khin found that the unfolding is most dramatic and rapid in the physical sensation within the body. His students were directed to place their concentrated attention on that and become sensitive to the process of change observable in the tactile reaction of heat, cold tingling, pain, numbness, pressure or whatever was there. Simply observe the changing nature of the phenomenon within you, he taught.

Continued practice of the method, as he points out in the following articles, yields spiritual and worldly results as well. He maintained that a householder could enjoy the fruit of the Nibbānic experience in this life time. And he encouraged men not to be content with ritual practice of simple book knowledge of the teachings. In addition, the practice, as his disciple S.N. Goenka terms it, is an art of living. So convinced was U Ba Khin of the power of this method for clearing the mind that he insisted that all of his employees in the Accounts Department take a course of meditation from him and that a portion of the office be set aside for a meditation space. Mr. Robert Hover recounts the story that his teacher told him. Sometimes U Ba Khin, attending particularly unfocused meetings of government with men of more biased minds, would in the midst of heated argument rise from his chair and stand for some moments gazing out of the window before returning to the conference table. His colleagues thought he was watching the world outside. In fact, U Ba Khin explained, he was busy within, re-establishing mindfulness to deal with the demands of life.

The Value of Buddhism for the Modern World

by

Dr. Howard L. Parsons

WHEEL PUBLICATION NO. 232/233

Copyright © Kandy; Buddhist Publication Society, (1976)

The Value of Buddhism for the Modern World

"Every living and healthy religion," Santayana has said, "has a marked idiosyncrasy. Its power consists in its special and surprising message and in the bias which that revelation gives to life." What is the special and surprising message of Buddhism? What is the lasting revelation of its leader, Gotama Buddha? We are concerned here not merely with Gotama's utility for past generations (though that has been great) but with the truth of his moral vision for all human times and hence for modern times.

Let us consider first his conception of the problem of human life, and second his conception of its solution.

I

The problem of our lives begins in the fact that we are always beset by problems. Human life is problematic. Scarcely do we achieve settlement and certainty than we are unsettled by new difficulties. Fixities and finalities elude us. In the words of Gotama's younger contemporary, Heraclitus of Ephesus, "All things flow; nothing abides." Heraclitus, like Gotama, must have been caught in that "urban revolution" that swept ancient civilizations, and he must have seen that no perspective, no culture, no standard ultimately stands: "we are and we are not."

The problem of human life can be expressed otherwise. Man is born without a fixed identity. He is born without instincts—except, if you will, the instinct to live and to learn and to grow. Man is indeterminate at birth. In consequence, his life is a quest; man is a wanderer and a pilgrim, seeking an identity, a role, and a home. Man's symbolism is both cause and result of this quest. For in virtue of the fact that he acquires and invents languages the continuous choice among many alternatives and roles forces itself upon him, and he lives, unlike the animals, in a tower of Babel; and his attempt to find a determination for his own life in the midst of myriad possibilities drives him to adopt this or that symbolic role for himself. Thus we go through life seeking, asking and knocking—trying to discover who we are, trying to fulfil our natures. The ultimate problem of life, which man has sought to solve through his religious activity, is just this: Who am I? How might I and others achieve the most abundant fulfilment possible?

This problem expresses itself at two levels. First of all, man is incomplete in so far as the basic hungers of his body and personality go unmet. The power of these needs is coercive; and when they are not fulfilled man experiences pain. Primitive religion is primarily an attempt to cope with such pain, through various techniques. But man is incomplete and consequently questing at another level. Not only do his appetites lack completion; something else cries out for fulfilment. Not only does man seek food, crops, game, a mate, children, a long and approved life; man wants an identity and a fulfilment greater than any of these particular fulfilments. Not only does man undergo privation and pain and eventual death; he knows, as Pascal says, that he dies. And so he enters into the realm of suffering. Suffering arises out of a sense of the difference between what is and what might be. It is the tragic sense. It is the realization that creative possibilities have not or will not be fulfilled: that man can never fully "find" or complete himself; that time is greater than one moment, and eternity vaster than time; that death conquers individual life, but that collective life transcends individual death; that no matter how rich or full a single life may be, it cannot begin to encompass the richness and fullness of the multiform cosmic life around it, and is destined to be singular and lonely in the midst of that great abundance. Even the primitive religions represent inchoate efforts to deal with this problem and to find a fully satisfying identity. The advanced religions of mankind give overt expression to this side of man's problem—his suffering—and endeavour to cope with it, in thought and action; and Gotama must be seen as one of those who thus struggled with the problem of suffering.

There is a secondary aspect to the problem of human suffering. Our deep desire to find an identity leads to the adoption of some role which at the outset seems to satisfy the need for identity yet at the same time frustrates that very need; for we are often not fully satisfied with one particular role, yet our very adoption of it, necessitated by our need, has led us to take it up with fervent loyalty and, perhaps, with idolatry. We continuously seek closure in our meanings and identities, yet we cannot tolerate the constrictions they lay upon us, for we demand newer and deeper identities. Moreover, if we live long enough, the processes of living crack open the closures we have built and force us to construct new meanings and roles. Thus our roles come to dominate us; we fain would let them go, yet we cannot. So we find that we are enslaved by our own desire for freedom. Our quest for identity seems doomed. For this inveterate desire for identity issues in habits and in character-structure which is well nigh impossible to break and which must yet be broken if we are to be liberated and saved from constriction and death. In Paul's language, "the good that I would, I do not; but the evil which I would not, that I do. O wretched man that I am! Who shall deliver me from the body of this death?"

We are doomed to this kind of death in life because we are caught up in a partial commitment and in the domination of a demonic good. This death is not physical annihilation but is on the contrary the torture which one must suffer who cannot die; it is, in the language of Gotama's India, karma and rebirth; it is the perpetuation of compulsive passion and the continuation of that fatal winding of a chain (*nidānas*) of events which begins in indigenous ignorance and issues always in suffering. For while in a sense we do die when the object of our devotion and the symbol of our identity changes or passes away—since "decay is inherent in all compound things"—yet our dispositions (*guṇas*, as the Saṅkhya calls them) persist and continue to give rise to the same old structures of habit of the same old Adam.

The whole doctrine of the non-existence of the soul (*anattavāda*) and that of "dependent origination" are designed to deal with the age-old problem of the past and to do so in a way that lends the problem to moral solution. To say that rebirth takes place without anything substantial migrating (after the manner of a seal being pressed upon wax) is to say that a man's past character is his fate but that he can moment by moment change his character. These doctrines have both a metaphysical and moral advantage, because they avoid the tyranny of eternalism and the hopelessness of nihilism. To describe our suffering as caused by dispositions and habits is to take the first step toward their removal.

Buddha's personal success and widespread appeal lie partly in the directness of his approach. He begins with the prime fact of unhappiness. Pain and suffering are recurrent and unceasing. We crave and yearn for what is or what is not; and when we obtain it, we yet yearn for more. We, like all things, change: health passes into sickness, youth into old age, and life into death. But we insist on setting our hearts or minds on something that does not seem to change—and we always suffer disappointment. Yet, even to have what we want is pain; for no matter what we want or what we get, we are never satisfied. Man oscillates, as Schopenhauer says, between the restlessness of need and the boredom of satiety, and his will is forever uneasy. Lacking a generic sense of satisfaction, man cannot help feeling that his life is a mistake and a miscarriage; he suffers, in Spinoza's language, the sadness that is deeper than any specific disappointment or ennui; that is the sadness of the life-urge itself, the sadness of impotence.

If we suffer, what are we, and what are the sources in us that lead to suffering? Much of traditional religious and philosophical thought directly contradicts the answer that Gotama gives to this question. That thought holds that in the midst of untruth, darkness, death, incompletion, change, and time, there abides a truth, light, life, completion, permanence, and eternity to which man must turn if he is to be saved from suffering; man's primal error, therefore, consists in his "fall" from this domain of permanence into the domain of change, which he mistakes for the permanent. But Gotama's analysis is different. He does agree with traditional Hindu thought in asserting that man's first major mistake is to take as real and important what is at bottom illusory, namely, the empirical self. But he radically departs from that tradition and indeed all the great religious traditions by holding, like Hume, that the self is nothing more than a complex of ingredients, a bundle or a stream of matter and of perception, a collection of body, mind, and formless consciousness. Here he typically rejects two logical extremes, materialism and idealism (and their uneasy compromise, dualism). Not only is there no permanent self; there is no permanent ātman, within or beyond, human or super-human; there is nothing permanent, here or hereafter, to which man can turn for guidance, succor or refuge.

The term "self", therefore, has no fixed referent, for what it commonly denotes is, in time, a changing stream, and, in space, an aggregate of five *khandhas* or "graspings" bound together in an interaction that forever changes. These graspings—the body, feelings, ideas based on sense-perception, instinctual and subconscious drives, and conscious evaluations—are the essence of the organism and its individuality, if we may speak of that. The organism and its parts clutches, selects, and organizes; it prehends, in Whitehead's sense, its world; it lays hold of, completes, forms, transforms, and retains its world. These *khandhas* are the seat of our loves and hates, hopes and fears, joys and sorrows; for they are polar, and as such participate in the pervasive and ceaseless opposition in the world. To act on the presupposition that our self is identical with these *khandhas* is to be clutched by their clutchings and to be caught up in their oscillations and to suffer the sadness or disappointment or the outworn satisfactions which they undergo. Man's problem is that, in the midst of incomplete meanings and values, he is driven to find and assert some form of completion, but his assertions, however satisfying and complete they seem to be, never ultimately satisfy and always remain partial and mutable. No matter what the self identifies itself with, it cannot seem to find a final and sovereign identity.

In time, the self is a stream, and with great penetration Gotama analyzes the causal chain that leads him backward from suffering to its ultimate source. We should not suffer had we not first been born as a result of our predisposition to birth and, behind that, our mental clinging to objects. Clinging is due to thirst or *taṇhā*—the consequence, in turn, of sense experience, sense-object contact, and the organs of knowledge. These led us back to the embryo and its cause in some incipient awareness—the product of experiences in some past life, which derive at last from ignorance or *avijjā*. *Avijjā* is the blindness of all organismic striving; it is the Greek eros, Hobbes' "appetite" and "aversion," Spinoza's "power," Schopenhauer's "will to live," Nietzsche's "will to power," and Bergson's "elan vital." We suffer. Why? We are driven blindly to hold what we have and to obtain what we have not. In our consciousness we keep and cling to what we are and have; in the depths of our unconsciousness we return to what we have lost or have imperfectly kept, and seek to grasp it firmly, re-enacting the tragic temptation of Faust: "Ah, still delay, thou art so fair." And why? We know not why. And this ignorance of ours is the root of the whole matter.

In a word, it is our own illusory habit-structure, taken as real and all-important, that destroys us. Behind that lies our tendency to grasp things and fasten upon them as final—our ignorance. We believe in the wrong things because we blindly grasp at any image that seems to promise closure, meaning, satisfaction, and fulfilment. For Gotama "what is impermanent is suffering, what is suffering is not I; what is not I is not mine, it is not I, it is not myself." Salvation is achieved by both an intellectual and active conquest over the craving or thirst that bedevils man. It is achieved by non-attached work, work which no more elicits self-destructive loyalties than the sowing of fried seeds elicits plants. Such work carries a double blessing. It saves the doer from involvement, and it ministers objectively and hence effectively to the person or situation.

Man "hankers" after the world, says the Buddhist literature, and as a result is "tainted" by lusts, by the desire for continued sensuous experience, and by ignorance. Passion, aversion, and confusion beset him. In the vivid words of the Dhammapada, "The thirst of a thoughtless man grows like a creeper; he runs from life to life, like a monkey seeking fruit in the forest." He is on fire with the fiery movement of the world. Buddhism has been criticized because in its attack on the "self" and "selfish" craving it has appeared to contradict its contention that the self is illusory and, further, that the self enjoys nirvana. But this criticism springs from the failure to understand that when Buddhism attacks selfish craving it attacks something partial, self-limiting, and demonic. The self of our desires and values does have power so long as we delegate it that power. The centre of this partial and illusory "self" is man's basic biotic tenacity as conditioned by culture—his craving for the things and values of the world. But "the world," as the Idealists have insisted, is always "my world"; the world which I have and cherish in apperception and action is my ego; it comprises my loyalties, my source of support and affection, my role, my identity. To crave, love, preserve, protect, and defend one's world, therefore, is to crave, love, preserve, protect, and defend one's self. Trespass on a man's property and you trespass on him; ridicule a man's ideas and his world-conception, and you ridicule him.

Craving entails clinging, and the root of clinging is demand. We not only want what we want; we demand it. We move heaven and earth to get it; we turn reason into rationalization, honour into chicanery, people into means, and opportunity into expediency, in order to get what we want. We cannot live without it, and if we must go without it we see to it that others will share our misery and go without it too. Why do we not only demand things but also demand that, once had, they must be kept? Here, Gotama's answer, by implication, is close to that of Jesus; we feel anxious for our life. Gotama put it positively: we are driven by an ignorant impulse to live and to build our lives around the forms of our values. Thus we tend to elaborate and integrate our way of life as though it were the be-all and the end-all of existence, and when it is threatened we fight desperately in its defense. We tend to weave the loose threads of meaning in our lives into some pattern of personal identification. We tend to bring into closure the qualities and forms of our experience and to endow that closure with some character of finality in importance. The closures we choose will vary with body-type, temperament, cultural tradition, and socio-economic condition. They will be predominantly personal and idiosyncratic or will reflect the dominant ideology of environment: idealism, vitalism, or materialism; aristocracy, or democracy; the authority of law, force, or sensuous satisfactions. We tend to invest such meanings with impervious or charismatic powers; at last it becomes difficult to undo our belief and loyalty toward them.

Anyone who has sought to change himself or others or the social order which sustains us knows the truth of the view expressed in *The Authoritarian Personality*[1]: "The transformation of our social system from something dynamic into something conservative, a status quo, struggling for its perpetuation, is reflected by the attitudes and opinions of all those who, for reasons of vested interests or psychological conditions, identify themselves with the existing set up. In order not to undermine their own pattern of identification, they unconsciously do not want to know too much and are ready to accept superficial or distorted information as long as it confirms the world in which they want to go on living." Thirst, craving, *taṇhā*, not only expresses itself

---

1. Adorno, Theodor W. (1950). *The Authoritarian Personality*, New York, Harper.

in the demand to have and to keep; it involves the "great refusal" to consider alternatives to one's beliefs and way of life and indeed positive resistance against what encroaches on what one views as all-important, namely, one's world, one's world view, one's self. And this stubbornness persists often in the face of great suffering.

II

What is the solution? We may mention four (among others) responses that are required on the part of man if he is to be delivered from the continuous wheel of unhappiness and to find fulfilment in this life. They are: understanding, renunciation, resolution and compassion.

(1) An indispensable attitude is understanding. This is indicated by the nature of our malady, *avijjā*, which is literally lack of vision or insight. Where there is no vision—spiritual vision—the people perish. For without vision we are blind, and our efforts to save others become the blind leading the blind. Blindness is the brute, unconsidered belief that what lies before us as the object of our appetite or aversion is real; that the whole complex of our sensuous experience is ultimate; that this complex comprises our being and that nothing more exists; that when this goes all goes; that our whole duty consists in preserving that complex of perception and self against change and decay; and that we ought properly to fear for its passing. Ignorance, in short, is not only impulsiveness, "a perpetual and restless desire of power which ceaseth only in death," in Hobbes' phrase; it is the blind demand for the sustenance and preservation of that impulsiveness.

To understand, therefore, is to understand this primal fact of the primate creature. To understand is to delay immediate response and belief; to check readiness and tendency to clutch; to transmute stimuli into signs and signals into symbols; in short, to see the world and ourselves for what they are, namely, appearances in passage. In detail, right understanding or right views involves a knowledge of the four noble truths: the problem of suffering, the cause of suffering, the solubility of the problem, and the solution or eightfold path. Understanding, therefore, is the master key which unlocks the door to liberation. But it is also a watchful eye which must be ever vigilant, since passion, aversion, and confusion ever dog our steps. For lest we be destroyed by ignorance and the craving and clinging which come from it, we must ourselves, with active understanding, destroy the source of our destruction.

Understanding is thus not to be theoretical or speculative; is not even to be theological, nor to develop the subtleties of psychology. It is to be directed to the immediate problem of the removal of the cause of suffering, as a physician would seek immediately to remove an arrow from a wounded man. This practicality characterizes many of the great religious founders and prophets; and this is why it is impossible to ascribe a definitive theology or creed to them; they plunged ahead, to sweat it out on the job before them. This is why, too, diverse theologies and psychologies have followed in their train: the same set of human values may be justified by a variety of theoretical schemes. The problem of human life is not to grasp the metaphysical secret of the world, as Gotama knew from personal experience, or to transcend it by mortification of the flesh. The problem is not merely to understand it, but, as Marx would say, to change it through understanding it. The problem, as Henry N. Wieman has put it, is for one to probe beneath the conscious beliefs and habits of the mind to the concrete reality that in fact sustains and fulfils one, and indeed to "relinquish every belief as the basis of his security", finding "what operates in human life with such character and power that it will transform man as he cannot transform himself, saving him from evil and leading him to the best that human life can ever reach, provided that he meets the required conditions." Thought, therefore, must pass beyond its abstract task of analysis and synthesis to the practical task of saving man from his suffering and carrying him over into fulfilment. This task of thought has not always been consistently or effectively pursued in Buddhism; it has tended to overestimate the power and importance of the conscious mind. But certainly its original aim was pragmatic, and the spirit of Gotama is existential rather than intellectual.

The importance of thought in the viewpoint of Buddhism, cannot be underestimated. It is stated in the very first verse of the Dhammapada: "All that we are is the result of what we have thought: it is founded on our thoughts, it is made up of our thoughts. If a man speaks or acts with an evil thought, pain follows him, as the wheel follows the foot of the ox that draws the carriage."

The source of our lives and hence of our happiness or unhappiness is, in Buddhism, entirely within our power; were this not at least partially so, then we should all be victims of personal karma or the arbitrary power of historical and natural processes. And the source of our lives is our thought. Since a good tree cannot bring forth evil fruit, neither can a corrupt tree bring forth good fruit, and since we all seek the good, the moral for human action is plain.

Understanding brings mastery and a sense of inner strength, not alone in the consequences it produces but also in its intrinsic quality. To understand is to see that "all forms are unreal … all created things are grief and pain … all created things perish"; it is to trace out the lineaments of things in their internal structure and their relations to other things in space and time; it is to acknowledge the paths of necessitation which things pursue as they come into being, change, and pass away. Truth in this sense induces tranquillity and strength in him who possesses it and whose mind is moulded and purified by a selfless acquiescence in the nature of things. For truth, as Spinoza observed, expels and purges that sense of impotence and sadness, that fear and hatred, which come when we are made slaves to the forces and fates of the world. Truth, by its power to lift us above what is circumstantial and passing, also lifts us free of those "passive" emotions which play upon our affections willy-nilly and undermine our integrity. When we can be like a Buddha who "by himself thoroughly knows and sees, as it were, face to face this universe—including the worlds above, the gods, the Brahmas, and the Māras, and the world below with its recluses and Brahmans, its princes and peoples," then we will indeed be liberated from human bondage and know what it means to speak of the truth as "lovely in its origin, lovely in its progress, lovely in its consummation." Understanding can issue in that fortitude which expresses itself as strength of mind and generosity (as Spinoza said) because it is an active attitude that clears up the confusion of blind impulse and its passion. While to some Western minds, influenced by the spirit of experimental science, understanding in this sense may seem to be passive and quiescent, it is in fact a tremendous act of labour, involving a penetration into the nature of human life; a continued mindfulness of what it has learned, discipline in speech, conduct, and livelihood, great resolve and effort, and concentration.

Not only is thought an inescapable ingredient in all action; it is necessary to man's salvation, for, as we have observed, man is born indeterminate, and salvation is not automatic. Some guide is needed, over and beyond the dispositions of the plastic body and the idiosyncrasies of culture. Buddhism is aware of this condition of man. There are no supernatural gods, a priori principles, or pre-existent, permanent souls on which man might, in his extremity, rely. But there is an observable psychic law of cause and effect; and there is the power of man's thought, whereby man determines who he is, what his world is, and whether he suffers hell or enjoys bliss. But thought (presumably the Buddhists here mean to include unconscious thought, or imagery) guides action; and since only positive action can neutralize negative actions, a change in man's thought is the one thing needful. In a similar way, man's emotions must be changed by him, that is, by his own thought. For hatred does not cease by inert passivity any more than it ceases by hatred; it ceases by love, and love arises out of man's truthful relation to his world.

Buddhism's emphasis on understanding may seem like a truism until one considers the vast numbers of people who labour under superstition and have never moved out of its half-light to face, progressively, the emergent truth about themselves and their world. They blindly and passionately pursue their objects and goals; they toil at their tasks with the brute patience of a bullock harnessed to a well wheel; and they become blind to the puniness, precariousness. and impermanency of their lives and objects of satisfaction. "A social system," said Whitehead, "is kept together by the blind force of instinctive actions, and of instinctive emotions clustered around habits and prejudices."

To understand this fact, in the Buddhist sense, is to be lifted above the level of the brute, and initiate a transformation that leads to liberation. Most of the time the mass of us live under the spell of the immediate, appetitive, and sensate, as if what is and has value for us always has been and always must be. We will fight to keep what we have; and if we have surplus time and energy, we may even go out of our way to impose our way of life on others. But to understand is to see that things are not thus necessitated. This misery, this suffering, this poverty, this oppression—they need not be! Things are everlastingly changing; it is man who saddles them with habit and custom and so, blindly and tyrannically, destroys himself and others. But as man has made himself, so he can, by unmaking himself, remake himself. By the intellectual realization of this truth, with its hope, man can begin to get out from under the burden of anxious compulsion, resignation and despair. He can acquire a sense of community with his fellow-men, and a sense of the possibility for human good. Neither social oppression nor personal unhappiness need to be; they can be undone and the blindness of animal passion and habit can be transcended. In the words of the Dhammapada, "The world does not know that we must all come to an end here; but those who know it, their quarrels cease at once."

Understanding has several aspects. It is, first, the perception of the world as flux and impermanence, and, with that, the realization that suffering comes in consequence of our attachments to the impermanent. It is, second, the detachment that arises with that realization—the release from the tyranny which our values exercise over us. The *khandha*s are essentially valuational processes, gripping or letting go of the world, and holding us in their grip so long as we identify ourselves with their processes and their products. To understand is to see, with detachment, that no single achievement, of ourselves, our families, our nations, our cultures, our race, is final, in fact or in value. Some interpreters of Buddha and Buddhism are inclined to rest their interpretation there; in such cases Buddha's lesson is at best a negative one. But beyond these meanings there is yet another, if only implicit in Buddha's teachings. That is not merely what E. A. Burtta calls "continuity of moral growth toward liberated integrity," though it includes and presupposes that. It is a wholehearted commitment to a way of life that is characterized by continuous and progressive transformation, of understanding, surrender, courage, and compassion. It involves detachment from specific goods but also an appreciation of the unique particularity of each good as it appears. This is the whole doctrine of "enjoyment without possession" lifted to its height. Understanding has its own value and power; but beyond that it fully humanizes us by releasing our emotional, active, and social powers from the dominations and dependencies of the world and enabling us to live richly through time with strength and joy.

Understanding requires a kind of resolute renunciation of itself. It must be touched by what the Ch'an masters called cultivation through non-cultivation. The intellect must not take itself too seriously. It must be sobered and softened by the realization that underneath all metaphysical or religious solemnity there is the sportive, childlike play of things; and that behind every square corner in the geometric world of the intellect, lurks the imp of particularity to upset every cart of a System. Yet often more than one "nasty little fact" (as Thomas Huxley put it) is needed to destroy "a beautiful theory" or a social system; an intellectual or social revolution may be required. We lead ourselves into traps of our own making because of our tendency to form stimulus-response bonds; and this tendency to habit gets ratified and fixed by the response of the intellect. Habits of body and of mind entrap us because they blind us to the unique quality of goodness inherent in every person, thing, and situation. Whitehead's advice, "Seek simplicity (of abstractions), but distrust it," finds favour with a Buddhist. For the Buddhist is a nominalist, and with Husserl cries, "To the things themselves!" Indeed, a Buddhist is only a nominalist "in name," for while we may name things, things are not the final realities. How effective might man's mind become, and how happy might man be, if he could form the habit that would free him from the tyranny of habituation.

For may we not ask ourselves: What remains after our emotional habits of distress, ill-temper, anxiety, and the rest have spent the greater part of our energies, and we have ground away our intellectual lives in the groove of wasteful habit? Understanding alone is not sufficient for liberation; as Gotama said, we must detach ourselves from detachment itself. We must be liberated from the repetitiveness of habit, which easily uses up our powers to respond sensitively and creatively. We must open ourselves to the forces of rejuvenation. We must cease taking the recurrent trifles of life seriously, and not consider that every cross-road is a major crisis. Our attachment needs must be to something deeper than the customary, the familiar, the established, and the known. It must be to those uncompelling leaves of grass that spring up between our feet as we walk. We must, as William Ernest Hocking has said, "combine an unlimited attachment with an unlimited detachment".

(2) This means that a second response man must make for his deliverance is renunciation. Renunciation occurs in the act of understanding. For understanding is an ascesis of awareness; it is a disciplining of our responses by the free manipulation and ordering of terms and symbols. It is the intellectual cleansing that produces moral integrity. When we understand we renounce the impulsive and the utilitarian attitudes toward things; we renounce the immediate and the technical for what is abiding and is an end in itself.

Specifically, what is renounced is sensuous attachment to the world (and hence to our "selves"), malice toward others, and our tendency to do harm to others. Is our love of the world so great that we can renounce it in order that the world might return to us, as the Gita puts it, in a transfigured way? Anyone who doubts that man's pride in his sensuous enjoyments and possessions hardens his heart as a miser's heart is hardened by his greed for his gold, and thus destroys that tenderness and plasticity needed for creative relations with others—anyone who doubts that should observe the world today. Many of the leaders of the imperialistic nations and evangelistic religions of the West, and many of the land lords, owners, and local authorities in Asia and Africa, are so obsessed with the threat of their loss of power that they cannot see clearly the situation that confronts them or the things they must do in order to deal with it and to be saved. They are blinded by the diffuse reactions of a deep anxiety—anxiety that stems from their attachment to their power, their satisfactions, their structure of beliefs, in a word, their whole way of life, and from an awareness that these values might be impaired or removed. They cannot adjust to change, let alone promote change, because they have staked their lives on the status quo.

There was a time when egoism was relatively harmless. Prior to the age of technological and industrial power, the roots of the self could not sink very deeply or widely into human affairs. The harm of ego-involvement was limited to the range of materials and of culture which the ego could command. But now a man's "world" may be very wide. A Hitler or Krupp, a Hearst or Rockefeller, can exercise control over millions: his word is their law, because the tentacles of his self and his world reach down into their lives and enwrap them like giant vines in a tropical forest. In this way the egoistic values of one man or a few men are imposed on a multitude, and in this way tenacious attachment to the ego can lead to mischief and disaster on a wide scale.

The evil that such men do is not merely the blind execution of the demands of some "system." Systems operate through individuals. To be sure, the system of imperialism is a set of exploitive relations: but it is only because men willingly or blindly submit themselves to those relations that the system continues. And that submission is possible because men do not understand their situation as human beings and cannot renounce the egoistic values to which they desperately cling. Such desperation is born of anxiety and panic, and is akin to the desperation of a man who, in his haste to get into a lifeboat, drowns his fellow-passengers as well as himself.

For certain persons to renounce their established values of capitalism, colonialism, white superiority, economic and military exploitation, and all the rest, would be to renounce their very gods. But they cannot, because they have invested too much of their lives in worship at the shrine of those gods, and they love them too dearly. The recent battle-cries of the West—"get tough," "massive retaliation," "operation killer," "war of extermination," "positions of overwhelming strength"—express the arrogance of certain people bent on defending and imposing their own values as well as their desperation in the face of a threat to those. Marx observed that successful and oppressing classes always blindly and violently defend what they have and are: they have become smitten by the power of their golden calves.

But the oppressed class has nothing to lose but its chains, and because its temptations and attachments are fewer it is apt to be more realistic and more disposed to relinquish the values of the present in favour of something greater in the future. Yet the oppressed class is possessed by a passion too, different in expression but similar in origin to that of the oppressors. A deprived man, once he has had a glimpse or a taste of goods, is apt to be overcome by hatred, indignation, contempt, envy, anger, and vengeance toward the ruling class. These attitudes are not evil in so far as they issue in action which rights wrongs; but they tend to become evil by a distortion of the power and the understanding which a man might wield. There is some indication that the social transformations now being wrought in Asia have been carried forward by men and women more realistic and less violent than those who conducted western revolutions. One of the reasons for this, I think, is the emphasis on detachment and renunciation propagated by Buddhism. Personal animosity, springing from oppression, and focused on specific persons, is not as effective as an intelligent understanding of the long-range causes and consequences of man's actions in history, and a diligent attempt with others to correct the causes of oppression. Personal animosity thus focused wastes one's fire and blinds one to the basic task that is to be done.

There is, moreover, the ever-present human problem: how may we all live most effectively once the wide gap between the haves and the have-nots is bridged. All of us are tempted to live by the world we "have" (be it expressed in tangible goods or the symbols of the psyche) rather than by the process of creative growth bringing with it the advance of understanding, mastery, and fellow-feeling. Failing to do so, we find the tables turned, and the world we have then has us. Never has the problem of possession and renunciation been so urgent as it is today; for as the domain of human wealth increases, men are more insistently forced to choose between freedom and suicide. Many Americans are sick with a satiety of goods, physical and mental; they refuse to be selective; they have, as Alan Watts says, a kind of omnivorous attitude toward the world: consumers and nothing more. They had best go back to their ancestor, Thoreau, who knew how to choose, reject, and simplify—who knew that the way to inner strength is renunciation and freedom from all that the world can give or take away. I read the other day of a wealthy American woman who took her own life and those of her children because, as she wrote, she was "second to TV and comic books." She is symbolic of the suicide that a whole nation can bring upon itself when it cannot renounce its wealth and control its leisure. So, also, are the many delinquents, criminals, neurotics, and psychotics of this and certain other wealthy lands. People will cheat, rob and kill in an economy of abundance. While such crimes are sharpened by the insecurities of local and world economies, they are also the consequences of a spiritual failure in the minds and hearts of men. The triumph of "property values" over "human values" does not mean that we must scorn materialistic advance, but it does mean that we will destroy ourselves with such advance if we are not prepared to produce and control material values for the benefit of what is best in human beings.

It may be asked, "What about the great mass of the world's population, who know only deprivation? Surely their problem is not renunciation." Their problem is and always will be renunciation, which is an integral aspect of human fulfilment. For they cannot achieve fulfilment if in the process of liberating themselves from physical poverty, starvation, and disease, they only fall victim on the other side to the depredations of accidie, greed, vanity, covetousness, violence, and all the other 'civilized' illnesses that beset modern, industrialized man. What about overpopulation? Is it not produced by ignorance, lust, and an unbridled attachment to the appetites? What about prejudice? What about violent racism, religion, and nationalism? While certainly influenced by man's physical environs, these are problems that are recurrently human ones, arising from man's outlook upon himself and his world, and they cannot be settled until man settles himself. Whether man is rich or poor, skilled or unskilled, educated or ignorant, well or ill, his problem is always uniquely this: how to manage his will in relation to what he has or does not have. Every man, if he would be a man, must be able to sweat it out, like the gods of earth, and to laugh, like the distant gods.

Is it so strange that in explaining renunciation Buddhism has coupled malevolence and harm to others with attachment to sensuous things? He who loves his world and his self overmuch always strives to keep it intact. He resists and resents its breakage, or the threat of its breakage. This entails a resistance to the transforming influences of the world, both consciously known and unconsciously felt. The egoist loves his status quo. Because this attachment prevents him from seeing that he could in fact open the way to much greater good for himself and others if he would renounce it, it also prevents him from creatively relating himself in sympathetic, appreciative, and cooperative ways to others. But the egoist is not just isolated. The very presence of others, vaguely apprehended, is a threat to him. Therefore in his unconscious compulsion to relieve his anxiety and protect his interests, he feels an urge to eliminate the gulf which separates him from others, and may do so by techniques of domination or submission.

Differences are always a threat to the egoist, and he deals with them by attempts to obliterate them. This involves treating others as fragments, as types, as stereotypes, as lifeless members of classes, as things, as commodities, as means to one's own ends. It involves ill-will toward others. An egoist necessarily "rejoices in iniquity" and not in the truth because the truth arises and grows in the interchange of diverse particulars, and the communal source of truth is a threat to the egoist who claims to have the whole truth and who can secure himself in that conclusion only by denying or undermining the existence and the perspectives of others. The total truth, in short, is the totality of mutually consistent, empirically correct perspectives, and we cannot really approach unto it unless we come to the realization that our own perspective with its values is one among a multitude, and are able to view it with the renunciation that is born of a detached mind and sane emotions. "If we think of our existence," said C. W. Holmes, Jr., "not as that of a little god outside, but as that of a ganglion within, we have the infinite behind us." When we give up speaking for or playing God, we can have the kindness of kinship with our fellow creatures; and the magnanimity of being one among (rather than over) many. If one has humility, is devoid of an overweening care for one's own life, and genuinely respects oneself, then one can have the strength to care about others. But if one hates oneself so completely that one must abnegate oneself in order to be more than one, then one must also hate others and do harm to them. In this way renunciation leads to true conquest, and weakness, in the words of Taoism, leads to strength. This is a profound truth in Buddhism, developed in the Mahāyana tradition.

 Psychologically, the status quo of a man is his established state of being; it is his "world" as he is able to feel, respond to, and find meaning in things. Our psychic "worlds" are the structures of belief and value selected out of our gross experiences by our sensitivities, needs, dispositions, and innumerable environmental factors. Thus what a man "is," at a given moment, is this structure; he is indeed a complex of such structures, cumulative, and hierarchical. Western psychoanalysis and Hindu psychology have shown that man consists of many such layers, or "sheaths", acquired by his experiences throughout time. But man is something more than these established structures: he is at the core of such layers a dynamic of "becoming", a continuous fountain of creativity which (in Bergson's figure) is forever throwing off its products. Man's "world" grows up around this dynamic centre and ever threatens to engulf it or to encase it in rigid walls; and so man, to retain his nature, must be vigilantly on guard against such self-strangulation. He must be always peeling away his created "worlds", separating himself from the constrictive bonds of his past; and giving heed to that faint and tender voice of creativity in the depths of his many-levelled "worlds." As Goethe said: "Would you live the happy way, keep the past out of today".

Egoism springs from a false belief in the permanence of one's self, a belief that masks the fear of its downfall and dissolution. More accurately, egoism is the secret desire for permanence, and the realization that this cannot be; and so the egoist, who seems so assured, is wrecked by this unresolved conflict. Precisely because he wishes to keep everything the egoist has nothing. But the opposite attitude is the relinquishment of one's self-concept and cherished values as final; and this brings home to one more than one could possibly ask for or imagine. "The way to get, is to forget." The honest facing of our transience carries us out of our egoistic illusions into bonds of fellowship which embrace us with a love in whose keeping transience seems acceptable, or unimportant.

One may ask: Does egoism spring from ignorance or from a deliberate refusal to acknowledge one's own finitude? Is "the illusion of individuality"—as a modern psychiatrist, Harry Stack Sullivan, calls it—something that is inherent or acquired? We have been assuming implicitly that it is both, as Buddhists seem to do: man has tendencies which can be turned in the direction of rigidity and isolation, and his psychological, social, and ecological situation can be decisive in this turning. The logic of Buddhism precludes that man is born totally bad; for Buddhism holds that man can be saved from evil, and if he can be saved from evil then he must possess at birth both the materials and the means for salvation. What is it that comprises the goodness of the new-born baby? It is the baby's capacity for transformation by way of the increase of linkages of meaning generated between its responses and the things and persons around it; it is the baby's capacity for continuous self-transcendence, for leaving, like the chambered nautilus, its "low-vaulted past," for spiralling out into progressive identity with the vast universe of qualities. Man's spirit, as Berkeley observed, moves, and, unlike those static perspectives to which it gives succession, cannot be perceived in the same way. The fabric of meanings woven on the moving loom of spirit is such that the strand which is my life is inseparable from the strands that constitute other lives and existences; and sharp boundaries are obliterated. But faults and disruptions in the machinery of weaving may occur: the parent communicates to the child its own anxieties, hostilities, and conflicts; the youth senses the ambiguities and injustices of the economy in which he lives and must make a living. What is the result? Retreat, separation, crystallization, individuality. The result is the isolationism and hidden terror which, in the Western world, reached its climax in World War II. The freezing of the spiritual fluids of love was thus described by W. H. Auden:

> And the living nations wait,
> Each sequestered in its hate
> And the seas of pity lie
> Locked and frozen in each eye.

In consequence of social orders which pit each against all and all against each—or, at best, pits the few against the many—men develop an unnatural concern with themselves. They "grasp" for particular securities instead of opening themselves to that one grand Security, that Supreme Identity, which can alone save. "Life is so short!" is our anguished cry, in this age of abundance and of promise of abundance. And when we experience sickness, injury, premature ageing, or the imminence of death, we are apt to protest, "Why me, why me?" Buddhism deals with this problem by turning the question around: if the meaning of life cannot be found in length of days, perhaps it lies in the death of the individual through his intellectual recognition of his transience and his emotional tenderness toward all suffering things. Life is surely short, measured against the movement of sidereal or cosmic time; but physical time is only one dimension of that quality and the qualitative rapport we may have with one another. We probably do not discover this dimension in its fullest richness until we have been separated from our loved ones or nearest possessions; then it is, with the realization of transience, that a deeper and freer love can possess us and woo and win us to its way of living.

In the place of clinging, therefore, Buddhism proposes to put the attitude of letting go; in the place of dominance, it proposes to put the attitude of non-interference. Such proposals are not mere dreamy idealism. There is a certain economy of nature that allows life to advance by the conditions of freedom and separation. The three factors that combine to produce progressive organic evolution, as Alfred E. Emerson has said, are "genetic variation, reproductive isolation, and natural selection." Similar factors are required for advance at the psychological and sociological levels in the affairs of men. Novelty, solitude, and the selectivity of interaction are all necessary for human creativity. Novelty and solitude mean that we must let each other alone; and selectivity means that we must deal with them compassionately and considerately. This implies, too, that the UN principles of the self-determination of the nations and the non-interference by one nation in the internal affairs of another nation, are not abstractions but are rather rooted in the nature of human societies.

Renunciation arises from understanding, and understanding is confirmed in renunciation. To see one's self as a temporary thing means to detach one's deepest desires from the structure and aims of the self. Self-knowledge always leads to humility; it is disenchantment with what is all leaf and illusion, and a return to the root of reality. What is the alternative to this relinquishment of the illusory self? It is either resignation or mania. Men either "live lives of quiet desperation", as Thoreau says, or they ride roughshod over others and leave the wrecks and ruins of history behind them. They either worship the external gods of a blind Nature, Fate, or Chance, or they create their own internal god out of their Self. But understanding can put in its proper perspective both the possibilities of the external situation and the limitations of man himself. Man is neither a passive pawn nor an autonomous king—his effective way is neither complete dependence nor complete dominance. It is rather the middle way between these: a way that can seek without finding, desire without having, have without keeping, renounce without despairing, and understand without withdrawing. In this process man must give himself to the creative transformation if he is to be given unto; he must forgive himself and others if he is to receive forgiveness. To be able to live in the present and yet live above the present, to suck the juice from immediate fruits and yet see both the roots of the past and the seeds of the future, to acknowledge one's presence and predicament in the world as important but not all-important: this is the most important thing. It is the meaning of intelligent renunciation, and it leads to the joy of nirvana.

Renunciation clears the ground for understanding. For it is our egoistic attachments which block our vision of what the world is and of who we are. "When a thing is not loved," says Spinoza, "no quarrels will arise concerning it—no sadness will be felt if it perishes—no envy if it is possessed by another—no fear, no hatred, in short no disturbances of the mind." Pain-provoking attachments arise from our anxieties, and our anxieties force us into beliefs which momentarily allay the unrest of those anxieties but at the same time prevent us from the transformation that might eradicate that unrest. Thus we come to adopt and hold fast certain illusions: "idealized images" about ourselves, and an unduly glorified or darkened picture of the working of the universe. Our egoism, blinding us to ourselves and to things, makes us prone to believe that stock of popular superstitions which impinges on us from all sides from birth to death. In this way our basic anxiety takes, as Epicurus observed, two fundamental forms: the fear of death, and the fear of the retribution of the gods. Then we wander about in the cave of our ignorance, guided only by shadows, frightened by them, and unsure of their reality. Once, however, we renounce our overweening sense of importance, we are freed to open our eyes to what lies within us. The phantasms of private and public sources fall away like ghosts at dawn; the universe ceases to be peopled with anthropomorphisms; and the way is cleared for the liberating venture of seeking, and of finding. It is self-absorption which prevents this initial step in our liberation; and once the step is taken, then it is courage that is required to carry us along the pathway to fulfilment.

(3) A third attitude needful to man is resolution. This embraces the act of aspiration, purposiveness, and earnestness, on the one hand; and the determination of one's destiny on the other. Man must be saved by his own efforts; he has none else as his refuge. If modern man is to have the Utopia of abundance and world peace

which now beckons him from the future where atomic power will do all his physical labour, he must achieve that freedom and security for himself; no rulers, no parliament of man, no United Nations, no gods from on high, no act of fate, will present it to him on a silver platter. The actualization of such an ideal, moreover, will not come to pass apart from man's wholehearted striving and unresting vigilance. A steadfastness and stubbornness of what is known in the West as "faith" is called for. "Those who are in earnest do not die; those who are thoughtless are as if dead already." Those brave and reassuring words of the Dhammapada have nerved the efforts of millions long before Goethe penned a similar sentiment in his Faust. To aspire in the right direction without wearying is the ultimate act that is required of man. What else could be asked? And "a good man" says Goethe, "in his dim urgency is still conscious of the right way." Buddhism holds that this urgency must be enlightened and directed into right mindfulness and other disciplines of the eightfold path.

To aspire earnestly and to determine one's own destiny are entailed by both understanding and renunciation. To be willing to know, to face the brute propensity of possessiveness which lies at the base of our distorted natures, to analyze and resolve our habits into their constituent parts—this requires great courage and steadfast faith. In the same way renunciation is an act of courage, for it means abandoning one's self and relinquishing one's hold on cherished values.

One cannot fully grasp the moral implications, or the fervent hope of Buddhism, I think, unless one first understands the stark existential predicament of man which lies at the centre of its concern and thought. What is man? He is nothing. He may think he is something; but when carefully analyzed everything that he thinks he is—fire-maker, tool-user, shaper of symbols, creator of culture, sublime intellect, immortal soul, son of God, Brahman himself; or doctor, lawyer, merchant, thief, or John Q. Jones—he is not. For "nothing is but what is not." Man's myriad series of "selves" comes and goes, and no substantial thread binds the selves together; the pattern of karma alone endures. "Thou carriest them away as with a flood; they are as asleep."

But while this is man's extremity, puzzle, and tragedy, it is also his opportunity. Precisely because he is not bound to a permanent self bearing down on him oppressively from the past, man can and must make and re-make himself. In the interstices of becomings, man has the opportunity for re-directing the past and freeing himself from its blind thrust. Buddhist philosophy was consistent with the intent of Gotama when it developed the doctrine that a given event does not pre-exist in its causes, and the subtle doctrine of momentariness. From moment to moment we are different, and the success of life is to see this and make the most of it. Not to see it is to be caught in the clutch of craving, habit, illusion, and suffering.

The doctrine of momentariness is implicitly the doctrine of creativity. Gotama rejects the common-sense view of substance, which lends itself easily to the lazy and irresponsible religious notion of an immortal "soul-substance." He also rejects the nihilistic view that things are utterly empty or illusory. What is illusory is the substantial appearance of events. (This is the point that Madhyamika philosophy has taken up and developed.) What is real is the qualitative creativity of experience—the nirvana to be appreciated in and through the passage of experience. Viewed in the dynamic span of the creative self, any given, achieved self is an abstraction. The substantive "I," accordingly, cannot be real; it cannot really "pass through" an experience, for to pass through means to be affected and to be changed, but by definition such an "I" cannot change. The fact is that our selves become. A child becomes an adult; the adult does not (contrary to Aristotle and others) pre-exist in the child. Similarly, a person becomes a mother by mothering, a farmer by farming, a writer by writing; the mother, the farmer, or the writer does not pre-exist and suddenly reveal himself. The self must be achieved, won, created. Anyone who has lived, i.e. has grown up progressively into new forms of reality, knows this. Earnestness is the moral attitude enjoined on us by the whole universe, since the whole universe in a sense is earnest. It is a popular saying that we should love people for what they are and respect them in their true being. But what is the being of man? Is it not that he forever changes and becomes, and that his character is the way he becomes—the energetic quality of his striving, in heart and mind, the courage and clarity of his aspiring, the depth of his compassion in helping others in their striving and aspiring? The courage to be is the courage to become. And this requires infinitely more courage than would be needed if our natures were already prepared and completed prior to experience. The emptiness of the universe is vast; and to fill our little portion of it with a creative act, moment after moment, and to find our immortality in that, is a large and noble task for finite man.

Creative becoming, as a norm for human life, represents an answer to David Hume's proposition that we have no direct evidence for the existence of the world, the soul, or God, and Hume's search for a guide to human life. Gotama's analysis is very similar to Hume's; and his answer is similar too; Kant, who was profoundly influenced by Hume, stated the nature of the self more clearly. The "self" or "soul" is only a regulative ideal, he maintained, for we have not lived out its full potentialities. We know it, as a dynamic process, only in part; it is forever becoming and incomplete. Moreover, the soul is an inner thing, hidden from sensuous perception.

Kant's view moves in the same direction as Buddhist thought. Ultimate reality or value is not confinable to any given experience or achievement of the self. It is not a created structure but is instead a power of creation. In this sense it is "void", non-sensuous, and indescribable.

It is the source of our specific qualities, forms, values, and "selves". Our suffering, therefore, lies in our ignorant, tenacious attachment to what is created; and our liberation, happiness, and fulfilment lie in living for that creative source. Salvation begins when we make the shift from one mode of orientation to the other. Sudden insight into the difference between these two modes is what Zen calls *satori*. To aspire for this kind of transformation and this kind of orientation is the highest aspiration one can undertake.

It would be impossible to recapture or state the deep reaction of gratitude and hope with which people in India must have first received the message of Buddha. To learn that the miseries of life need not be; that one's history or past could not doom one to eternal suffering; that regardless of one's place or condition one could, by one's own efforts and intelligence, achieve freedom: what a sense of liberation and hope this must have generated among vast numbers of people! Buddha's was a call for resolute courage and self-reliance. It was a reaction against religion as an opiate of the people, and against all of man's self-made opiates which permit corruption, parasitism, empty ritual, and superstition to flourish in religion and outside of religion.

Resolution entails understanding and renunciation. We cannot really live lives of courage unless we understand the ultimate issues of life and hold clearly in our vision the right path. Nor can our action be effectual unless we strip ourselves of useless impediments and run with patience the race that is set before us. Two-thirds of the world's population live in hunger, poverty, and disease; the other third enjoy the abundance of modern technology and industry. Aside from its general emphasis on understanding and compassion, Buddhism lacks the socio-economic perspective and method which can minister directly and curatively to the problem of hunger, though it has been alleviative in its mental effects. But Buddhism has a profound insight relevant to the age of material abundance. For as Lewis Mumford has pointed out, man has become overmastered and mechanized by the multitude of material processes and things which his technology has produced. His means have become ends in themselves; and man, as an integrative, creative spirit, has ceased to be the centre of his personal life and his culture. The cure for this is Thoreau's simplify, simplify, simplify. This is a Buddhist principle, for to simplify means to renounce and to put first things first, to restore man's attitude of self-mastery to the driver's seat. The spirit of Gotama's thought is that man ought to be the determiner of his destiny, so far as he can, and that to abdicate control of his life to kings, cartels, armies, editors, advertisers, pathogenic organisms, or any other force other than his own mind and spirit is slavery and needless suffering. This does not mean retirement from the world, nor does it mean mere action under the illusion that to act on one's world is to be self-determining. It means rather that man must act resolutely to organize his life so as to increase progressively what he can think, feel, control, and communicate.

(4) A fourth attitude, already implied in the previous three, is compassion. Understanding implies compassion, for to understand is to comprehend, to see suffering and mortality as the common condition of all, to be familiar with the family of living creatures. One cannot really and completely know all unless one knows that all are saved, and assist in that enterprise. Renunciation implies

compassion too, for to give up one's attachments means to open oneself to the multifarious needs and perspectives of the huge world-community. Resolution implies compassion, for one cannot seek to determine one's own destiny and aspire to what is right without considering the tragedy and the struggle of innumerable others. The earnest man, purged of lust and self-seeking, surely cannot interfere with the lives of others; and at his purest state, having helped himself, he will have the overflowing strength to help others. This is expressed in the magnificent Bodhisattva ideal of selfless love, "infinite compassion," and "universal redemption."

> "At all costs I must bear the burdens of all beings ... The whole world of living beings I must rescue, from the terrors of birth, of old age, of sickness, of death and rebirth, of all kinds of moral offence, of all states of woe, of the whole cycle of birth-and-death, of the jungle of false views, of the loss of wholesome dharmas, of the concomitants of ignorance—from all these terrors I must rescue all beings ... And why? Because it is surely better that I alone should be in pain than that all these beings should fall into the states of woe ... There has arisen in me the will to win all-knowledge, with all beings for its object, that is to say, for the purpose of setting free the entire world of beings."

Compassion is the opposite of sensuous attachment and illusion, of craving and lust, ignorance and confusion. Compassion has a depth which carries it beyond the beguilements of surface appearance. In the same way that knowledge penetrates beneath the changing phenomena of things, and seeks to discover the real nature of things, so compassion seeks to go below the level of smiles or tears which people may wear, the masks of position and repute which are taken as real by so many, the characters which they have built, the habits which dominate them, the desires which determine their habits, and, ultimately, the potential means of their liberation. Compassion is a fellow-feeling for the plight and possibilities which we share with others. Such a feeling is not mere sympathy; it is sympathy qualified by a positive sense of clear distance between ourselves and others; it is what Nietzsche called "the pathos of distance." Compassion is impossible unless we ourselves have been purified of egocentric drives and obsessive cravings: otherwise what passes as compassion is only an attempt on the part of the self to embrace, dominate, and swallow up the object of our interest. Compassion then is mistaken for what is only the extension of the ego's needs; the object of interest is not seen for what it is, in itself, as a living, suffering, and striving subject; it is not seen with genuine "respect" but becomes only an item in a perceptual field to be organized and used. Compassion of that kind is only the velvet glove for the iron hand or the acquisitive palm. This is why "love," in the West, has been called "blind"; it is passion and lust, devoid of the detachment which can emerge only when we have conquered our own desires and freed ourselves from the distortions in knowledge caused by coercive needs.

Compassion begins at home. "Let each man first direct himself to what is proper, then let him teach others." To reverse this is to have the blind leading the blind. When we grow in our own integrity to a greatness and magnanimity of soul; when we can scorn personal injury and death as incidents in the destined progression of man; when we can cast off the fetters of fear and hatred of our enemies; when we shed like a heavy burden the unmet demands we make upon others and the world, and are able to have all that is worth having because we want nothing; when we live in each moment grateful for its blessings and responsive to the unmerited wealth of value left in the wake of time as it passes: then we are truly free, and are able to discover others and help them because we have first discovered and helped ourselves. This is something which our "other-directed" cultures tend to forget.

Compassion begins in solitude—in that "sweetness of solitude" that is the distillation of inner victory. "We must be our own," says Emerson, "before we can be another's." Compassion arises out of a clarified trust of one individual for another. But man is a huddling animal. He huddles, not because he is solitary, like some animals, but because he is lonely. Loneliness is the felt isolation from the object of some desire; and man, being conscious, is able to desire many things—the moon, the sun, the cosmos, and eternal life—and hence to experience deep loneliness. The pathology of human life is to be seen in man's efforts to overcome this loneliness; and most of those efforts are social. Man seeks to exact recompense from his fellows. He believes not only that the world owes him a living, but also that it should provide for him a cure for his loneliness. So he forces himself into communion with others, and gains a vague sense of assurance there. But as loneliness arises in the self it must find its essential cure in the self. While the self takes its origin and data from a social context, it is also, on the other side, a solitary thing. What we do, what we think, what we become, are consequences of personal acts. After we have received the insights of a providential grace, the ultimate decisions are ours alone to make; the ultimate freedom is ours alone to fashion. And these decisions, this creative freedom, must be achieved in solitude. When this is accomplished, then we can see others for what they are and can see the loveliness that lies in them. This clear-eyed perceptiveness, from which the subtleties of exploitation have been expunged, carries us then on to compassion.

A vast majority of men live under the dominance of food, sex, other material goods, and money. This is true in Los Angeles no less than in Lucknow. It is a fact which ruling economic groups, politicians, advertisers, and charlatans of various kinds universally recognize and tend to exploit for their own selfish ends. But we could not be victimized by others if we were not first our own victims. Men are lured and betrayed by gold and pleasures, by social power and arms, because in the first instance they set up and assert those values. Such traps are of their own making; and it requires both predator and prey to spring the trap. A sociologist of knowledge, however, might say that man is not entirely made by his own habits or decisions, since these are influenced by his social context; and that is a truth that needs to be added to Buddhism. At the same time, it is men who help to make their social context.

Compassion is the opposite of self-indulgence. It should be distinguished from the mystical feeling which one may have in being identified with a family, a nation, a culture, or a mob. Such exaltations or phobias are a far cry from genuine sympathy. They are egoistic sentiments expanded, projected, and glorified on a social scale. One does not really see or understand others as individuals: what one sees is one's own inner world, filled with needs and ideals, and one then gives oneself the illusion of objectivity and charity. Indeed, it is necessary for men driven by cravings to seek this sort of security; any other sort they could not tolerate. The egoist is devoted to the status quo; he could not bear to have it broken down by the intrusion of other personalities with their problems. This is why, as Dr. Elsa A. Whalley has recently discovered, gregarious and active persons who take a "live and let live" attitude are often "inflexible at the core." Their many social contacts and gay camaraderie are only false fronts for an unregenerate individualism.

We cannot exercise compassion until this self-concern is broken; we cannot give ourselves to others until we first have given up ourselves. The story of Kisā Gotamī illustrates this. When we weep at the passing of others, do we not weep for ourselves, or a portion of ourselves? Yet this kind of painful separation of the self from itself is a recurrent thing that has no cessation. "Decay is inherent in all compound things." We may, however, reply: "No, I weep for life that might have been, that might have enjoyed itself, that might have grown up and fulfilled itself." Even so death is a final fact from which there is no reprieve. The past is done, and the present ever presses upon us and presents itself before us, as a continuing gift. The only satisfying response to death is to lose oneself in a new life—to find, as Kisā Gotamī did, an end of sorrow through an open-heartedness to all her fellow-sufferers, whereby her own private grief is transformed into deeper understanding. More sacrificial renunciation, braver resolution, and broader compassion. The only effective way to cope with individual disappointment, diminution, and death is to find new affirmations; for death is not overcome by mourning anymore than hatred is overcome by hatred—it is overcome by life and by love. If one's child dies, one must find new children, now living, who need the ministrations of a humble, wise, and compassionate heart. If one's self and its ideals, loyalties, and attachments die, as indeed they must, one must find another self, chastened by the lesson that what is deeper and more dear than any individual self is the process that progressively transforms the self toward new levels of integrity in understanding, power, sympathy, courage, and faith. In this process, in time, one may find a qualitative peace and assurance that endures through time.

Buddhism is not simply a religion of compassion. For its compassion is not ignorant, passive, or selfish, but is guided by understanding, carried out by earnest action, and directed toward all sentient creatures. Buddhism is just the opposite of self-indulgence; and if anyone believes that man is "naturally selfish," he should consider how Buddhism over a period of 2,500 years has profoundly influenced millions of people. Self-indulgence has two sides, apathy and license, and Buddhism opposes the first by its emphasis on "receptivity and sympathetic concern," and the second by its "self-control." Both of these attitudes involve understanding and renunciation. Some Buddhists have stressed the first attitude (the Bodhisattva ideal) and others the second (the Arahatta ideal). Thus Buddhism is simple in that it comes to grip with the basic, recurrent tendencies and attitudes of human nature: but it is complex because it considers that one must counter dependence with the attitudes of understanding and resolute action; dominance, with the attitude of non-interference or renunciation; and detachment, with the attitude or compassion. All of these attitudes, along with their opposites, must, in Buddhism, be transcended by the Maitreyan ideal, described by Charles Morris as "detached-attachment:" one must live within, but rise beyond, all bonds, all cravings, all thoughts; one must find liberation in and through the creative transformation of experienced qualities. This is the whole meaning of "the middle way" and its consequence and reward, Nibbāna.

Conclusion

Buddhism has shaped the lives of countless millions through the centuries because what people need is compassion; they need to give it no less than to receive it, for unless we can receive it we cannot achieve the self-acceptance of maturity, with its full capacity to feel, think, and act; and unless we can give it we cannot know the full significance of a life devoted to something higher than itself. In referring to this lesson, Oliver Wendell Holmes, Jr., has said that a man "may put it in the theological form of justification by faith or in the philosophical one of the continuity of the universe. I care not very much for the form if in some way he has learned that he cannot set himself over against the universe as a rival god, to criticize it, or to shake his fist at the skies, but that his meaning is its meaning, his only worth is as a part of it, as a humble instrument of the universal power."

Compassion, cleansed of provincialism and the drive for power, gives man a sense of such super-personal participation. Indeed, it may be questioned whether without an initiating and continuing sense of compassion man may rise to any worthy philosophy, religion, or heroism at all. For compassion is the most intimate and primary binding power which we can experience; if we cannot feel a sense of at-oneness with our fellow beings, surely we cannot feel the same toward the universe. And, conversely, communion with our kind radiates out into every detail of our experience and communicates its assurance and good feeling to the whole of history, the creatures of nature, and the universe itself. This sense is very powerful in the full flowering of Buddhism. More important, Buddhism has realized only implicitly that man is more than what he thinks, that his thought cannot be the only thing therefore that will save him, and that unconscious powers lying below and beyond the reach of his conscious mind (in the psyche and society) must continuously transform his conscious mind to release it from its limitations and from the suffering which man undergoes when he lives by its structures. Buddhism acknowledges the ultimate fact of change; it conceives of its problem as that of breaking the grip of the causal series which forms our self and the apperceptive world. This is to be accomplished by knowledge, conduct, and concentration.

Suffering itself is an experience that comes to us and stimulates us to change, in spite of our conscious efforts to prevent it; and we cannot cope with it completely, once it has come, by mere understanding, resolution, or any other conscious attitude. Indeed, to explain the transformation in the lives of many Buddhists we should have to look below the level of conscious belief to a creative power into whose keeping these persons were led to give themselves, and which led to a qualitative poise in passage that no mere belief could generate. The Buddhist emphasis on renunciation of all clingings would carry a person part of the way in that self-giving, but it does not indicate explicitly the positive creativity that easily transforms man once the grip of his devotion upon created form has been relinquished and other conditions have been provided.

The effects of Buddhism, like those of all religions, go far beyond its explicit doctrines. These effects have not depended on the literal truth of the doctrines. The doctrine of universal change, whether or not it is the whole truth about the world, is humanistically useful in opening up the possibility for men to change themselves. Similarly, the doctrine that the soul does not exist, while in dispute among philosophers, has functioned to facilitate non-egoistic thought, feeling, and action; if you really believe that the soul is illusory, then you are not apt to lust, drink, lie, cheat, steal, fight, and kill in its behalf. Again, if you believe that the only karma which you carry is the causal law of Dhamma—whereby your present state arises from the conditioning of some past state, then you are simultaneously freed of the yoke of Determinism and the gambling of Chance—you can undertake to change your state with resolution, confidence, and hope. Moreover, the Buddhist doctrine of rebirth, while difficult to understand as the mental or dispositional inheritance that passes from one body to another save as we inherit our constitutions and hence our temperaments from our parents—has undoubtedly generated in men a deep sense of kinship and communion with all creatures. It has given men a "world loyalty." Gotama Buddha himself is "one of an endless line of Enlightened Beings, reaching from remotest times into immeasurable cycles of futurity." Likewise, every Buddhist can think of himself as having been incarnated in an indefinite number of races of men and conditions of life, and as one participant now in dynamic spiritual evolution.

Through its teachings of understanding, renunciation, resolution, and compassion, Buddhism has helped large numbers of people to deal effectively with the problems of change and suffering, anxiety and identity. It has given them a sense of identity with something important, in a world that undermined their identity. It has enabled men to live with equanimity in a world of time and disappointment and to live creatively in a world of transience and destruction. This has been its contribution to man, and this is Buddha's and Buddhism's value for the modern world.

The Miracle of Being Awake

A Manual on Meditation
for the Use of Young Activists

by
Thich Nhat Hanh

Translated from the Vietnamese by
Mobi Quynh Hoa

WHEEL PUBLICATION NO. 234/235/236

Copyright © Kandy; Buddhist Publication Society, (1976, 1983)

Editor's Preface

The lines that follow are meant to introduce to the readers of *The Wheel* series the author of this inspiring essay, my esteemed friend the Venerable Thich Nhat Hanh. He is a Mahayana monk originally from South Vietnam residing now for the last several years living in Plum Village in France.

Thich Nhat Hanh's abilities and activities show the rare combination of his being a scholar and a poet, a meditator and a social worker; and, as far as I can judge, he has not been superficial in any of these. As a scholar he was active as a Professor of Religions and Director of Social Studies at Van Hanh Buddhist University in Saigon. Sensitive and stirring poems of his have been published in the United States. His meditative bent appears in the present essay, devoted to the everyday application of mindfulness. He also conducts meditation classes. As a dedicated social worker, he established in South Vietnam the School of Youth for Social Service, which was inspired by a deeply Buddhist spirit of compassion and non-violence, and meditation was an integral part of the life of that community. This essay, in fact, takes the form of letters addressed to one of its members. Not subscribing to either of the two warring ideologies in Vietnam, Nhat Hanh and the School drew upon themselves the antagonism of both sides.

In 1966 Thich Nhat Hanh was invited to Cornell University (USA) as a guest lecturer. After concluding his assignment there, he went on lecture tours throughout the United States and many countries of Europe. In these lectures he told of the plight of the long-suffering Vietnamese people, pleading for peace in that country to be achieved through its neutralisation. While in Paris, he wrote the book which was to have a strong impact on public opinion in the US, widening the circle of those who morally and politically disapproved of America's military involvement in Vietnam. The title of that influential book was *Vietnam: Lotus in a Sea of Fire* (Hill and Wang, New York). Its Vietnamese version ran an edition of 200,000 copies before it was banned.

It was quite clear to Thich Nhat Hanh that his lecture tour and book had closed the doors to his return to South Vietnam. So he then settled in Paris (later in the suburb of Sceaux), where he founded the 'Vietnamese Buddhist Peace Delegation,' in order to plead the cause of peace in Vietnam among international and inter-religious peace organizations. Along with his devoted band of helpers he also did splendid work in organising support and sponsorships for a large number of orphans and refugee children in South Vietnam. This compassionate and successful activity lasted for many years, as long as political conditions allowed contact with South Vietnam.

The undersigned Editor is grateful to the Venerable Thich Nhat Hanh for his permission to reproduce his essay in *The Wheel* series, and he is also thankful to him for his consent to the abridgements required for this edition.

Nyanaponika
March 1976

A Few Words

by the translator, Mobi Quynh Hoa

The other day I received a letter from a friend in Saigon saying he was about to be drafted and this letter would probably be the last one he could send me before being forced into the army. "These last few days I have been full of anxiety, but I am glad that peace is coming soon to our country. I hope that I shall be able to return and devote all my efforts to easing the hatred between brothers of both sides after twenty years in which they have been forced to carry guns against each other."

At that time, Thay Nhat Hanh and Chi Phuong (Thay means Teacher and Chi means older Sister) were in Thailand for a gathering of young Asian social workers. They were also able to contact friends in Vietnam almost every day by telephone to find out what work was being done to ease the situation of the refugees. With Thay and Chi Phuong gone, I found it hard to practise mindfulness, yet I knew that practising mindfulness was the only way I could continue to live in those days and have anything to offer to anyone else. The phone rang constantly, usually insistent persons who wanted to adopt a Vietnamese orphan. I had to explain many times why we felt it was best to help the children in Vietnam where they could remain with an aunt or uncle rather than being torn from their relatives and culture. I never answered the phone on the first or second ring in order to give myself a few seconds to watch my breath and smile before picking up the receiver. Before saying "Hello", I tried to give rise to the thought: "May I be aware of all that this person asks for and how and what I reply, treating this conversation as though it is the most important conversation I will ever have." The doorbell buzzed many times a day. Often it was Vietnamese friends who came to share their worries or sometimes to share news they'd just received from members of their families. Before I opened the door I tried to watch my breath and relax my body. I let a half-smile rise on my face and as I opened the door I tried to keep in mind the thought: "Let me make this person feel at once welcomed and refreshed when they enter this door." But without the presence of Thay and Chi Phuong I often forgot to practise these methods of mindfulness.

One evening, several days after I had received my friend's letter, I stood for a long while in front of Thay's window looking out in the night air at the poplar tree which stands there. I thought about my friend and all the other young men forced to carry guns. A few weeks previously I had watched a television special on Cambodia which showed young boys and men shooting each other and being shot. Their eyes were still fresh like the eyes of young deer, and their hands were slender as shoots of bamboo. I was filled with anxiety as I stood looking out the window. I began to watch my breath. After a few inhalations and exhalations my breathing was slow and even. I said my friend's name silently and looked at the poplar tree as though looking into my own heart. Its leaves fluttered lightly in the night breeze. A kind of peace arose in me. I knew my friend was not far away. If I looked closely, I could see him in the leaves blown lightly by the breeze, I could see him in my own heart. My worry did not disappear but I had the feeling that I could see my friend for the first time, could see that he and I were one.

I often speak of trying to be a bridge between Vietnamese and Americans, between Easterners and Westerners, between Buddhists and Christians. But the time I spent time in Italy I saw that a bridge is perhaps not the best image, for it implies a separation between two shores. Yet while in Italy, the separation between two cultures seemed no longer to exist. If both cultures nourish my life, can they really be two and not one? By practising mindfulness, perhaps the worry about being from a different culture disappears, and more importantly, there is no longer any fear to experience the differences in another culture or religion. We are free to be nourished by the differences. In fact, they are no longer differences—they are simply another part of our lives and experience of the world. Instead of bridges we become like fish who can swim from one current to another with ease.

Some of you may be familiar with the work of the School of Youth for Social Service (SYSS) in Vietnam. The workers are mostly young Buddhists who have left the more comfortable life in the cities to share the difficulties of the peasants and refugees in the countryside. For many years they have been trying to keep hope alive in the people. Once they rebuilt a village four times after it had been bombed four times. "Why don't you just move to a safer area or go to the city with the villagers to avoid the bombs?", they were asked. "We are building more than huts and irrigation ditches," they answered. "If we abandon the village, we let down the villagers. At least if we stay here, we can demonstrate that hope is still possible." Many of you who read Thay's words in this essay will identify closely with the SYSS workers, because you have been trying to keep hope alive in people, too. Perhaps situations differ, for instance the Vietnamese countryside and an American inner city differ greatly; the SYSS workers come from an Eastern and Buddhist culture, whereas most of us come from a Western and Christian culture. But we have recognized each other. When Thay Nhat Hanh began to write this letter on mindfulness for the SYSS workers, he told me, "You must translate it into English and write a Foreword. We will give it to friends in the US who are doing work like the SYSS workers, such as the Catholic Workers." I know that I do not need to write a Foreword which places Thay's words, coming from a Vietnamese Buddhist context, into an American Christian context. The language is often different but I know you will understand anyway. For instance, when Thay says that the half-smile is the smile you see on the face of Buddhas, many of us might also think of the half-smiles we have seen on the faces of Madonna and Christ figures. It makes no difference who smiles; the smile is there. The thing you might find different, however, is that Thay tells us to smile to ourselves. Let go of everything except your breath. Then let a half-smile arise.

As I have translated Thay's words I have felt the presence of several friends. One group of friends are a community of young Buddhists in Thailand who have begun the kind of work the SYSS workers do in Vietnam. Yesterday a letter came from one of their members named Wisit. When Thay and Chi Phuong came home from Thailand, they told me about Wisit and his friends. Translating Thay's words have helped me to practise mindfulness, and knowing that I also translate this letter for Wisit and his friends has helped me to translate more mindfully. I have tried to think of my translating as a way of being with our friends in Thailand, which means that I have translated not in order to finish the translation to send to them, rather I have translated to live and preserve a Way with them.

Because you friends have been with me as I translate, if you look closely as you read Thay's words, I think you will also see and recognize each other. If we can discover and apply the methods of mindfulness, then whether we live in Vietnam, Sri Lanka, Thailand, Holland, France, or America, I think we will began to see each other in every action we undertake. Perhaps we will all become bridges to one another (or fish who swim together!). And whatever we do to preserve life, in the Thai countryside or in an American inner city, we will help each other. We will meet each other on the bridge of our service and there share a communal meal.

If we do not practice mindfulness, will we be able to continue our work which grows more and more difficult and seemingly more and more invisible in our present world where the violence of partisan conflicts burns everywhere? Let us at least not be invisible to each other. If we do not practise mindfulness we will not be able to see and help each other across the stretches of ocean and land. We will not be able to share humble meals (of coconut and cabbage) with each other in our hearts. If we cannot see each other, if we cannot make our work one for the human family, will any of the seeds we now sow bear fruit?

Sceaux (France), 18 June 1975

The Miracle of Being Awake

Having a Lot More Time

Dear Quang,

Yesterday Steve came over to visit with his son, Tony. Tony's grown so quickly! He's already seven years old and is fluent in French and English.

I gave him several picture books for children but he barely glanced at them before tossing them aside and interrupting our conversation again. He demands the constant attention of grown-ups.

Later, Tony put on his jacket and went outside to play with a neighbour's child.

Then Steve said, "I've just discovered a way to have a lot more time." I asked how. He answered, "In the past, I used to look at my time as if it were divided into several parts. One part I reserved for Tony, for helping him with school work, reading him stories, giving him a bath. Another part was for Ann, helping her with Zoe, going to the market for her, taking the clothes to the laundromat, talking with her when the children were in bed. I still see Ann and Zoe as one person because Zoe's breath is Ann's breath; if one of them stopped breathing, the other one would as well. The time left over, I considered my own. I could read, write, do research, go for walks. My work at the office was yet another time slot.

"But now I try not to divide time into parts anymore. I consider my time with Tony and Ann as my own time. When I help Tony with his homework, I try not to keep the thought in the back of my mind that 'This is the time I reserve for Tony. Afterwards I'll have some time for myself.' I try to find ways of seeing his time as my own time. I go through his lesson with him, sharing his presence and finding ways to be interested in what we do during that time. That way the time for him becomes my own time. The same goes with Ann, and the remarkable thing is that now I have unlimited time for myself."

Steve smiled as he spoke. I was surprised. I knew that Steve hadn't learned this by reading any books. This was something he'd discovered for himself in his own daily life.

Over the past few months I've been going through the Sūtra on Mindfulness with a small group each Saturday evening. After I explain a section, the young people in the group ask questions about how to apply the principles spoken of in the Sūtra to their own daily lives. We've considered the use of time. Although Steve, not speaking Vietnamese, has never attended one of these sessions, he has attained an understanding on his own which those in the group have been discovering by studying the Sūtra.

Last Saturday I related what Steve told me to those in the meditation group. One of the young men said, "Steve has discovered the principle, but how do we know he's found the method yet?" I answered, "If you can find the principle, you should be able to find the method as well." If Steve knows how to really share Tony's presence and be interested in Tony's lesson, Steve has already found out how to apply methods of his own. The Sūtra on Mindfulness is certainly not the only source which can offer us the methods. Although Steve has studied Buddhism and reads Sanskrit, Steve is not a Buddhist himself. But it's not only the people who claim to be Buddhist who realize the methods of Buddhism.

One of the young women in the group said, "I think we should invite Steve to come to one of our sessions to share with us some of his own experiences. Maybe we could learn something from him." I think that she recognized something important: a Buddhist can easily learn from the experience of non-Buddhists and, more importantly, can learn a lot about Buddhism through people who are not Buddhists themselves. I remembered a sentence repeated often in the Mahayana tradition: "The methods of Buddhism are the methods of life." We could also say, "The methods in the Sūtra of Mindfulness have something in common with Steve's awakening."

If he wishes, Steve could also apply the methods taught in the Sūtra of Mindfulness. However the methods which Steve has found out on his own are probably not enough yet to allow him to realize his goal entirely.

I'm sure our workers in the School of Youth for Social Service would like to know, as well, how far Steve's methods have been able to take him. I know that there isn't one worker who doesn't feel that his or her own time is far too lacking. I'm a worker also.

As are you, Quang. I know we'd both like to know how Steve has acquired his 'unlimited time.' But has he really acquired unlimited time, or is he just beginning to see the principle?

Washing the Dishes to Wash the Dishes

In the US I have a close friend named Jim Forest, who came to visit me last winter. I usually wash the dishes after the evening meal before sitting down and drinking tea with everyone else. One night Jim asked if he might do the dishes. I said, "Go ahead, but if you wash the dishes you must know the way to wash them." Jim replied, "Come on, Thay, you think I don't know how to wash the dishes?" I answered, "There are two ways to wash the dishes. The first is to wash the dishes in order to have clean dishes and the second is to wash the dishes in order to wash the dishes." Jim was delighted with this reply and said, "I choose the second way—to wash the dishes to wash the dishes." From then on, Jim knew how to wash the dishes. I transferred the 'responsibility' to him for an entire week. Afterwards, he made a great deal of propaganda for 'washing the dishes to wash the dishes' and published the saying in several journals. Even at home he brought it up so much that one day Laura laughed and said to him, "If you really like washing the dishes to wash the dishes so much, there is a cupboard full of clean dishes in the kitchen. Why don't you go and wash them?"

Thirty years ago, when I was still a novice at Tu Hieu Pagoda, washing the dishes was hardly a pleasant task. During the Season of Retreat when all the monks returned to the monastery, two novices had to do all the cooking and wash the dishes for sometimes well over 100 monks. There was no soap. We had only rice or coconut husks and ashes, and that was all. Cleaning such a high stack of bowls was a chore, especially during the winter when the water was freezing cold. Then you had to heat up a big pot of water before you could do any scrubbing. Nowadays one stands in a kitchen equipped with liquid soap, special scrub-pads, and even running hot water, which makes it all the more agreeable. It is easier to enjoy washing the dishes now. Anyone can wash them in a hurry, then sit down and enjoy a cup of tea afterwards. I even know of a lot of women who have asked their husbands to buy a dishwashing machine. Quang, I can see a machine for washing clothes, although I wash my own things out by hand, but a dishwashing machine is going just a little too far! I'm sure the women back home would cluck their tongues in disapproval: "Good grief, how on earth can anyone be so lazy?" According to the Sūtra on Mindfulness, while washing the dishes one should only be washing the dishes, which means that while washing the dishes one should be completely aware of the fact that one is washing the dishes. At first glance that might seem a little silly: why put so much stress on a simple thing? But that's precisely the point, Quang. The fact that I am standing there and washing these bowls is a wondrous reality. I'm being completely myself, following my breath, conscious of my presence and conscious of my thoughts and actions. There's no way I can be tossed around mindlessly like a bottle bobbing up and down on the waves. My consciousness cannot be dispersed like the foam on the tips of waves when the waves dash against the cliffs.

If, while washing the dishes, we think only about the cup of tea that awaits us, or about anything else which pertains to the future, thus hurrying to get the dishes out of the way, as if they were a nuisance, then we are not 'washing the dishes to wash the dishes,' and what's more we are not alive during the time we are washing the dishes. In fact, we are completely incapable of realizing the miracle of life while standing at the sink. If we can't wash the dishes, then chances are we won't be able to drink our tea either. During our cup of tea, we will only be thinking about other things, barely aware of the cup in our hands. Thus we are sucked away into the future, and what that really means is that we are incapable of living even one minute of life.

Finding Time for Practising Mindfulness

More than 30 years ago, when I first entered the monastery, the monks gave me a small book called *The Essential Discipline for Daily Use*, written by the Buddhist monk Doc The from Bao Son Pagoda, and they told me to memorize it. It was a thin book; it couldn't have been more than 40 pages, but it contained all the thoughts Doc The used to awaken his mind while doing any task. For example, when he woke up in the morning, his first thought was, "Just awakened, I hope that every person will attain great awareness and see clearly in all ten directions." When he washed his hands, he used this thought to place himself in mindfulness:

"Washing my hands, I hope that every person will have pure hands to receive Reality." The book is comprised only of sentences like that, the goal being to help the beginner practitioner take hold of his own consciousness. Zen Master Doc The helped all of us young novices to practise, in a relatively easy way, those things which are taught in the Sūtra of Mindfulness. Each time you put on your robe, wash the dishes, go to the bathroom, fold your mat, carry buckets of water, brush your teeth, etc., you could use one of the thoughts from the book in order to take hold of your own consciousness.

The Sūtra of Mindfulness says: "When walking, the practitioner must be conscious that he is walking, when sitting, the practitioner must be conscious that he is sitting, when lying down, the practitioner must be conscious that he is lying down ... No matter what position one's body is in, the practitioner must be conscious of that position. Practicing thus, the practitioner lives in direct and constant mindfulness of the body." The mindfulness of the positions of one's body is not enough, however. The Sūtra of Mindfulness says that we must be conscious of each breath, each movement, every thought and feeling—in short, everything which has any relation to ourselves.

But what is the purpose of the Sūtra's instruction? Where are we to find the time to practise such mindfulness? If a worker spends all day practising mindfulness, how will there ever be enough time to do all the work that needs to be done to change and build an alternative society? How does Steve manage to work, study Tony's lesson, take Zoe's diapers to the laundromat, and practise mindfulness at the same time?

The Miracle is to Walk on Earth

Steve said that since he's begun to consider Tony and Ann's time as his own, he has unlimited time. But perhaps he has it only in principle. There are doubtless times when Steve forgets to consider Tony's time as his own time while going over Tony's homework with him; and thus Steve may lose that time. Steve might hope for the time to pass quickly, or he may grow impatient because that time seems wasted to him, because it isn't his own time. And so, if he really wants "unlimited time" (which means more than just in principle), he will have to keep alive the thought 'this is my time' throughout the time he's studying with Tony. But during such times, one's mind is inevitably distracted by other thoughts, and so if one really wants to keep one's consciousness alive (from now on I'll use the term 'mindfulness' to refer to keeping one's consciousness alive to the present reality), then one must practise right now in one's daily life, as well as practise during meditation sessions.

When a worker walks along a red dirt path leading into a village, he can practise mindfulness. As he walks along the dirt path, surrounded by patches of green grass, if he practises mindfulness, he will know that he is walking along that path, the path leading into the village. He practises by keeping this one thought alive: 'I'm walking along the path leading into the village.' Whether it's sunny or rainy, whether the path is dry or wet, he keeps centered on that one thought. But he doesn't just repeat it like a machine, over and over again. Machine thinking is the opposite of mindfulness. There are some people who recite the name of the Buddha like a machine while in the meantime their mind scatters in a thousand different directions. I think that reciting the name of Buddha like that is worse than not reciting it at all. If we're really engaged in mindfulness while walking along the path to the village, then we will consider the act of each step we take as an infinite wonder, and a joy will open in our hearts like a flower, enabling us to enter the world of reality. I like to walk alone on country paths, rice plants and wild grasses on both sides, putting each foot down on the earth in mindfulness, knowing that I walk on the wondrous earth. In such moments, existence is a miraculous and mysterious reality. People usually consider walking on water or in thin air a miracle, but I think the real miracle is not to walk either on water or in thin air but to walk on earth. Everyday we are engaged in a miracle which we don't even recognize. Just think, Quang: a blue sky, white clouds, green leaves and the black, curious eyes of your little daughter Hai Trieu Am. Your two eyes, Quang, are also a miracle, like that sky, those clouds, those leaves and her young eyes.

Zen Master Doc The says that when sitting in meditation, one should sit upright, giving birth to this thought: "Sitting here is like sitting on the Bodhi spot". The Bodhi spot is the spot where Lord Buddha sat when he obtained Enlightenment. If any person can become a Buddha, and the Buddhas are without number, that means persons who have obtained enlightenment, who are Buddhas themselves, have sat on the very spot I sit on now. Sitting on the same spot as a Buddha gives rise to happiness; and sitting in mindfulness means itself to have become a potential Buddha. The poet Nguyen Cong Tru experienced the same thing when he sat down on a certain spot, and suddenly saw how others had sat on the same spot countless ages ago, and how in ages to come others will also come to sit there:

> On the same spot I sit today
> Others came, in ages past, to sit
> One thousand years, still others will come
> Who is the singer, and who the listener?

That spot and the minutes he spent there became a link in eternal reality.

But our workers do not have time to spend leisurely, walking along paths of green grass and sitting beneath trees. A worker must prepare projects, consult with the villagers, try to resolve a million difficulties that arise, work in the fields, and deal with every kind of hardship. During all that, the worker must keep his or her attention focused on the work, must be alert and ready to handle any situation ably and intelligently. You might well ask: "Then how are we workers to practise mindfulness?" My answer is to keep one's attention focused on the work, to be alert and ready to handle any situation which arises—this is mindfulness itself. There is no reason why mindfulness should be different from focusing all one's attention on one's work, and using one's best judgement. During the moment one is consulting, resolving and dealing with whatever arises, a calm heart and self-control are necessary if one is to obtain good results. Any worker can see that. If we are not in control of ourselves but instead let our impatience or anger interfere, then our work is no longer of any value.

Mindfulness is the miracle by which we master and restore ourselves.

Consider, for example, a magician who cuts his body into many parts and places each part in a different region—hands in the south, arms in the east, legs in the north, etc., and then by some miraculous power lets forth a cry which reassembles whole every part of his body. Mindfulness is like that—it is the miracle which can call back in a flash our dispersed mind and restore it to wholeness so that we can live each minute of life.

Taking Hold of One's Breath—Arriving at Mindfulness

Thus mindfulness is at the same time a means and an end, at the same time the seed and the fruit. When we practise mindfulness in order to build up concentration, mindfulness is a seed. But mindfulness itself is the life of awareness: the presence of mindfulness means the presence of life, and therefore mindfulness is also the fruit. Mindfulness frees us of forgetfulness and dispersion; mindfulness makes it possible to live each minute of life. Mindfulness enables us to live as fully as possible.

The worker should know how to breathe to maintain mindfulness, as breathing is a natural and extremely effective tool which can prevent dispersion. Breath is the bridge which connects life to consciousness, which unites one's body to one's thoughts. Whenever one's mind becomes scattered, the worker should use his breath in order to take hold of his mind again. Breathe in lightly a fairly long breath, Quang, conscious of the fact that you are inhaling a deep breath. Now breathe out all the breath in your lungs, remaining conscious the whole time of the exhalation. The Sūtra of Mindfulness teaches the method to take hold of one's breath in the following manner: Ever mindful he breathes in, and mindfully he breathes out.

Breathing in a long breath, he knows "I am breathing in a long breath," breathing out a long breath, he knows "I am breathing out a long breath," breathing in a short breath, he knows "I am breathing in a short breath," breathing out a short breath, he knows "I am breathing out a short breath." "Experiencing the whole (breath) body, I shall breathe in," thus he trains himself. "Experiencing the whole (breath) body, I shall breathe out," thus he trains himself. "Calming the activity of the (breath) body, I shall breathe in," thus he trains himself. "Calming the activity of the (breath) body, I shall breathe out," thus he trains himself.

In a Buddhist monastery, everyone learns to use his breath as a tool to stop dispersion and to build up concentration power. Concentration power is the strength which comes from practising mindfulness. It is concentration which can help one obtain the

Great Awakening. But the Great Awakening is also an awakening—when a worker takes hold of his own breath, he has already become awakened to that extent, and in order to maintain mindfulness throughout a long period, we must continue to watch our breath.

It is autumn here and the golden leaves falling one by one are truly beautiful. Taking a ten-minute walk in the woods, watching my breath and maintaining mindfulness, I feel refreshed and restored. Like that, I can really enter into a communion with each golden leaf. Walking alone on a country path, Quang, it is easier to maintain mindfulness if there's a friend by your side, not talking but also watching his breath, then you can continue to maintain mindfulness without difficulty. But if the friend at your side begins to ask you questions, it becomes a little more difficult.

If in your mind, you think, "I wish this fellow would quit asking questions, so I could concentrate," you have already lost your mindfulness, but if you can think, instead, "If he wishes to ask questions. I will answer, but I will continue in mindfulness, aware of the fact that we are walking along this path together, aware of the questions he asks and the answers I give. I can continue to watch my breath as well." If you can give rise to that thought, Quang, you will be continuing in mindfulness. It is harder to practise in such situations than when one is alone, but if you continue to practise nonetheless, you will develop the ability to maintain much greater concentration. There is a line from one of our folk songs that says: "Hardest of all is to practise the Way at home, second in the crowd, and third in the pagoda." It is only in an active and demanding situation that mindfulness really becomes a challenge!

Counting One's Breath and Following One's Breath

In the Sūtras, Buddha usually teaches that one should use one's breath in order to achieve concentration. There is one particular Sūtra which speaks about the use of one's breath to maintain mindfulness, and that is the Ānāpānasati Sutta. This Sūtra was translated and commentated on by a Vietnamese Zen Master of Central Asian originally named Khuong Tang Hoi, around the beginning of the third century C.E. *Ānāpāna* means in and out breath and *sati* means mindfulness. Tang Hoi translated it as 'Guarding the Mind.' The Ānāpānasati Sutta is the Sūtra on using one's breath to maintain mindfulness. The Discourse on Breath to Maintain Mindfulness is the 118th in the Majjhima Nikāya collection of Suttas and it teaches sixteen methods of using one's breath.

In the meditation sessions I conduct for non-Vietnamese, I usually suggest various methods that I myself have tried, methods that are quite simple. For example, I suggest to beginners the method of 'following the length of the breath.' I invite a student to lie down on his back and breathe normally. Then I invite all of the participants to gather around so I can show them a few simple points.

Although inhaling and exhaling are the work of the lungs, and take place in the chest area, the stomach area also plays a role. The stomach rises in conjunction with the filling of the lungs. You can see how at the beginning of the breath the stomach begins to push out. But after you've inhaled about two thirds of the breath, it starts to lower again. Why? Between your chest and stomach there is a muscular membrane called the diaphragm. When you breathe in correctly the air fills the lower part of the lungs first, before the upper lungs fill with air. When the lower lungs are filled with air, the diaphragm pushes down on the stomach, causing the stomach to rise. When you have filled your upper lungs with air, the chest pushes out and causes the stomach to lower again. That is why, in former times, people spoke of the breath as originating at the navel and terminating at the nostrils.

For beginners, lying down to practise breathing is very helpful. The important thing is to guard against making any kind of effort. Making too great of an effort could be dangerous for the lungs, especially in the case where the lungs are weak from lack of correct breathing. In the beginning, the practitioner should lie on his or her back on a thin mat or blanket, the two arms loosely at the sides. You should not prop your head on a pillow. Focus your attention on your exhalation and watch how long it is, you might measure it by slowly counting in your mind: 1, 2, 3. After several times, you will know the 'length' of your breath. Perhaps it is 5. Now try to extend the exhalation by one more count (or 2) so that the exhalation's length becomes 6 or 7. Begin to exhale counting from 1 to 5. When you reach 5, rather than immediately inhaling as before, try to extend the exhalation to 6 or 7. Like that, you will empty your lungs of more air. When you have finished exhaling, pause for an instant to let your lungs take in fresh air on their own. Let them take in just as much air as they want without making any effort. The inhalation will normally be shorter than the exhalation. Keep a steady count in your mind to measure the length of both. The beginner should practise several weeks like this, remaining mindful of all his exhalations and inhalations while lying down. (If you have a clock with a loud tick you can use it to help you keep track of the length of your inhalation and exhalation.) You should continue to measure your breath while walking, sitting, standing and especially whenever you are outdoors. If while walking, you can use your steps to measure your breath, it is a very good method.

After a month or so, the difference between the length of your exhalation and inhalation will lessen. Gradually they will even out until they are of equal measure. So if the length of your exhalation is 6, the inhalation will also be 6. If you feel at all tired while practising, stop at once. But even if you do not feel tired, you should not prolong the practice of long, equal breaths beyond short periods of time. For example, from 10 to 20 breaths is enough. As soon as you feel the least bit of fatigue, return your breath to normal. Fatigue is an excellent mechanism of our bodies and the best advisor as to whether we should rest or continue. In order to measure your breath you can count or you can use a rhythmic phrase that you like. For example, if the length of your breath is 6, instead of counting numbers you might use the 6 syllables of 'My heart is now at peace,' or 'My being is wondrous'; if the length is 7 you might use: 'I walk on the new green earth,' or 'Take refuge in the Buddha,' etc. When you are walking, each step should correspond to one syllable.

Your breath should be light, even, and flowing like a thin stream of water running through the sand. Your breath should be very quiet, so quiet that a person sitting next to you cannot hear it. Your breathing should flow gracefully like a river, like a water snake crossing the water, not like a chain of rugged mountains or the gallop of a horse. To master our breath is to be in control of our bodies and minds. Each time we find ourselves dispersed and find it difficult to gain control of ourselves by different means, the method of watching the breath should always be used. The instant the practitioner sits down to meditate, he should begin watching his breath. At first he should breathe normally, gradually letting his breathing slow down until it is quiet, even, and the length of the breaths is fairly long. From the moment he sits down to the moment his breathing has become deep and silent, the practitioner should be conscious of everything that is happening internally. As the Sutta on Mindfulness says:

> Breathing in a long breath, the practitioner knows, "I am breathing in a long breath," breathing out a long breath, he knows, "I am breathing out a long breath," breathing in a short breath, the practitioner knows "I am breathing in a short breath," breathing out a short breath, he knows "I am breathing out a short breath."
>
> "Experiencing the whole (breath) body, I shall breathe in," thus he trains himself. "Experiencing the whole (breath) body, I shall breathe out," thus he trains himself. "Calming the activity of the (breath) body, I shall breathe in," thus he trains himself. "Calming the activity of the (breath) body, I shall breathe out," thus he trains himself.

After about 10 to 20 minutes, the practitioner's thoughts will have quieted down like a pond on which not even a ripple stirs.

The method to make one's breath calm and even is called the method of following one's breath. If the method of following one's breath seems hard at first, one can substitute it by the method of counting one's breath. As you breathe in, count 1 in your mind, and as you breathe out count 1. Breathe in, count 2. Breathe out, count 2. Continue counting through to 10, then return to 1 again. This counting is like a string which attaches your mindfulness to your breath. This exercise is the starting point in the process of becoming continuously conscious of your breath. Without mindfulness, however, you will quickly lose count. When the count is lost, simply return to 1 and keep trying until you can keep the count correctly. Once you can truly focus your attention on the counts, you have reached the point at which you can begin to abandon the counting method and begin to concentrate solely on the breath itself.

In those moments when you are upset or dispersed and find it difficult to practise mindfulness, return to your breath. Taking hold of one's breath is itself mindfulness. Your breath is the wondrous method of taking hold of your consciousness. The seventh discipline of the Tiep Hien order is especially devoted to the use of the breath. One should not lose oneself in mind-dispersion or in one's surroundings. Learn to practise breathing in order to regain control of body and mind, to practise mindfulness and to develop concentration and wisdom.

Every Art is a Rite

I once heard a good simile, Quang, for one's breath. Suppose there is a towering wall from the top of which one can see vast distances, but there is no apparent means to climb it, only a thin piece of thread hanging over the top and coming down both sides. A person who is clever enough will tie a thicker string onto one end of the thread, walk over to the other side of the wall, then pull on the thread, pulling the string to the other side. Then he will tie the end of the string to a strong rope and pull the rope over. When the rope has reached the bottom of one side and is secured on the other side, the wall can be easily scaled.

Our breath is such a fragile piece of thread. Yet once we know how to use it, it can become a wondrous tool to help us surmount situations which would otherwise seem hopeless. Our breath is the bridge from our body to our mind, the element which reconciles our body and mind and which makes possible oneness of body and mind. Breath is aligned to both body and mind and it alone is the tool which can bring them both together, illuminating both and bringing both peace and calm.

There are a lot of people and quantities of books which discuss the immense benefits that result from correct breathing. They say that a person who knows how to breathe is a person who knows how to build up endless vitality: breath builds up the lungs, strengthens the blood and revitalizes every organ in the body. They say that proper breathing is more important than food. And all of these statements are correct.

You know, Quang, several years ago, I was extremely ill. After several years of taking medicine and undergoing medical treatment, my condition did not improve. So I turned to the method of breathing and, thanks to that, was able to heal myself.

What I wish to speak about, Quang, is how the breath is a tool and how the breath is itself mindfulness. The use of breath as a tool might help one obtain immense benefits but these cannot be considered as ends in themselves. These benefits are only the by-products of the realization of mindfulness.

In Paris I guide a small class in meditation for non-Vietnamese, among whom are many young people. I've told them: if you can meditate an hour each day, that's good, but it's nowhere near enough. You've got to practise meditation when you walk, stand, lie down, sit, and work. I've told them how to practise mindfulness while washing their hands, washing the dishes, sweeping the floor, talking to friends, or wherever they are. I said, "While washing the dishes, you might be thinking about the tea afterwards, and so try to get them out of the way as quickly as possible in order to sit and drink tea. But that means that you are incapable of living during the time you are washing the dishes. When you are washing the dishes, washing the dishes must be the most important thing in your life. Just as when you're drinking tea, drinking tea must be the most important thing in your life. When you're using the toilet, let that be the most important thing in your life, and so on." Chopping wood is meditation. Carrying water is meditation. The practitioner must be mindful all through the day, and certainly not just during the one hour allotted for formal meditation or reading scripture and reciting Sūtras. Each act must be carried out in mindfulness. Each act is a rite, a ceremony. Raising your cup of tea to your mouth is a rite. Perhaps the word 'rite' is a bit too solemn, but I use that word in order to jolt people into the realization of the life-and-death matter of awareness.

The Half-Smile

Every day and every hour, we should be practising mindfulness. That's easy to say, but to carry it out in practice is not. That's why I suggest to those who come to the meditation sessions that each person should reserve one day in the week to devote entirely to their practice of mindfulness. Although, in principle, every day should be that day, and every hour the hour of practice, the fact is that very few of us have yet reached such a point: we have the impression that our family, place of work and society rob us of all our time, and so I urge everyone to select a day each week as their own practice day. If it is Saturday, then Saturday must be entirely your day, a day during which you are completely the master. Then

Saturday will be the lever to hold on to in order to form the habit of practising mindfulness. Every worker in our community of service must also have the right to such a day, for if we do not, we will lose ourselves quickly in a life full of worry and action. Whatever the day chosen, it can be considered as the day of mindfulness.

If you want to set up a day of mindfulness, you should figure out a way to remind yourself at the moment of waking that this day is your day of mindfulness. You might hang something on the ceiling or on the wall, a paper with the word 'mindfulness' or a pine branch—anything that will suggest to you as you open your eyes and see it that today is your day of mindfulness.

Today is your day. Remembering that, you should smile a smile that affirms that you are in complete mindfulness, a smile that nourishes that perfect mindfulness.

While still lying in bed, begin to follow your breath—slow, long and conscious breaths. Then slowly rise from bed (instead of jumping out all at once as usual), and nourishing mindfulness by every motion. Once up, brush your teeth, wash your face, and do all your morning activities in a calm and relaxing way, each movement done in mindfulness. Follow your breath, take hold of it, and don't let your thoughts scatter. Each movement should be done relaxingly. Measure your steps with quiet, long breaths. Maintain a half-smile.

At the very least, you should spend a half hour taking a bath. Bathe relaxingly and mindfully so that by the time you have finished, you feel light and refreshed. Afterwards, you might do household work, such as washing clothes, dusting and wiping off the tables, scrubbing the kitchen floor, arranging books on their shelves. Whatever the tasks, they must be done slowly and with ease, and in mindfulness. In any case, don't do these tasks in order to get them over with. Resolve to do them relaxingly, with all your attention focused on them. Enjoy them, be one with them. If not, then the day of mindfulness will be of no value at all. The feeling that these tasks are a nuisance will soon disappear if they are done in mindfulness. Take the example of the Zen Masters: no matter what task or motion they undertake, they do it slowly and evenly, without reluctance.

For those who are just beginning to practise, it is best to maintain a spirit of silence throughout the day. That doesn't mean that on the day of mindfulness, you shouldn't speak at all. You can talk, you can even go ahead and sing, but if you talk or sing, do it in complete mindfulness of what you are saying or singing. And keep talking and singing to a minimum. Naturally, it is possible to sing and practise mindfulness at the same time, just as long as one is conscious of the fact that one is singing and aware of what one is singing. But one should be warned that it is much easier, when singing or talking, to stray from mindfulness if your meditation strength is still weak.

At lunchtime, prepare a meal for yourself. Cook the meal and wash the dishes in mindfulness. In the morning, after you have cleaned and straightened up your house, and in the afternoon, after you have worked in the garden or watched clouds or gathered flowers, prepare a pot of tea to sit and drink in mindfulness. Allow yourself a good length of time to do this. Don't drink your tea like someone who gulps down a cup of coffee during a work break. Drink your tea slowly and reverently as if it were the axis on which the earth revolves: slowly, evenly, without rushing towards the future. Live the actual moment. For only this actual moment is life. Don't be attached to the future. Don't worry about things you have to do. Don't think about getting up or taking off to do anything, don't think about 'departing.' Do you remember the lines in my poem "Butterfly Over the Field of Golden Mustard Flowers"?

> Be a bud sitting quietly in the hedge
> Be a smile, one part of wondrous existence
> Stand here. There is no need to depart.
> This homeland is as beautiful as the homeland of our childhood
> Do not harm it, please, and continue to sing...

In the evening, you might read scriptures and copy passages, write letters to friends, or do anything else you enjoy outside of your normal duties during the week. But whatever you do, do it in mindfulness. Eat only a little for the evening meal. Later, around 10 to 11 o'clock, when you sit in meditation, you will be able to sit more easily on an empty stomach. Afterwards you might take a slow walk in the fresh night air, following your breath in mindfulness and measuring the length of your breaths by your steps. Finally, return to your room and sleep in mindfulness.

Quang, somehow we must find a way to allow every social worker a day of mindfulness. Once a week, such a day is crucial. Its effect on the other days of the week is immeasurable. Ten years ago, thanks to such a day of mindfulness, Chu Van and our other sisters and brothers in the Tiep Hein order were able to guide themselves through many difficult times. After only three months of observing such a day of mindfulness once a week, I know that you will see a significant change in your life. The day of mindfulness will begin to penetrate the other days of the week, enabling you eventually to live seven days a week in mindfulness. I'm sure you agree with me on the importance of a weekly day of mindfulness!

Awakening in Plum Village

Our workers need not only one day out of the week, but they also need one month out of the year. I'm sure you remember the letter I wrote to Thay Chau Toan about the project for Plum Village. Plum Village was to be a spiritual home for social workers, just as Phuong Boi was a spiritual home for us in the past.

We need a Plum Village to return to after months of work, a place to plant vegetables, grow herbs, walk, play with the children who live in the village, and practise mindfulness and meditation. Thay Chau Toan had written to me about this project, suggesting the name 'School of Youth for Social Service Village.' He said that he hoped to find a spot in the highlands to build it where the climate might also be suitable for growing plums. Thus I suggested the name Plum Village, a prettier and lighter name for this spiritual homeland than the School of Youth for Social Service Village.

Because Thay Chau Toan was an artist, I anticipated the beauty of the village he would plan and build. I asked him to leave every rock he found in place, whether in the streams or on the hillsides, and to try to leave as many trees, large and small, as he could. The village was to have a community building, groves of trees and many paths for walking. And it was to have gardens of plum, from which it would take its name. You must be smiling at me, Quang, for living in the future, and I am, but I'm also living in the present. Here in France, I also grow several kinds of herbs. (Tuyet recently sent me several more seeds but I can only plant them once the warm weather returns.) So I have a kind of Plum Village already, and I know that Plum Village has also begun to exist in you.

Quang, you and our friends must go ahead with the project to build Plum Village. Plum Village will be a refreshing and warming image alive in our hearts. All the workers who get married and have children must also continue to return to Plum Village each year with their families. Plum Village will bring us together. We will take care of our village, organize activities for the children, and create an atmosphere of love and renewal for every person. Each worker, when she or he returns to the village, will feel immediately welcomed. During the month of retreat in Plum Village, a worker will be able to play with children (I'm sure the number of Hai Trieu Ams will be sizeable), read, sit in the sun, grow vegetables, meditate, unload oneself of the burdens of worries and anxieties that have built up, replacing them with understanding and love.

The Pebble

Why should a worker meditate? First of all, to be able to realize total rest. You know, Quang, even a night of sleep does not provide total rest. Twisting and turning, the facial muscles tense, all the while dreaming—this can hardly be considered rest. Nor is lying down rest, at least when you feel restless, you can twist and turn. Lying on your back, with your arms and legs straight but not stiff, your head unsupported by a pillow—this is a good position to practise breathing and to relax all the muscles, but this way it is also easier to fall asleep. You cannot meditate lying down as well as when you are sitting; moreover, it is possible to find total rest in a sitting position, and in turn to advance deeper in meditation in order to resolve the worries and troubles that upset and block your consciousness.

I know that among our workers there are many who can sit in the lotus position, the left foot placed on the right thigh and the right foot placed on the left thigh. Others can sit in the half lotus, the left foot placed on the right thigh, or the right foot placed on the left thigh. In our meditation class in Paris, there are people who do not feel comfortable in either of the above two positions and so I have shown them how to sit in the Japanese manner, the knees bent, resting on their two legs. By placing a pillow beneath one's feet, it is possible to sit that way for more than an hour and a half. Even so, anyone can learn to sit in the half lotus, though at the beginning it may be somewhat painful, but after a few weeks of practice, the position gradually becomes quite comfortable. During the initial period, when the pain is bothersome, alternate the position of the legs or change to another sitting position. If one sits in the lotus or half-lotus position, it is necessary to use a cushion to sit on so that both knees touch the floor. The three points of bodily contact with the ground created by this position provide an extremely stable position.

Keep your back straight. This is very important. The neck and head should be aligned with the spinal column; they should be straight but not stiff or wood-like. Keep your eyes focused about two metres in front of you. Maintain the half-smile.

Now begin to follow your breath and relax all of your muscles. Concentrate on keeping your spinal column straight and follow your breath. As for everything else, let it go. Let go of everything. If you want to relax the muscles in your face tightened by worry, fear or sadness, let the half-smile come to your face. As the half-smile appears, all the facial muscles begin to relax. The longer the half-smile is maintained, the better. It is the same smile you see on the face of the Buddha image.

Place your left hand, palm side up, in your right palm. Let all the muscles in your hands, fingers, arms and legs relax. Let go of everything, like the water plants which flow with the current, while beneath the surface of the water, the riverbed remains motionless. Hold on to nothing but your breath and the half-smile.

For beginners, it is better to sit no longer than 20 or 30 minutes. During that time, you must be able to obtain total rest. The technique for obtaining this rest lies in two things: watching and letting go, watching your breath and letting go of everything else. Release every muscle in your body. After about 15 minutes or so, it is possible to reach a deep quiet filled with inner peace and joy. Maintain this quiet and peace.

Some people look on meditation as a toil and want the time to pass quickly in order to rest afterwards. Such persons do not know how to sit yet. If you sit correctly, it is possible to find total relaxation and peace right in the position of sitting. Often

I suggest to such people that they meditate on the image of a pebble thrown into a river, in order to find joy and rest in the position of sitting.

How does one use the image of the pebble? Sit down in whatever position suits you best, the half lotus, or lotus, back straight, the half-smile on your face. Breathe slowly and deeply, following each breath, becoming one with the breath. Then let go of everything. Imagine yourself a pebble which has been thrown into a river. The pebble sinks through the water effortlessly. Detached from everything, it slowly sinks down by the shortest distance possible, finally reaching the bottom, the point of perfect rest. You, the practitioner, are like a pebble which has let itself fall into the river, letting go of everything else. At the centre of your being is your breath. You don't need to know the length of time it takes before reaching the point of complete rest on the bed of fine sand beneath the water. When you feel yourself as much at rest as a pebble which has reached the riverbed, that is the point you begin to find your own rest. You are no longer pushed or pulled by anything else. You know that if you cannot find joy and peace in these very moments of sitting, then the future itself will only flow by as a river flows by, you will not be able to hold it back, you will be incapable of living the future when it has become the present. Joy and peace are the joy and peace possible in this very hour of sitting. If you cannot find it here, you won't find it anywhere. Don't chase after your thoughts as a shadow follows its object. Don't run after your thoughts as a stolen soul runs after the magic amulet. Don't postpone it, but find joy and peace in this very moment.

This is your own time, this spot where you sit is your own spot. It is on this very spot and in this very moment that you can become a Buddha and certainly not beneath some bodhi tree off in some distant life. Practise like this for a few months, and you will begin to know what the Delight of Dhyāna is. Dhyāna Delight is the joy that one experiences while sitting in meditation. (Several years ago when we still had Phuong Boi, Thay Thanh Tu constructed a small meditation hut on the top of Phuong Boi's hill and named it the Hut of Dhyāna Delight.)

You know, the ease of sitting depends on whether one practises mindfulness a little or a lot each day, and it depends on whether or not one sits regularly. At Phap Van Pagoda we should organize an hour of sitting each night for the workers, say from 10 to 11. Whoever wishes could come and sit for a half hour, or if they like for the entire hour.

Recognition

Someone might well ask: Is relaxation then the only goal of meditation? In fact the goal of meditation goes much deeper than that. While relaxation is the necessary point of departure, once one has realized relaxation, it is possible to realize a tranquil heart and clear mind. To realize a tranquil heart and clear mind is to have gone far along the path of meditation.

We should remember that the mindfulness of one's breath is a wondrous method at all times. It isn't only a method for beginners. In the third century, Zen Master Tang Höi wrote in his commentary on the Ānāpānasati Sutta: "The mindfulness of one's breath is Buddha's great vehicle to save all beings caught in the cycle of birth and death." Measuring, following and taking hold of the breath are the wondrous methods to take hold of your own mind.

Of course, to take hold of our minds and calm our thoughts, we must also practise mindfulness of our feelings and perceptions. To take hold of your mind, you must practise mindfulness of the mind. You must know how to observe and recognize the presence of every feeling and thought which arises in you. Zen Master Thuong Chieu, near the end of the Ly dynasty, wrote: "If the practitioner knows his own mind clearly he will obtain results with little effort. But if he does not know anything about his own mind, all of his effort will be wasted." If you want to know your own mind, there is only one way: to observe and recognize everything about it. This must be done at all times, during your day to day life no less than during the hour of meditation.

During meditation, various feelings and thoughts may arise. If we do not practise mindfulness of the breath, these thoughts will soon lure us away from mindfulness. But the breath isn't simply a means by which to chase away such thoughts and feelings. Breath remains the vehicle to unite body and mind and to open the gate to wisdom. When a feeling or thought arises, one's intention should not be to chase it away, even if by continuing to concentrate on the breath the feeling or thought passes naturally from the mind.

The intention isn't to chase it away, hate it, worry about it or be frightened by it. So what exactly should one be doing concerning such thoughts and feelings? Simply acknowledge their presence. For example, when a feeling of sadness arises, immediately recognize it: "A feeling of sadness has just arisen in me." If the feeling of sadness continues, continue to recognize: "A feeling of sadness is still in me." If, for example, a thought like "It's late but the neighbours are sure making a lot of racket" appears, recognize that this thought has appeared. If the thought continues to exist, continue to recognize it. If a different feeling or thought arises, recognize it in like manner. The essential thing is not to let any feeling or thought arise without recognizing it in mindfulness, like a palace guard who is aware of every face that passes through the front corridor.

If there are no feelings or thoughts present, then recognize that there are no feelings of thoughts present. Practising like this is to be mindful of one's feelings and thoughts. By practising in this way, you will soon arrive at taking hold of your mind. One can join the method of mindfulness of the breath with the mindfulness of feelings and thoughts.

Deluded Mind Becomes True Mind

Quang, let me stress that while practising mindfulness, one should not be dominated by the distinction between good and evil, thus creating a battle within oneself. Whenever a wholesome thought arises, acknowledge it: "A wholesome thought has just arisen." And if an unwholesome thought arises, acknowledge it as well: "An unwholesome thought has just arisen." Don't dwell on it or try to get rid of it, even if you don't like it. To acknowledge it is enough. If you have departed, then you must know that you have departed, and if you are still there, you must know that you are still there. Once you have reached such an awareness, there will be nothing you need fear anymore.

When I mentioned the guard at the emperor's gate, Quang, you might have imagined a front corridor with two doors, one entrance and one exit, with your mind as the guard. Whatever feeling or thought enters, you are aware of its entrance, and when it leaves, you are aware of its exit. But the image has a shortcoming: the idea that those who enter and exit the corridor are different from the guard, whereas our thoughts and feelings are us, are a part of us. There is a temptation to look upon them, or at least some of them, as an enemy force which is trying to disturb and lay siege on the concentration and understanding of your mind, but in fact when we are angry, we ourselves are anger. When we are happy, we ourselves are happiness. When we have certain thoughts, we are those thoughts. We are both the guard and the visitor at the same time. We are both the mind and the observer of the mind. Therefore, chasing away or dwelling on any thought isn't the important thing. The important thing is to be aware of the thought. This observation is not an objectification of the mind: it does not establish distinction between subject and object. Mind does not grab on to mind, mind does not push mind away. Mind can only observe itself. This observation isn't an observation of some object outside and independent of the observer.

Remember the koan of Zen Master Bach An who asked: "What is the sound of one hand clapping?" Or take the example of the taste the tongue experiences: what separates taste and taste bud? The mind experiences itself directly within itself. This is of special importance, and so in the Sūtra of Mindfulness, the Buddha always uses the phrasing "mindfulness of feeling in feeling, mindfulness of mind in mind." Some people have said that the Buddha used this phrasing in order to put emphasis on such words as feeling and mind, but I don't think they have fully grasped the Buddha's intention. Mindfulness of feeling in feeling is mindfulness of feeling directly in feeling directly while experiencing feeling, and certainly not contemplation of some image of feeling which one creates to give feeling some objective, separate existence of its own outside of oneself. Mindfulness of mind in mind is the mind experiencing mindfulness of the mind in the mind. The objectivity of an outside observer to examine something is the method of science, but it is not the method of meditation. Therefore the image of the guard and the visitors entering and leaving the front corridor of mind fails to adequately illustrate the mindful observation of mind.

The mind is like a monkey swinging from branch to branch through a forest, says the Sūtra. In order not to lose sight of the monkey by some sudden movement, we must watch the monkey constantly. The Sūtra says to be one with it. Mind contemplating mind is like an object and its shadow—the object cannot shake the shadow off. The two are one. Wherever the mind goes, it still lies in the harness of the mind. The Sūtra sometimes uses the expression 'bind the monkey' to refer to taking hold of the mind, but the monkey image is only a means of expression. Once the mind is directly and continually aware of itself, it is no longer like a monkey. There are not two minds: one which swings from branch to branch and another which follows after to bind it with a piece of rope.

The person who practises meditation usually hopes to "see into his own nature," in order to obtain awakening. But if you are just beginning, don't wait to "see into your own nature." Better still, don't wait for anything. Especially don't wait to see the Buddha or any version of "ultimate reality" while you are sitting. In the first six months, try only to build up your power of concentration, to create an inner calmness and serene joy. The social worker must practise like that. You will shake off anxiety, enjoy total rest and quiet your mind. You will be refreshed and gain a broader, clearer view of things, and deepen and strengthen the love in yourself. Sitting in meditation is nourishment for your spirit and nourishment for your body, as well. Through sitting, our bodies obtain harmony, feel lighter and are more at peace. The path from the observation of your mind to seeing into your own nature won't be too rough. Once you are able to quiet your mind, once your feelings and thoughts no longer disturb you, at that point your mind will begin to dwell in mind. Your mind will take hold of mind in a direct and wondrous way which no longer differentiates between subject and object. Drinking a cup of tea, the seeming distinction between the one who drinks and the tea being drunk evaporates. Drinking a cup of tea becomes a direct and wondrous experience in which the distinction between subject and object no longer exists.

Dispersed mind is also mind, just as waves rippling in water are also water. When mind has taken hold of mind, deluded mind becomes True mind.

One Is All, All Is One

Quang, I'd like to devote a few lines here to talk about the methods a worker might use in order to arrive at liberation from narrow views, and to obtain the fearlessness and great compassion of the

Bodhisattvas. These are the contemplations on interdependence, impermanency and compassion.

While you sit in meditation, after having taken hold of your mind, you can direct your concentration to contemplate on the interdependent nature of certain objects. This meditation is not a discursive reflection on a philosophy of interdependence; rather, it is a penetration of mind into mind itself, using one's concentration power to cause the objects contemplated to reveal their real nature.

Those who have studied the teaching of Vijñānavāda know that the term *vijñāna* (consciousness) denotes both the subject and object of knowledge. The subject of knowledge cannot exist independently from the object of knowledge. To see is to see something, to hear is to hear something, to be angry is to be angry over something, to hope is hope for something, thinking is thinking about something, and so forth. When the object of knowledge (the something) is not present, there can be no subject of knowledge. The practitioner meditates on mind and, by so doing, is able to see the interdependence of the subject of knowledge and the object of knowledge. When we practise mindfulness of breath, then the knowledge of breath is mind; when we practise mindfulness of the body, then the knowledge of body is mind; when we practise mindfulness of objects outside ourselves, then the knowledge of these objects is also mind. Therefore the contemplation on the nature of interdependence of all objects is also the contemplation of the mind.

Every object of the mind is itself mind. In Buddhism, the objects of mind are called the dharmas. Dharmas are usually grouped into five categories:

1. bodily and physical forms,
2. feelings,
3. perceptions,
4. mental functionings, and
5. consciousness.

These five categories are called the five aggregates. The fifth category, consciousness, however, contains all the other categories and is the basis of their existence.

Contemplation on interdependence means looking deeply into all dharmas in order to pierce through to their real nature, in order to see them as parts of the great body of reality, and in order to see that the great body of reality is indivisible. It cannot be cut into pieces with separate existences of their own.

The first object of contemplation is our own person, the assembly of the five aggregates in ourselves. The practitioner contemplates on the five aggregates which makes up the person.

In his or her own body the practitioner is conscious of the presence of bodily form, feeling, perception, mental functionings and consciousness. He observes these 'objects' until he sees that each of them has intimate connection with the world outside himself: if the world did not exist, then the assembly of the five aggregates could not exist either. Consider the example of a table. The table's existence is possible due to the existence of things which we might call the 'non-table world': the forest where the wood grew and was cut, the carpenter, the iron ore which became the nails and screws, and countless other things which have relation to the table, from the parents and ancestors of the carpenter, to the sun and rain which made it possible for the trees to grow. If we grasp the table's reality, then we see that in the table itself are present all those things which we normally think of as the non-table world. If you took away any of those non-table elements and returned them to their sources—the nails back to the iron ore, the wood to the forest, the carpenter to his parents—the table would then no longer exist.

A person who looks at the table and can see the universe is a person who can see the Way. The practitioner meditates on the assembly of the five aggregates in him- or herself in the same manner. He meditates on them until he is able to see their presence in himself, and can see that his own life and the life of the universe are closely interrelated. If the five aggregates return to their sources, the self no longer exists. Each second, the world nourishes the five aggregates. The self is no different from the assembly of the five aggregates themselves. In addition, the assembly of the five aggregates plays a crucial role in the formation, creation and destruction of all things in the universe.

Liberation from Suffering

People normally cut reality into sections and divide it into compartments, and so are unable to see the interdependence of all phenomena. To see one in all and all in one is to break through the great barrier which narrows one's perception of reality, a barrier which Buddhism calls the attachment to the false view of self. Attachment to the false view of self means belief in the presence of unchanging entities which exist on their own. To break through this false view is to be liberated from every sort of fear, pain and anxiety. The Prajñāpāramitā Hṛdaya Sūtra says that when the Bodhisattva Quan-The-Am saw into the reality of the five aggregates giving rise to emptiness of self, he was liberated from every suffering, pain, doubt and anger. The same applies to you, Quang, to me and to all the workers. If we contemplate the five aggregates in a stubborn and diligent way, we too will be liberated from suffering, fear and dread. The Bodhisattva Avalokita is recognized as the one who offers the gift of fearlessness to others. The nature of this gift should not be foreign to us. It is realized through contemplation of the interdependent nature of the five aggregates. We must realize, however, that if the giver gives with all his or her heart, the receiver must also receive with all his or her heart. Only thus can the gift be received.

The practitioner must strip away all the barriers in order to live as part of the universal life. A person is not some private entity travelling unaffected through time and space as if sealed off from the rest of the world by some thick shell. Living for 100 or for 100,000 lives sealed off like that, not only isn't living, but it isn't also possible. In our lives are present a multitude of phenomena, just as we ourselves are present in many different phenomena. We are life, and life is without limits. Perhaps one can say that we are only alive when we live the life of the world, and so live the sufferings and joys of others. The suffering of others is our own suffering, and the happiness of others is our own happiness. If our lives have no limits, the assembly of the five aggregates which makes up our self also has no limits. The impermanent character of the universe, the successes and failures of life can no longer manipulate us. Having seen the reality of interdependence and penetrated deeply into its reality, nothing can oppress you any longer.

The meditation on interdependence is to be practised constantly. We might naturally devote time to meditate on it while sitting, but it must become an integral part of our involvement in all ordinary tasks. We must be able to see that the person in front of us as oneself and that we are that person. We must be able to see the process of inter-origination and interdependence of all events, both those which are happening and those which will happen.

A Ride on the Waves of Birth and Death

Quang, if I talk to the workers, I cannot leave out the problem of life and death. Serving in a situation like Vietnam right now, we encounter death daily. How many of our brothers and sisters have already given their lives? Lien, Vui, Tuan, Tho, Lanh, Mai, Hung, Hy, Toan, and our eight brothers who were kidnapped nine years ago. While working in the fire zones, while burying the bodies of children and adults, it is impossible to ignore death.

Many young people and many monks and nuns have come out to serve, through their love for those who are suffering. They are always mindful of the fact that the most important question in Buddhism is the question of life and death. Once having realized that life and death are but two faces of one reality, we will have the courage to encounter both of them. When I was only 19 years old, I found the meditation on the corpse in the cemetery, a meditation to which I was assigned, very hard to take, and I resisted meditating on it, but now I no longer feel that way. I thought that such a meditation should be reserved for older monks, say 35 or 40. Since then, I have seen many young soldiers lying motionless beside one another, some only 13, 14 and 15 years old. They had no preparation, no readiness for death. Now I see that if one doesn't know how to die, one can hardly know how to live. Because death is a part of life. Just two days ago, Quynh Hoa told me that she thought at 20 one was old enough to contemplate on the corpse. Quynh Hoa is able to say that because she has only turned 21 herself. We must look death in the face, recognize and accept it, just as we look at and accept life.

The Sūtra on Mindfulness speaks about the meditation on the corpse: meditate on the decomposition of the body; how the body bloats and turns violet; how it is eaten by worms until only bits of blood and flesh still cling to the bones; meditate up to the point where only white bones remain which in turn are slowly worn away and turn into dust. Meditate like that, knowing that your own body will undergo exactly the same process. Meditate on the corpse until you are calm and at peace, until your mind and heart are light and tranquil and a smile appears on your face. Thus, overcoming revulsion and fear, life will be seen as infinitely precious, every second of it worth living. And it is not just our own lives that are recognized as precious, but the lives of every other person, every other being, every other reality. We can no longer be deluded by the notion that the destruction of others' lives is necessary for our own survival. We see that life and death are but two faces of life and that without both, life is not possible, just as two sides of a coin are needed for the coin to exist. Only now is it possible to rise above birth and death, and to know how to live and how to die. The Sūtra says that the Bodhisattvas who have seen into the reality of interdependence have broken through all narrow views, and have been able to enter birth and death as a person takes a ride in a small boat without being submerged or drowned by the waves of birth and death.

Quang, some people have said that if you look at reality with the eyes of Buddhist, you become pessimistic, but to think in terms of either pessimism or optimism oversimplifies the truth. It is about seeing reality as it is. A pessimistic attitude can never create the calm and serene smile which blossoms on the lips of the Bodhisattvas and all others who follow the Way.

The Sound of the Rising Tide

When your mind is liberated, your heart floods with compassion. Compassion for yourself, for having undergone countless sufferings because you were not yet able to relieve yourself of false views, hatred, ignorance, and anger; and compassion for others because they do not yet see and so are still imprisoned by false views, hatred and ignorance, and continue to create suffering for themselves and for others. Now you know how to look at yourself and at others with the eyes of compassion, "Look at every being with the eyes of compassion."

Practise looking at all beings with the eyes of compassion: this is the meditation called 'the meditation on compassion.'

The meditation of compassion must be realized during the hours you sit and during every moment you carry out service for others. No matter where you go, where you sit, remember the call of the Bodhisattva Quan-The-Am in the Lotus Sūtra (*Saddharma Puṇḍarika*): "Look at all beings with the eyes of compassion."

Quang, there are many subjects and methods for meditation, so many that I could never hope to write them all down for our friends. I've only mentioned a few, simple but basic methods here. A social worker is like any other person. She or he must live her own life. Work is only a part of life, and work is life only when done in mindfulness. Otherwise, one becomes like the person 'who lives as though he were dead.' Each of us needs to light his own torch in order to carry on, but the life of each one of us is connected with the life of those around us. If we know how to live in mindfulness, if we know how to preserve and care for our own mind and heart, then thanks to that, our brothers and sisters will also know how to live in mindfulness.

Meditation Reveals and Heals

When we sit in mindfulness both our body and mind can be at peace and total relaxation, and this state of peace and relaxation differs fundamentally from the lazy, semi-conscious state of mind that one gets while resting and dozing, which is like sitting in a dark cave, far from being mindful. In mindfulness we are not only restful and happy, but also alert and awake. Meditation is not evasion; it is a serene encounter with reality. The person who practises mindfulness should be as awake as the driver of a car: if he is not awake he will be possessed by dispersion and forgetfulness, just as the driver who is not awake could easily cause a grave accident. You should be as awake as a person who walks on high stilts—any misstep could fling him to his death. You should be like a medieval knight walking weaponless in a forest of swords, or like a lion, going forward in slow, gentle and firm steps. Only with this kind of vigilance can you realize total Awakening.

For beginners, the method of pure recognition is recommended. I have said that this recognition should be done without judgement: both feelings of compassion and irritation should be welcomed, recognized and treated on a absolutely equal basis, because both are us.

When we are possessed by a sadness, an anxiety, a hatred, or a passion, or whatever, we may find the method of pure observation and recognition difficult to practise, in which case it is helpful to turn to the method of Meditation on a Fixed Object, using our very state of mind as the subject of meditation, as this meditation reveals and heals. The sadness or anxiety, hatred, or passion, under the gaze of our concentration and meditation, reveals its own nature. That revelation leads naturally to healing and emancipation. The sadness, or whatever, having been the cause of pain, can be used as a means of liberation from torment and suffering. We call this using a thorn to remove a thorn. We should treat our anxiety, our pain, our hatred and passion gently, respectfully, not resisting it, but living with it, making peace with it, penetrating into its nature by the meditation on interdependence. A thoughtful practitioner knows how to select subjects of meditation that fit the situation. Subjects of meditation like interdependence, compassion, self, emptiness, non-attachment, all these belong to the categories of meditation which have the power to reveal and to heal.

Meditation on these subjects, however, can only be successful if we have a certain power of concentration. We get this power of concentration by the practice of mindfulness in everyday life, by the observation and recognition of all that is going on. The object of meditation should be a reality that has real roots in yourselves; it can't be just a subject for philosophical speculation. It should be like a kind of food that must be cooked for a long time over a hot fire. We put it in a pot, cover it, and light the fire. The pot is ourselves and the heat used to cook is the power of concentration. The fuel comes from the continuous practice of mindfulness. Without enough heat the food will never be cooked, but once cooked, the food reveals its true nature and helps lead us to liberation.

The Water is Clearer, the Grass is Greener

Quang, the Buddha once said that the problem of life and death is itself the problem of mindfulness. Whether or not one is alive depends on whether one is mindful. In a Saṃyutta Nikāya Sūtra (47.20), he tells a story which took place in one village: a famous dancer had just come to the village and the people were swarming the streets to catch a glimpse of her. At that same moment, a condemned criminal was obliged to cross the village carrying a bowl of oil filled to the very brim. He must concentrate all his might on keeping the bowl steady; for if even one drop of oil were to spill from the bowl to the ground, the soldier directly behind him had orders to whip his sword out and cut off the man's head. Having reached this point in the story, Gotama asked: "Now, brothers, do you think our prisoner was able to keep all his attention so focused on the bowl of oil that his mind did not stray to steal a glimpse of the famous dancer in town, or to look up at the throngs of villagers making such a commotion in the streets, any of whom could bump into him at any moment?"

Another time the Buddha recounted the following story, which made me suddenly see the supreme importance of practising mindfulness by one's own self, that is, to protect and care for one's self, not worrying about the way another looks after himself, a habit of mind which gives rise to resentment and anxiety. The Buddha said,

> "There once was a couple of acrobats. The teacher was a poor widower and the student was a small girl, named Medakathālikā. The two of them performed in the streets in order to earn enough to eat. They used a tall bamboo pole which the teacher balanced on the top of his head while the little girl slowly climbed to the top. There she remained balanced while the teacher continued to walk along the ground.
>
> "Both of them had to devote all their attention to maintain perfect balance and to prevent any accident from occurring. One day the teacher instructed the pupil: 'Listen, Medakathālikā, I will watch you and you watch me, in order for us to help each other maintain concentration and balance so that no accident will occur. That way we will be sure to earn enough to eat.' But the little girl was very wise and answered, 'Dear Master, I think that it would be more correct to say that each of us must watch himself. To look after oneself means to look after both of us. That way I am sure we will avoid any accidents and will earn enough to eat.' The Buddha said: 'The child spoke correctly.'" (Saṃyutta Nikāya Sutta 47-19).

In a family, if there is one person who practises mindfulness, the entire family will be able to do likewise thanks to that one person. Because of the presence of one member who lives in mindfulness, the entire family will be reminded to live in mindfulness. If in one class, one student lives in mindfulness, the entire class will be influenced, thanks to the constant reminder of that one student. The presence of such a person can be considered as the presence of a Buddha.

In the School of Youth family, we must follow that principle. Don't worry that those around you aren't doing their best. Only worry about how to make yourself worthy. If you do your best, that is the surest way to remind those around you to do their best. If we want to be worthy, we must practise mindfulness. That is a certainty. Only by practising mindfulness will we not lose ourselves and will acquire a bright joy and peace. Only by practising mindfulness will we be able to look at every one else with the open mind and eyes of love.

I was just invited downstairs for a cup of tea, into an apartment where a friend who helps us has a piano, to wet my throat before coming back upstairs to continue writing. As Kirsten poured the tea for me, I looked at her pile of work and said, "Why don't you stop translating orphan applications for a minute and play the piano for me?" Kirsten was glad to put down her work for a moment and sat down at the piano to play a selection of Chopin she has known since she was a child. The piece has several measures which are soft and melodic but others which are loud and quick. Her pet dog was lying beneath the tea table and when the music became excited, it began to bark and whine. I knew that it felt uneasy and wanted the music to stop. Kirsten's dog is treated with the kindness one treats a small child, and perhaps it is much more sensitive to music than most ordinary children. Perhaps it is because its ears can pick up certain vibrations that human ears cannot. Kirsten continued to play while trying to console the dog at the same time, but it continued to bark and protest. She finished the piece and began to play another one by Mozart which was light and harmonious. During this piece, the dog lay quietly and appeared to be content and at peace. When Kirsten finished, she came over and sat down beside me and said, "Often when I play a piece of Chopin that is the least bit loud, the dog comes and grabs hold of my pants trying to force me to leave the piano. Sometimes I have to put it outside before I can continue playing. But whenever I play Bach or Mozart, it lies quietly and content."

Kirsten read somewhere that in Canada people experimented with playing Mozart for their plants during the night and these plants grew quicker than normal, and the flowers inclined towards the direction the Mozart was played from. Others played several tracks of Mozart every day in wheat and rye fields and these fields grew quicker than in other fields where no music was played.

As Kirsten spoke, I thought about conference rooms where people argue and debate with each other, where angry and reproachful words are thrown back and forth. If one placed flowers and plants in such rooms, chances are they would not continue growing if the angry words continued to fly day after day.

I thought about the garden tended by a monk living in mindfulness. His flowers are fresh and green, nourished by the peace and joy which emanate from his mindfulness. One of the ancients said, "When a great Master is born, the water in the rivers turns clearer and the plants grow greener." At the beginning of any gathering to study or discuss our work, we ought to listen to music or sit and practise breathing, don't you think, Quang?

Three Wondrous Answers

To end this letter, I'd like to retell a short story of Tolstoy's which you and our friends in the School will enjoy. It is the story of the emperor's three questions. (Tolstoy did not know the emperor's name.) One day it occurred to a certain emperor that if he only knew the answers to the following three questions, he would never stray in any matter, and these questions were:

> What is the most opportune time to do each thing?
> Who are the most important people to work with?
> What is the most important thing to do at all times?

The emperor issued a decree throughout his kingdom announcing that whoever could answer these three questions would receive a great reward. Many who read the decree made their way to the palace at once. Each person had a different answer to offer the emperor.

In reply to the first question, one person advised that the emperor make up a thorough time schedule, consecrating every hour, day, month and year for certain tasks and then follow the schedule to the letter. Only then could he hope to do every task at the right time. Another person replied that it was impossible to plan in advance and that the emperor should put all vain amusements aside and remain attentive to everything in order to know what to do at what time. Someone else insisted that, by himself, the emperor could never hope to have all the foresight and competence necessary to decide when to do each and every task and what he really needed was to set up a 'Council of Wise Men' and then to act according to their counsel.

Yet someone else said that certain matters require immediate decision and could not wait for consultation, but if he wanted to know in advance what was going to happen he should consult magicians and soothsayers.

The responses to the second question also lacked accord. One person said that the emperor needed to place all his trust in administrators, another urged reliance on priests and monks, while others recommended physicians. Still others put their faith in warriors.

The third question drew a similar variety of answers. Some said science was the most important pursuit. Others insisted on religion. Yet others claimed the most important thing was military skill.

Because all the answers were different from one another, the emperor was not pleased with any of them and no reward was given.

After several nights of reflection, the emperor resolved to visit a hermit who lived up on the mountain and was said to be an enlightened man. The emperor wished to find the hermit to ask him the three questions, though he knew the hermit never left the mountain and was known to receive only the poor, refusing to have anything to do with persons of wealth or power. So the emperor disguised himself as a simple peasant and ordered his attendants to wait for him at the foot of the mountain while he climbed the slope alone to seek the hermit.

Reaching the holy man's dwelling place, the emperor found the hermit digging a garden in front of his small hut. When the hermit saw the stranger, he nodded his head in greeting and continued to dig. The labour was obviously hard on him for he was an old man, and each time he thrust his spade into the ground to turn the earth, he heaved heavily.

The emperor approached him and said, "I have come here in order to ask your help with three questions: When is the most opportune time to do each thing? Who are the most important people to work with? What is the most important thing to do at all times?"

The hermit listened attentively but did not reply. He only patted the emperor on the shoulder and then continued digging. The emperor said, "You must be tired. Let me give you a hand with that." The hermit thanked him and handed the emperor the spade and then sat down on the ground to rest.

After he had dug two beds, the emperor stopped and turned to the hermit and repeated his three questions. The hermit still did not answer, but instead stood up and pointed to the spade and said, "Why don't you rest now? I can take over again." But the emperor did not hand him the spade and continued to dig. One hour passed, then two hours. Finally the sun began to set behind the mountain. The emperor put down the spade and said to the hermit, "I came here to ask if you could answer my three questions, but if you can't give me any answer, please let me know so that I can get on my way home."

The hermit lifted his head and asked the emperor, "Do you hear someone running over there?" The emperor turned his head and suddenly they both saw a man with a long white beard emerge from the woods. He ran wildly, pressing his hands against a bloody wound in his stomach. The man ran towards the emperor before falling unconscious to the ground, where he lay groaning. Opening the man's clothing, the emperor and hermit saw that the man had received a deep gash. The emperor cleaned the wound thoroughly and then used his own shirt to bandage it, but the blood completely soaked it within minutes. He rinsed the shirt out and bandaged the wound a second time and continued to do so until the flow of blood had stopped.

The wounded man regained consciousness and asked for a drink of water. The emperor ran down to the stream and brought back a jug of fresh water. Meanwhile, the sun had disappeared and the night air had begun to turn cold. The hermit gave the emperor a hand in carrying the man into the hut where they lay him down on the hermit's bed. The man closed his eyes and lay quietly. The emperor was worn out from a long day of climbing the mountain and digging the garden. Leaning against the doorway, he fell asleep. When he woke up, the sun had already risen over the mountain. For a moment he forgot where he was and what he had come here for. He looked over to the bed and saw the wounded man also looking around him in confusion. When he saw the emperor, he stared at him intently and then said in a faint whisper, "Please forgive me."

"But what have you done that I should forgive you?" the emperor asked.

"You do not know me, your Majesty, but I know you. I was your sworn enemy, and I had vowed to take vengeance on you, for during the last war you killed my brother and seized my property. When I learned that you were coming alone to the mountain to meet the hermit, I resolved to surprise you on your way back and kill you. But after waiting a long time there was still no sign of you, and so I left my ambush in order seek you out, but instead of finding you, I came across your attendants who recognized me and grabbed me, giving me this wound. Luckily, I escaped their hold and ran up here. If I hadn't met you I would surely be dead by now. I had intended to kill you, but instead you saved my life! I am ashamed and grateful beyond words. If I live, I vow to be your servant for the rest of my life, and I will bid my children and grandchildren to do the same. Please grant me your forgiveness, your Majesty."

The emperor was overjoyed to see that he was so easily reconciled with a former enemy. He not only forgave the man but promised to return all the man's property and to send his own physician and servants to wait on the man until he was completely healed. After ordering his attendants to take the man home, the emperor turned to see the hermit. Before returning to the palace the emperor wanted to repeat his three questions one last time. He found the hermit sowing seeds in the earth they had dug the day before.

The hermit stood up and looked at the emperor, "Your questions have already been answered."

"How's that?" the emperor asked, puzzled.

"Yesterday, if your Majesty had not taken pity on my age and given me a hand with digging these beds, you would have been attacked by that man on your way home. Then you would have sorely regretted not staying with me. Therefore the most important time was the time you were digging the beds, the most important person was myself, and the most important pursuit was to help me. Later when the wounded man ran up here, the most important time was the time you spent dressing his wound, for if you had not cared for him he would have died and you would have lost the chance to be reconciled with him. Likewise, he was the most important person, and the most important pursuit was taking care of his wound Remember that there is only one important time and that is Now. The present moment is the only time over which we have dominion. The most important person is always the person with whom you are, who is right before you, for who knows if you will have dealings with any other person in the future. The most important pursuit is making that person, the one standing at your side, happy, for that alone is the pursuit of life."

Quang, Tolstoy's story is like a story out of a Buddhist scripture: it doesn't fall short of any Sūtra. We talk about social service, service to the people, service of humanity, service for others who are far away—but often we forget that it is the very people around us that we must live for first of all. If you cannot serve your wife, Muoi, and little Hai Trieu Am, how are you going to serve society? If you cannot make Hai Trieu Am happy, how do you expect to be able to make anyone else happy? If all our friends in the School of Youth do not love and help one another, whom can we love and help? Are we working for other humans, or are we just working for the name of our organization?

Social service. The word 'service' is so immense and the word 'social' is just as immense. Let's return first of all to a more modest scale: our families, our classmates, our friends, our own community. We must live for them, for if we cannot live for them, who else do we think we are living for?

Tolstoy is a Bodhisattva. But was the emperor himself able to see the meaning and direction of life? How can we live the present moment, live right now with the people around us, helping to lessen their suffering and making their lives happier? How? The answer, Quang, is this: We must practise mindfulness. The principle that Tolstoy gives appears easy; but if we want to put it into practice we must use the methods of mindfulness in order to seek and find the Way of the Buddha. Quang, I've written these pages for our friends to use. There are many people who have written about these things without having lived them, but I've only written down those things which I have lived and experienced myself. I hope you and our friends will find these things at least a little helpful along the path of our seeking: the path of our return.

Alkmaar, February 1975

Thirty Exercises to Practise Mindfulness

Note: Here are a number of exercises and methods in meditation which I have often used, adapting them from various methods to fit my own circumstances and preferences. Select the ones you like best and find the most suitable ones for you. The value of each method will vary according to each person's unique needs. Although these exercises are all relatively easy, they form the foundations on which everything else is built.

1. The Half-Smile

a) *Half-smile when you first wake up in the morning:* Hang a branch or any other sign, or even the word 'smile' on the ceiling or wall so that you see it right away when you open your eyes. This sign will serve as your reminder. Use these seconds before you get out of bed to take hold of your breath. Inhale and exhale three breaths gently while maintaining the half-smile. Follow your breaths.

b) *Half-smile during your free moments:* While in a waiting room, or on a bus, standing in line at the post office, or anywhere you find yourself sitting or standing, half-smile. Look at a child, a leaf, a painting on the wall, anything which is relatively still, and smile. Inhale and exhale quietly three times. Maintain the half-smile and consider the spot of attention as your own true nature.

c) *Half-smile while listening to music:* Listen to a piece of music for two or three minutes. Pay attention to the words, music, rhythm and sentiments. Smile while watching your inhalations and exhalations.

d) *Half-smile when irritated:* When you realize you are irritated, half-smile at once. Inhale and exhale quietly, maintaining the half-smile for three breaths.

2. Letting Go/Relaxation

a) *Letting go in a lying down position:* Lie on your back on a flat surface without the support of mattress or pillow. Keep your two arms loosely by your sides and your two legs slightly apart, stretched out before you. Maintain a half-smile. Breathe in and out gently, keeping your attention focused on your breath. Let go of every muscle in your body. Relax each muscle as though it were sinking, down through the floor or as though it were as soft and yielding as a piece of silk hanging in the breeze to dry. Let go entirely, keeping your attention only on your breath and half-smile. Think of yourself as a cat, completely relaxed before a warm fire, whose muscles yield without resistance to anyone's touch. Continue for 15 breaths.

b) *Letting go in the sitting position:* Sit in the half or full lotus, or cross-legged, or your two legs folded beneath you, or even on a chair, your two feet touching the floor. Half-smile. Let go as in 2a.

3. Breathing

a) *Deep breathing:* Lie on your back (as in 2a). Breathe evenly and gently, focusing your attention on the movement of your stomach. As you begin to breathe in, allow your stomach to rise in order to bring air into the lower half of the lungs. As the upper halves of your lungs begin to fill with air, your chest begins to rise and your stomach begins to lower. Don't tire yourself. Continue for 10 breaths. The exhalation will be longer than the inhalation.

b) *Measuring your breath by your footsteps:* Walk slowly and leisurely in a garden, along a river or on a village path. Breathe normally. Determine the length of your breath, the exhalation and the inhalation, by the number of your footsteps. Continue for a few minutes. Begin to lengthen your exhalation by one step. Do not force a longer inhalation. Let it be natural. Watch your inhalation carefully to see if there is a desire to lengthen it. Continue for 10 breaths.

Now lengthen the exhalation by one more footstep. Watch to see whether the inhalation also lengthens by one step or not. Only lengthen the inhalation when you feel that it will give delight. After 10 breaths return to your normal pattern of breathing. About 5 minutes later, you can begin the practice of lengthened breaths again. When you feel the least bit tired, return to normal breathing.

After several sessions of the practice of lengthening the breath, your exhalation and inhalation will grow equal in length. Do not practise long, equal breaths for more than 10 to 20 breaths before returning to normal breathing.

c) *Counting your breath:* Sit in the half or full lotus or take a walk. As you inhale, be mindful that "I am inhaling, one." When you exhale, be mindful that "I am exhaling, one." Remember to breathe from the stomach (3a). When beginning the second inhalation, be mindful that "I am inhaling, two." And slowly exhaling, be mindful that "I am exhaling, two." Continue one up through 10. After you have reached 10, return to one. Whenever you lose count, return to one.

d) *Following your breath while listening to music:* Listen to a piece of music. Breathe long, light and even breaths. Follow your breath, be master of it while remaining aware of the movement and sentiments of the music. Do not get lost in the music, but continue to be master of your breath and yourself.

e) *Follow your breath while having a conversation:* Breathe long, light and even breaths. Follow your breath while listening to a friend's words and to your own replies. Continue as in 3d.

f) *Following the breath:* Sit in a full or half lotus or go for a walk. Begin to inhale gently and normally (from the stomach), mindful that "I am inhaling normally." Exhale in mindfulness, "I am exhaling normally." Continue for three breaths. On the fourth breath extend the inhalation, mindful that "I am breathing in a long inhalation." Exhale in mindfulness, "I am breathing out a long exhalation." Continue for three breaths.

Now follow your breath carefully, aware of every movement of your stomach and lungs. Follow the entrance and exit of air. Be mindful that "I am inhaling and following the inhalation from its beginning to its end. I am exhaling and following the exhalation from its beginning to its end."

Continue for 20 breaths. Return to normal. After five minutes, repeat the exercise. Remember to maintain the half-smile while breathing. Once you have mastered this exercise, move on to 3g.

g) *Breathing to quiet the mind and body to realize joy:* Sit in the full or half lotus. Half-smile. Follow your breath (3d). When your mind and body are quiet, continue to inhale and exhale very lightly, mindful that "I am breathing in and making the breath-body light and peaceful. I am exhaling and making the breath-body light and peaceful." Continue for three breaths, giving rise to the thought in mindfulness, "I am breathing in and making my entire body light and peaceful and joyous." Continue for three breaths and in mindfulness give rise to the thought, "I am breathing in while my body and mind are peace and joy. I am breathing out while my body and mind are peace and joy."

Maintain this thought in mindfulness from 5 to 30 minutes, or for an hour, according to your ability and to the time available to you. The beginning and end of the practice should be relaxed and gentle. When you want to stop, gently massage your eyes and face with your two hands and then massage the muscles in your legs before returning to a normal sitting position. Wait a moment before standing up.

4. Mindfulness of the Position and Movements of the Body

a) *Mindfulness of the positions of the body:* This can be practised at any time and place. Begin to focus your attention on your breath. Breathe quietly and more deeply than usual. Be mindful of the position of your body, whether you are walking, standing, lying or sitting down. Know where you walk; where you stand; where you lie; where you sit. Be mindful of the purpose of your position. For example, you might be conscious that you are standing on a green hillside in order to refresh yourself, to practise breathing or just to stand. If there is no purpose, be mindful that there is no purpose.

b) *Mindfulness of the preparation of tea:* Prepare a pot of tea to serve a guest or to drink by yourself. Do each movement slowly, in mindfulness. Do not let one detail of your movements go by without being mindful of it. Know that your hand lifts the pot by its handle. Know that you are pouring the fragrant warm tea into the cup. Follow each step in mindfulness. Breathe gently and more deeply than usual.

Take hold of your breath if your mind strays.

c) *Mindfulness while washing the dishes:* Wash the dishes relaxingly as though each bowl is an object of contemplation. Consider each bowl as True-Reality. Follow your breath to prevent your mind from straying. Do not try to hurry to get the job over with. Consider washing the dishes the most important thing in life. Washing the dishes is meditation. If you cannot wash the dishes in mindfulness, neither can you meditate while sitting in silence.

d) *Mindfulness while washing clothes:* Do not wash too many clothes at one time. Select only three or four articles of clothing to wash at any one time. Find the most comfortable position to sit or stand so as to prevent a backache. Scrub the clothes relaxingly. Hold your attention on every movement of your hands and arms. Pay attention to the soap and water. When you have finished scrubbing and rinsing, your mind and body should feel as clean and fresh as your clothes. Remember to maintain the half-smile and take hold of your breath whenever your mind wanders.

e) *Mindfulness while cleaning house:* Divide your work into stages: straightening things and putting away books, etc., scrubbing the toilet, scrubbing the bathroom, sweeping the floors and dusting, etc. Allow a good length of time for each task. Move slowly, three times more slowly than usual. Fully focus your attention on each task. For example, while placing a book on the shelf, look at the book, be aware of what book it is, know that you are in the process of placing it on the shelf, intending to put it in that specific place. Know that your hand reaches for the book and picks it up. Avoid any abrupt or harsh movement. Maintain mindfulness of the breath, especially when your thoughts wander.

f) *Mindfulness while bathing:* Allow yourself 30 to 45 minutes to take a bath. Don't hurry for even one second. From the moment you prepare the bath water to the moment you put on clean clothes, let every motion be light and slow. Be attentive of every movement. Place your attention to every part of your body, without discrimination or fear. Be mindful of each stream of water on your body. By the time you've finished, your mind should feel as peaceful and light as your body. Follow your breath. Think of yourself as being in a clean and fragrant lotus pond in the summer.

g) *Mindfulness on a pebble:* Sit in the full or half lotus. Regulate your breath as in 3c. When your breathing is slow and even, begin to relax all your muscles while maintaining the half-smile as in 2a. Think of yourself as a pebble which is falling through a clear stream. While sinking, there is no intention to guide your movement. Sink towards the spot of total rest on the gentle sand of the riverbed. Continue meditating on the pebble until your mind and body are at complete rest: a pebble resting on the sand. Maintain this peace and joy for half an hour while watching your breath. No thought about the past or future can pull you away from your present peace and joy. The universe exists in this present moment. No desire can pull you away from this present peace, not even the desire to become a Buddha or the desire to save all beings. Know that to become a Buddha and to save all beings can only be realized on the foundation of the pure peace of the present moment.

h) *Plan a day of mindfulness:* Select one day of the week, any day that accords with your own situation. Forget the work you do during the other days. Do not organize any meetings or have friends over. Do only such simple work as house cleaning, cooking, washing clothes and dusting. Follow the methods described in 4e. Once the house is neat and clean, and all your things are in order, take a bath as described in 4c. Afterwards, prepare and drink tea (4b). You might read a scripture or write letters to close friends. Afterwards take a walk to practise breathing (3b, 3c, and 3e). While reading scripture or writing letters, maintain your mindfulness, don't let the Sūtra or letter pull you away to somewhere else. While reading the sacred text, know what you are reading; while writing the letter, know what you are writing. Follow the same procedure as listening to music or conversing with a friend (3d, 3e). In the evening prepare yourself a light meal, perhaps only a little fruit or a glass of fruit juice. Sit in meditation for an hour before you go to bed.

Follow the method described in 4g, 3e, or 3g. During the day, take two walks of 30 to 45 minutes long. Do not read before you go to sleep. Instead of reading, practise total relaxation (2a) for 5 to 10 minutes. Be master of your breathing. Breathe gently (the breath should not be too long), following the rising and falling of your stomach and chest, with your eyes closed. Every movement during this day should be at least two times slower than usual.

5. Contemplation on Interdependence

a) *Contemplation on the five aggregates:* Find a photo of yourself as a child. Sit in the full or half lotus. Begin to follow your breath as in 3e. After 20 breaths, begin to focus your attention on the photo in front of you. Recreate and live again the five aggregates of which you were made up at the time the photo was taken: the physical characteristics of your body, your feelings, perceptions, mind functioning and consciousness at that age. Continue to follow your breath. Do not let your memories lure you away or overcome you. Maintain this contemplation for 15 minutes. Maintain the half-smile. Turn your mindfulness to your present self. Be conscious of your body, feelings, perceptions, mind functioning and consciousness in the present moment. See the five aggregates which make up yourself.

Ask the question, "Who am I?" The question should be deeply rooted in you, like a new seed nestled deep in the soft earth and damp with water. This question should not be an abstract question to consider with your discursive intellect, for it will not be confined to your intellect, but to the care of the whole of the five aggregates. Don't try to seek an intellectual answer. Contemplate for 10 minutes, maintaining light but deep breathing to prevent being pulled away by philosophical reflection.

b) *Contemplation of your own skeleton:* Lie on a bed, or on a mat or on the grass in a position in which you are comfortable. Don't use a pillow.

Be aware of your breath. Contemplate that all that is left of your body is a white skeleton lying on the face of the earth. Maintain the half-smile and continue to follow your breath. Imagine that all your flesh has decomposed and is gone, that your skeleton is now lying in the earth 80 years after burial. See clearly the bones of your head, back, your ribs, your hip bones, leg and arm bones, finger bones. Maintain the half-smile, breathe very lightly, your heart and mind serene. See that your skeleton is not you.

Your bodily form is not you. Nor feelings, thoughts, actions and knowledge. Maintain this contemplation from 20 to 30 minutes.

c) *Contemplation on your true face before you were born:* In the full or half lotus, follow your breath. Concentrate on the point of your life's beginning (A). Know that it is also the point of beginning of your death. See that both your life and death are manifested at the same time: *this is* because *that is,* this could not have been if that were not. See that the existence of your life and death depend on each other, one being the foundation of the other. See that you are at the same time your life and your death, that the two are not enemies but two aspects of the same reality. Then concentrate on the point of ending of the twofold manifestation (B), which is wrongly called death. See that it is the ending point of the manifestation of both your life and your death.

See that there is no difference before A and after B. Look for your true face in the periods before A and after B.

d) *Contemplation on a loved one who has died:* On a chair or bed, sit or lie in a position in which you feel comfortable. Follow your breath as in 3e. Contemplate the body of a loved one who has died, whether a few months or several years ago. Know clearly that all the flesh of the person has decomposed and only a skeleton remains lying quietly beneath the earth. Know clearly that your own flesh is still here and in yourself are still combined the five aggregates of bodily form, feeling, perception, mental functioning and consciousness. Think of your interaction with that person in the past and right now. Maintain the half-smile and stay with your breath. Contemplate in this way for 15 minutes.

6. Contemplation on Compassion

a) *Contemplation on the person you hate or despise the most:* Sit in the full or half lotus. Breathe and maintain the half-smile as in 2b. Contemplate the image of the person who has caused you the most suffering. Use this person's image as the subject of your contemplation. Contemplate on the bodily form, feelings, perceptions, mind functioning and consciousness of this person. Contemplate on each aggregate separately. Begin with bodily form. Contemplate the features you hate or despise the most or find the most repulsive. Continue with the person's feelings. Try to examine what makes this person happy and suffer in his daily life. When contemplating perception, try to see what patterns of thought and reason this person follows. As for mind functioning, examine what motivates this person's hopes and aspirations and what motivates his actions. Finally consider his consciousness. See whether his views and insights are open and free or not, and whether or not he has been influenced by any prejudices, narrow-mindedness, hatred or anger. See whether or not he is master of himself. Contemplate like this until you feel compassion rise in your heart like a well filling with fresh water, and your anger and resentment disappear. Practise this exercise many times on the same person.

b) *Contemplate on the suffering caused by the lack of wisdom*: Sit in the full or half lotus. Begin to follow your breath as in 3e. Choose the situation of a person, family or society which is suffering the most of any you know. This will be the object of your contemplation.

In the case of a person, try to see every suffering which that person is undergoing. Begin with the suffering of bodily form (sickness, poverty, physical pain) and then proceed to the suffering caused by feelings (internal conflicts, fear, hatred, jealousy, a tortured conscience). Consider next the suffering caused by perceptions (pessimism, dwelling on his problems with a dark and narrow viewpoint). See whether his mind functionings are motivated by fear, discouragement, despair or hatred. See whether or not his consciousness is shut off because of his situation, because of his suffering, because of the people around him, his education, propaganda, or a lack of control of his own self. Meditate on all these sufferings until your heart fills with compassion like a well of fresh water, and you are able to see that that person suffers because of circumstances and ignorance. Resolve to help that person get out of his present situation through the most silent and unpretentious means possible.

In the case of a family, follow the same methods as above. Go through all the sufferings of one person and then on to the next person until you have examined the sufferings of the entire family. See that their sufferings are your own sufferings. See that it is not possible to reproach even one person in that group. See that you must help them liberate themselves from their present situation by the most silent and unpretentious means possible.

In the case of a society, take the situation of a country suffering war or any other situation of injustice. Try to see that every person involved in the conflict is a victim. See that no person, including all those in warring parties or in what appear to be opposing sides, desire the suffering to continue. See that it is not only one or a few persons who are to blame for the situation. See that the situation is possible because of the clinging to ideologies and to an unjust world economic system which is upheld by every person through ignorance or through lack of resolve to change it. See that the two sides in a conflict are not really opposing, but two aspects of the *same* reality. See that the most essential thing is life and that killing or oppressing one another will not solve anything. Remember the Sūtra's words:

> In the time of war
> Raise in yourself the mind of compassion
> Helping living beings
> Abandon the will to fight.
> Wherever there is furious battle
> Use all your might
> To keep both sides' strength equal
> And then step into the conflict to reconcile
>
> (Vimalakīrti Nirdeśa Sūtra)

Meditate until every reproach and hatred disappears, and compassion and love rise like a well of fresh water in your heart. Vow to work for awareness and reconciliation by the most silent and unpretentious means possible.

c) *Contemplation on detached action:* Sit in the full or half lotus. Follow your breath as in 3e. Take a project in rural development or any other project which you consider important, as the subject of your contemplation. Examine the purpose of the work, the methods to be used, and the people involved. Consider first the purpose of the project. See that the work is to serve, to alleviate suffering, to respond to compassion, not to satisfy the desire for praise or recognition. See that the methods used encourage cooperation between humans. Don't consider the project as an act of charity. Consider the people involved. Do you still see in terms of ones who serve and ones who benefit? If you can still see who are the ones serving and who are the ones benefiting, your work is for the sake of yourself and the workers, and not for the sake of service. The Prajñāpāramitā Sūtra says: "The Bodhisattva helps row living beings to the other shore but in fact no living beings are being helped to the other shore." Determine to work in the spirit of Prajñāpāramitā, the spirit of detached action.

d) *Contemplation on detachment:* Sit in the full or half lotus. Follow your breath as in 3e. Recall the most significant achievements in your life and examine each of them. Examine your talent, your virtue, your capacity, the convergence of favourable conditions that have led to success. Examine the complacency and the arrogance that have arisen from the feeling that you are the main cause for such success. Shed the light of interdependence on the whole matter to see that the achievement is not really yours but the convergence of various conditions beyond your reach. See to it that you will not be bound to these achievements. Only when you can relinquish them can you really be free and no longer assailed by them.

Recall the bitterest failures in your life and examine each of them. Examine your talent, your virtue, your capacity, and the absence of favourable conditions that led to the failures. Examine to see all the complexes that have arisen within you from the feeling that you are not capable of realising success. Shed the light of interdependence on the whole matter to see that failures cannot be accounted for by your inabilities but rather by the lack of favourable conditions. Contemplate to see that you have no strength to shoulder these failures, that these failures are not your own self. See to it that you are free from them. Only when you can relinquish them can you really be free and no longer be assailed by them.

e) *Contemplation on non-abandonment:* Sit in the full or half lotus. Follow your breath as in 3e. Apply one of the exercises 5a, 5b, or 5c. See that everything is impermanent and without eternal identity. Contemplate to see that although things are impermanent and without lasting identity, they are nonetheless wondrous. While you are not bound by the conditioned, neither are you bound by the non-conditioned. Contemplate that the bodhisattva, though not caught by the five aggregates and by conditioned dharmas, neither does he get away from the five aggregates and conditioned dharmas. Although he can abandon the five aggregates and conditioned dharmas as if they were cold ashes, still he can dwell in the five aggregates and all conditioned dharmas and not be drowned by them. He is like a boat upon the water. Contemplate to see that awakened people, while not being enslaved by the work of serving living beings, never abandon the work of serving living beings.

The Psychology of Emotions in Buddhist Perspective

The Sir D. B. Jayatilleke
Commemoration Lecture,
Colombo, 1976

by
Dr. Padmasiri de Silva

Copyright © Kandy; Buddhist Publication Society, (1976)

Introduction

Let me first thank you for inviting me to deliver the Sir D. B. Jayatilleke Commemoration Lecture. The invitation was accepted with mixed feelings of diffidence and hope—diffidence because our own thinking sometimes reflects the very conditions that generates the turmoil around us; hope because in the message of the Buddha there is a ray of light that will help us to emerge out of this predicament with clarity of thought and purpose. There is a need for clarity not only in the way we think, but in the way we feel, and incidentally the affective dimension of man provides thematic content of today's lecture. In this context Sir D. B. Jayatilleke is to us basically a nation builder, and a nation builder who firmly stood on the soil of our cultural traditions. This lecture is presented as a tribute to this great national leader of Sri Lanka.

We shall first raise the question, "What is the place of emotions in Buddhism?", then move on to an analysis of specific emotions—fear, hatred, sorrow and grief—and finally to the four sublime states. Having discussed the negative and positive aspects of emotions within the ethics and the psychology of Buddhism, we shall raise some questions regarding the aesthetic aspect of emotions in Buddhism.

The Place of Emotions in Buddhism

Emotions are generally regarded in the mind of the Buddhist as aspects of our personality that interfere with the development of a spiritual life, as unwholesome states ethically undesirable, and roadblocks to be cleared in the battleground between reason and emotion. In keeping with this perspective emotions are described as states of "agitation" or "imbalance."[1]

While a large number of emotional states discussed in Buddhist texts fit in to this description, are we to accept that all the emotions are of this sort? Within the field of experimental psychology, some accept that emotions can be both organizing (making behaviour more effective) and disorganizing. In the field of ethics, the place of emotions in the moral life is a neglected subject, but a few voices in the contemporary world have expressed opinions which bring out the relevance of the psychology of emotions to moral assessment, reminding us of the very refreshing discussions in Aristotle's *Nichomachean Ethics*. In these discussions too there is an acceptance of the creative role of emotions in the moral life of man. It may be that there is an emotional aspect of man that distorts his reasoning, feeds his prejudices and darkens his vision, but should we not look for an emotional facet in man that expands one's horizons of thinking, breaks through our egotism, sharpens a healthy sense of the tragic and evokes the ennobling emotions of sympathy and compassion for fellow man?

There are young people all over the world today torn between the world of the senses with its excitement and boredom and "path of renunciation" about which they are not clear, as it combines a sense of rebellion, escape, mystery, and a search for the exotic East. I am sure the message of the Buddha presents to them a philosophy of life that will combine non-attachment with zest for doing things. This evening, let us turn our minds towards an aspect of this modern predicament, with the hope of discovering a little light in the ancient wisdom of the Buddha, a light that may help us to see clearly the nature of the little world of turmoil that surrounds us.

---

1. See Rune Johansson, *The Psychology of Nirvana* (London, 1969), p. 24.

Our discussion today is not a matter of mere academic interest. The recent drama competition organized by the Kandy Y.M.B.A., an attempt to present a drama based on the Buddhist Jātaka stories, is the kind of venture that makes us think that the "education of the emotions" is not alien to the Buddhist tradition. This talk will be concerned with the psychological, the ethical and, to a limited extent, the aesthetic dimension of emotions.

What Are Emotions?

An emotion is the meaning we give to our felt states of arousal. Psychologists consider emotions to be complex states involving diverse aspects. On the one hand an emotion is a physiological state of arousal; on the other, it also involves an object as having a certain significance or value to the individual. Emotions are dynamically fed by our drives and dispositions; they are also interlocked with other emotions, related to an individual's beliefs, a wide-ranging network of symbols and the "cultural ethos" of a society.

Emotions basically involve dispositions to act by way of approach or withdrawal. Let us take an example to illustrate this. A man who walks a long distance across a forest track feels thirsty; he is attracted by the sight of water in a passing stream and he approaches, but there is a fierce animal close to the stream and he is impelled to withdraw or fight; if he withdraws he might then have a general feeling of anxiety, and if he gets back home safely he will be relieved. Thus perception of objects and situations is followed by a kind of appraisal of them as attractive or harmful. These appraisals initiate tendencies to feel in a certain manner and an impulse to act in a desirable way. All states of appraisal do not initiate action; for instance, in joy we like a passive continuation of the existing state and in grief we generally give up hope. Though there may be certain biologically built-in patterns of expressing emotions, learning plays a key role. Learning influences both the type and intensity of arousal as well as the control and expression of emotions.

The emotional development of people has been the subject of serious study. There are significant differences in the emotional development of people depending on the relevant cultural and social variables. In fact, certain societies are prone to give prominence to certain types of emotions (a dominant social ethos). There are also differences regarding the degree of expressiveness and control of emotions. The important point is that each of us develops a relatively consistent pattern of emotional development, coloured by the individual's style of life.

The Psychology of Emotions in Buddhism

An emotion occurs generally when an object is considered as something attractive or repulsive. There is a felt tendency impelling people towards suitable objects and impelling them to move away from unsuitable or harmful objects. The individual also perceives and judges the situation in relation to himself as attractive or repulsive. While a person feels attraction (*sārajjati*) for agreeable material shape, he feels repugnance (*byāpajjati*) for disagreeable material shapes. An individual thus possessed of like (*anurodha*) and dislike (*virodha*) approaches pleasure-giving objects and avoids painful objects.[2]

Pleasant feelings (*sukhā vedanā*) and painful feelings (*dukkhā vedanā*) are affective reactions to sensations. When we make a judgment in terms of hedonic tone of these affective reactions, there are excited in us certain dispositions to possess the object (greed), to destroy it (hatred), to flee from it (fear), to get obsessed and worried over it (anxiety), and so on. Our attitudes which have been formed in the past influence our present reactions to oncoming stimuli, and these attitudes are often rooted in dynamic personality traits. These attitudes, according to Buddha, are not always the result of deliberations at a conscious level, but emerge on deep-rooted proclivities referred to as *anusaya*. Pleasant feelings induce an attachment to pleasant objects, as they rouse latent sensuous greed (*rāgānusaya*), painful feelings rouse latent anger and hatred (*paṭighānusaya*). States like pride, jealousy, elation, etc., can also be explained in terms of similar proclivities (*anusaya*).[3] It is even said that such proclivities as leaning towards pleasurable

---

2. M I 226 (MN 38).
3. There are seven such proclivities: *kāma-rāga, paṭigha, diṭṭhi, vicikicchā, māna, bhava-rāga, avijjā*.

experience (*kāma-rāgānusaya*) and malevolence (*byāpādānusaya*) are found latent even in "an innocent baby boy lying on his back."[4]

The motivational side of the emotions can be grasped by a study of the six roots of motivation (*mūla*). They fall into two groups, wholesome (*kusala*) and unwholesome (*akusala*). The unwholesome roots are greed (*lobha*), hatred (*dosa*), and delusion (*moha*), while the wholesome roots are non-greed, non-hatred, and non-delusion. Greed generates the approach desires in the form of the drive for self-preservation (*bhava-taṇhā*) and the drive for sensuous pursuits (*kāma-taṇhā*); hatred generates the avoidance desires in the form of the drive for annihilation and aggressive tendencies (*vibhava-taṇhā*).[5] In keeping with our initial observations, non-greed, non-hatred, and non-delusion should be considered as the springs of wholesome or ethically desirable emotions. In fact, in a study of the impact of the wholesome roots on the forms of wholesome consciousness, the following significant observations has been made by the Venerable Nyanaponika Mahā Thera:

> "Non-greed and non-hate may, according to the particular case, have either a mainly negative meaning signifying absence of greed and hate; or they may posses a distinctly positive character, for example: non-greed as renunciation, liberality; non-hate as amity, kindness, forbearance. Non-delusion has always a positive meaning: for it represents the knowledge that motivates the respective state of consciousness. In their positive aspects, non-greed and non-hate are likewise strong motives of good actions. They supply the non-rational, volitional or emotional motives, while non-delusion represents the rational motive of a good thought or action."[6]

In the light of this analysis it is plausible to accept non-greed and non-hatred as the sources of healthy and positive emotions. It is also interesting to note that non-delusion is the basis of good reasons for ethical behaviour. A wrong ethical perspective also

---

4. M I 433 (MN 64).
5. For an analysis of *vibhava-taṇhā*, see Padmasiri de Silva, *Buddhist and Freudian Psychology* (Sri Lanka, 1973).
6. Nyanaponika Thera, *Abhidhamma Studies* (Sri Lanka, 1965), p. 79

may be conditioned by one's desires and emotions. In the light of the Buddha's analysis, a materialistic ethics, influenced by the annihilationist view (*uccheda diṭṭhi*),[7] may itself be conditioned by desires. On account of desire there is clinging (*taṇhā-paccayā diṭṭhi-upādānaṃ*), and clinging is said to be of four forms, one of which is clinging to metaphysical beliefs.[8] Thus there can be rational motives for good actions as well as rationalizations influenced by emotions. What is of importance in the observation we cited is that the Buddhist psychology of emotions does provide a base for creative emotional response, a point which, if accepted, has significant implications for Buddhist ethics, social theory and even art and aesthetics.

While we shall come to the role of the creative emotions as we proceed, let us now examine in detail the specific emotions discussed by Buddha. First we shall discuss the nature of fear, anger, guilt, and grief, and then move on to the four sublime states of loving-kindness, compassion, sympathetic joy, and equanimity.

Regarding the range of our analysis, our study of emotions is basically limited to the psychodynamics of emotional states. However, there is a significant range of factors emerging out of socio-economic structure of a particular society. Differing economic and social structures stimulate differing types of psychological drives. Sometimes, even when the socio-economic conditions change, the character structure of individuals is slow to change. In general, whether it be the desire to acquire or desire to share and care for others, these desires are in truth dependent on certain social structures for nourishment and existence. The desires to save and hoard, to protect and accumulate, to spend and consume, to share and sacrifice, have significant relations to the values embedded in a certain society. The emergence of greed and hatred or compassion and sympathy is related to the value system of a society.

---

7. M I 65 (MN 11).
8. The four kinds of clinging are sensuous clinging (*kamūpādāna*), clinging to views (*diṭṭhūpādāna*), clinging to rules and rituals (*sīlabbatūpādāna*) and personality belief (*attavadūpādāna*).

Fear

If we glance through the discourses of the Buddha as preserved in the Pali canon, the available material on the nature of emotions appears to be dispersed and coloured by the nature of the diverse contextual situations where emotions are discussed. However, in general there appear to be four types of situations where the nature of emotions is discussed: emotions obstructing the ideal of good life sought by the layman, emotions that interfere with the recluse seeking the path to perfection, emotions enhancing the layman's ideal of good life, and emotions developed by the recluse seeking the path of perfection. The grouping of emotions in this manner brings an ethical and spiritual dimension to the psychology of emotions in Buddhism. In the context of the psychology of the West, the undesirable emotions are those that create adjustive problems and impair our mental health, and those desirable are valuable as an adaptive resource. Delineation of mental health merely in terms of adjustment is being questioned in some psychological groups in the West, and new horizons have emerged, a trend which might help to bridge the gap between the psychology of Buddhism and the currently dominant psychology of the West.[9]

Fear generally arises as a response to a danger which is of a specific nature, whereas anxiety arises as a reaction to a danger which is not clearly seen. In anxiety, both the nature of the object and one's attitude to it are not clearly recognized. However, these states fade off into each other in certain contexts. *Bhaya* in Pali can be rendered as fear, fright, or dread.

Regarding the genesis of the emotion of fear, there are at least two clear types of situations which cause fear. Fear is often caused by strong desires (*taṇhāya jāyati bhayaṃ*).[10] Strong desires and attachment to either persons or things cause fear because if we cling to some precious and valuable object, we have to defend it against loss or theft; thieves can even be a serious threat to one's life. If one is tremendously attached to a person, and if the person is struck by a serious sickness, a concern for his well-being turns

---

9. See *Buddhist and Freudian Psychology*, Chapter V.
10. Dhp 216.

into a fear. The possibility of death causes anguish and anxiety. It is the same with the attachment to one's own self: a threat to one's life, sickness, the threat of losing one's job or reputation—all these situations are conditions for the emergence of fear. It is due to the strong self-preservative drive (*bhavataṇhā*) which in turn is fed by the *bhavarāga anusaya* (the lurking tendency to crave for existence) that fear becomes such an agitating condition. Apart from the drive for self-preservation, the desire for power, lust, jealousy and pride are intimately related to the emergence of fear. As we mentioned earlier, some emotions are interlocked with other emotions, as is the cause, for instance, with jealousy, pride, and fear.

The second type of fear is the consequence of leading an undesirable life. Here the emotion of fear is related to the emotion of guilt. In this context the emotion of fear has an unhealthy destructive aspect and a positive healthy aspect. If a person is burdened with a heavy sense of pathological remorse, it has a bad effect; it creates worry and restlessness. On the other hand a lively sense of moral dread and shame (*hiri-ottappa*) prevents man from taking to an evil life and forms the basis of responsibility and a civic sense.

The damaging aspect of a heavy conscience in respect to morals has been the subject of discussion since the work of Sigmund Freud. In admonishing both the laymen and the recluse regarding the bad effects of a pathological sense of guilt, the Buddha refers to a person who is subject to anxiety, fear and dejection thus: a person who has done the wrong thing fears that other people talk about him, and if he is in a place where people meet together, he fears that others are talking about him. When he sees others being punished by the king, he thinks that the same will happen to him and is disturbed by this possibility. Finally, when he is resting on a chair or the bed, these thoughts come to him and he fears that he will be born in a bad place. "Monks, as at eventide the shadows of the great mountain peaks rest, lie and settle on the earth, so, monks, do these evil deeds... lie and settle on him."[11] The kind of fear and guilt that disturbs the man here is different from a healthy and productive sense of shame and fear (*hiri-ottappa*). In

---

11. M III 164 (MN 129).

the Aṅguttara Nikāya there is a reference to four types of fears: fear of self-reproach (*attānuvāda-bhaya*), fear of others' reproach (*parānuvāda-bhaya*), fear of punishment (*daṇḍa bhaya*) and fear of lower worlds (*duggati-bhaya*). In this context these fears have a good effect on the person: "he abandons evil," and "develops the practice of good."

Fear is often found mixed with hatred (even self-hate) and discontent, and this is often so in the emergence of pathological guilt. *Kukkucca*, which can be rendered as uneasiness of conscience, remorse or worry, is considered a hindrance to spiritual development. It is associated with a hateful and discontented consciousness, similar to the Freudian superego consisting of aggressive elements. Among people who are disappointed with the way that they have lived in the past, some successfully change into better and productive men; others who take a more unrewarding line display a complex admixture of fear, hatred, and guilt.[12] The religious melancholy, the self-punishing ascetics, and similar types have an unproductive sense of fear and dread. Restlessness and worry are described in the Nikāyas with an apt analogy: if a pot of water were shaken by the wind so that the water trembles, eddies, and ripples, and a man were to look there for his own reflection, he would not see it. Thus restlessness and worry blind one's vision of oneself, and form an obstruction to the development of tranquility and insight.[13]

Hiri-ottappa (shame and dread), however, is a positive and healthy sense which must be cultivated and developed. In the words of Mrs. Rhys Davis, "Taken together they give us the emotional and conative aspects of the modern notion of conscience, just as *sati* represents it on its intellectual side."[14] He who lacks these positive emotions lacks a conscience.

In a recent study of "Morality and Emotions,"[15] Bernard Williams says that if we grasp the distinction made in Kleinian psychoanalytical work between "persecutory guilt" and "reparative guilt" we do not neglect the possibility of a creative aspect for

---

12. J. C. Flugel, *Man, Morals and Society* (London, 1955), p. 197.
13. AN 5.193.
14. Mrs. Rhys Davis, *Dhammasaṅgaṇī* (Trans.) (London, 1900), p. 20, n. 1.
15. Bernard Williams, *Problems of the Self* (London, 1973), p. 222.

remorse or guilt: "He who thinks he has done wrong may not just torment himself, he may seek to put things together again. In this rather evident possibility, we not only have in general a connection between the emotions and the moral life, we also have something that illustrates the point... about the interpretation of a set of actions in terms of an emotional structure."

It is also of interest to note that a student of Buddhism in the West has made an analysis of the "Dynamics of Confession in Early Buddhism."[16] Teresine Havens too says that in place of the external rites of purification (like bathing in the river, etc.) advocated by existing religions, the Buddha advocated a radical inner transformation of the affective side of man. According to Havens, the Buddha was as realistic as Freud or St. Paul in accepting and "recognizing the egocentric, lustful, hostile and grasping proclivities in unawakened man."[17] While advocating a method to uproot these traits, the Buddha "condemned worry over past offences as a hindrance to concentration and found a religion which in general seems to have produced far fewer neurotic guilt feelings than has Judaism and Christianity."[18] The Buddha has thus presented the principles of the catharsis of emotions, which have certainly caught the eyes of many contemporary students of Buddhism in the West.

Fear and Anxiety

Often we make a distinction between fear and anxiety. Fear is a response to a specific situation or a particular object. It is specific and demonstrable, whereas dread is objectless, diffuse, and vague. In anxiety both the nature of the object and one's attitude to it are not clearly recognized.

Anxiety is generally caused by ego-centered desires of diverse types. There are some anxieties or vague apprehensions which under clear analysis can be reduced to some specific fear. For instance, a person approaching the possibility of marriage

---

16. J. Tilakasiri, ed., *Añjali, Wijesekera Felicitation Volume* (Sri Lanka, 1970), pp. 20-27.
17. Ibid.
18. Ibid.

may feel some fear due to financial problems or a sense of apprehension whether the marriage would be success, but such vague apprehension could again under analysis be explained in a specific form. The Buddha says that there is a more basic type of anxiety due to our deep-rooted attachment to the ego. Thus in the words of Conze there is a type of "concealed suffering"[19] which lies behind much of everyday apprehensions. These emerge from the nature of the basic human condition: something which, while pleasant, is tied up with anxiety, as one is afraid to lose it. Here anxiety is inseparable from attachment; something while pleasant binds us to conditions which are the grounds on which a great deal of suffering is inevitable, like the possession of a body; and finally the five aggregates (khandha) have a kind of built-in anxiety.

Inability to face the inner vacuity of the so-called ego results in a flight from anxiety: some facets symptomatic of this overt anxiety are the frantic effort of people to join clubs, compulsive gregariousness, seeking to fill one's leisure by frantic activity such as motoring, and such diversions which will help people to avoid being alone.[20] The love of solitude and the way of silence advocated by the Buddha is anathema to large numbers of people who live in the "lonely crowd"!

The Buddha traces this predilection of the "anxious" man to his inability to grasp the basic truth of egolessness, which is the key to understand any form of anxiety. The belief in "I" and "mine," though it gives a superficial feeling of security, is the cause of anxiety, fear, and worry. The discourse on The Snake Simile refers to anxiety (paritissanā) about unrealities that are external and those that are internal; external unrealities refer to houses or gold that one possesses, or children and friends, and internal to the non-existing "I".

The Bhaya-bherava Sutta (Discourse on Fear and Dread) says that purely subjective conditions can cause fear in a recluse who has gone to the forest. If a recluse who has gone to the forest has not mastered his emotions like lust and covetousness, is corrupt in heart, etc., the rustling of fallen leaves by the wind or the breaking of the twig by an animal can cause fear and dread. Thus, whether

---

19. Edward Conze, *Buddhism* (London, 1957), pp. 46-48.
20. See Rollo May, *The Meaning of Anxiety* (New York, 1950), p. 8.

we are dealing with the fears of man attached to his possessions, the anxieties of one torn between conflicting desires, the fear and dread arising in the recluse gone to the wilderness, or the fears consequent on leading a bad life—in all these senses, the Buddha is for us a "dispeller of fear, dread, and panic."[21]

Now the most important question is, "Is there no creative existential stirring that awakens man to his real predicament?" There are references to authentic religious emotions caused by the contemplation of miseries in the world. The emotion of *saṃvega*, translated as "stirring" or "deeply moving," can be an invigorating experience which enhances one's faith and understanding of Dhamma.[22] The *saṃvega* that is referred to here as an emotional state of existential stirring should be distinguished from *paritassanā*, which is a kind of anxiety.

The doctrine of the Buddha is compared to a lion's roar.[23] In the forest, when the lesser creatures hear the roar of the king of the beast, they tremble. In the same way when the devas who are long-lived and blissful hear the doctrine of conditioned origination they tremble, but they yet understand the Buddha's doctrine of impermanence. This should be compared with the state *paritassanā*, where a person finds his eternalism challenged, but sees the doctrine of the Buddha through the eyes of an annihilationist, and laments, "'I' will be annihilated." When *saṃvega* is kindled in a person, he sticks to the doctrine with more earnestness.

Fear and Emotional Ambivalence

Fear is something which by its very nature entails "avoidance," but there is a strange phenomenon which may be described as "flirting with fear." There are people who search for forms of entertainment and sports which excite a mild degree of fear, like participating in mountain climbing that can be dangerous, motor sports, fire walking, etc.; there are others who like to read, see, and talk about gruesome incidents. A person who goes to see wildlife

---

21. D III 47 (DN 25).
22. See Padmasiri de Silva, *Tangles and Webs* (Sri Lanka, 1974).
23. Ibid. [And see MN 11.]

would like a little excitement rather than plainly see the animals at a distance. This kind of ambivalent nature is found in behaviour where a mild degree of fear created by situations helps people to break through monotony and boredom. Also disgust with life and one's own self can make people court situations, which are a danger to their life. Freud's study of the death instinct (which we have elsewhere compared with *vibhava taṇhā*) might shed some light on this rather dark facet of human nature. Even in ancient Rome it was said that people wanted both bread and circuses. It is possible that situations of disorder, turmoil, and violence, etc., are fed by this ambivalent nature.

Another facet of this compulsion to "flirt with fear" is found in the strange delight people find in violating taboos, laws, and commands. When desires are curbed through fear they are repressed and emerge through other channels. The coexistence of states which are condemned at the conscious level and approved at the unconscious level partly explain this compulsion to violate taboos. There are other types of irrational fears presently unearthed in the field of abnormal psychology,[24] which stresses that an undesirable situation has to be avoided on the basis of understanding rather than by an irrational fear or a process of drilling.

The Control and Expression of Fear

This brings us to the final aspect of the questions regarding the emotion of fear. The Buddha was not much directly concerned with the question whether the spontaneous expression of an emotion is good or whether it should be inhibited. He held that, rather, by a process of self-understanding, diligent self-analysis, and insight one can come to the point where emotions will not overwhelm him.

A recent study which attempts to work out a technique of living based on Buddhist principles has something significant to say on this problem.[25] Leonard Bullen says that there are three

---

24. Some of the irrational fears related to behaviour disorders have been the subject of psychological analysis: they are the fear of high places, fear of small places, fear of dark places, fear of animals, etc. These are called phobias.
25. Leonard A. Bullen, *A Technique of Living*, B.P.S. (Sri Lanka, 1976).

aspects to the disciplining of emotions: first is the development of a habit of self-observation with regard to one's emotional condition (a detailed observation of the mental state); the second involves the control of emotional manifestations as they arise; and finally the development of a new set of values, so that the situations which earlier elicited the responses of fear will fail to do so. As Bullen himself points out, the disciplining of emotions at the level of the individual has social implications.

If we begin with ourselves we do not excite the emotions of fear, hatred, jealousy, and pride in others. If others do not excite them in us, we are not impelled to see the shadows of our own fears and jealousies in the bosom of their own hearts. Self-analysis and understanding when practised with within a community has a reciprocal effect.

The emotion of fear when it is generated at the social level creates mutual mistrust, suspicion, and hatred. The roots of racial prejudices, for instance, can be understood in the light of this phenomenon of mutual fear.

The problem of the young has to be dealt with at the level of the family. It may be said in this connection that ambivalent feelings of love and hatred within the family, irrational fears and guilt complexes, have a very bad impact on children. At the school level the medium of art, literature, and drama could do much to honestly encounter the problem emerging out of the affective side of man.

If young people do not get a glimpse of their own emotional facets, there is the possibility that they create their own forms of rebellion and defiance. There are already in the West today emerging marginal faiths of a highly exotic nature, some of which are generated by fears and impulsion of immature minds; some of these "marginal faiths" may be described as forms of *sīlabbataparāmāsa* (rite and ritual clinging). On the other hand, there may be an unexpected ray of hope in the rebellion of the young mind trying to break through certain forms of conventional thinking, which to them lack the warmth, ardour, and sincerity of a dynamic faith. It is by a spirited rejuvenation of our own traditions that we respond to this challenge with sympathy and understanding. Let our reflections this evening be a very humble attempt to pursue the problem in this direction.

Hatred

Emotions often create a kind of fog between the subject and the object. In "approach desires," like greed, there is an infatuation due to which the person is blind to the undesirable aspects of the objects which he longs to possess. In the case of "avoidance desires" generated by fear, and more so by hatred, the subject projects his hatred in perceiving the object; in extreme anger his vision is blinded, like the fury of a serpent. Thus there is a positive attitude regarding things we like and a negative aversion for those we dislike. If we desire to avoid a situation or a person we dislike, and we cannot do so, there is excited in us an urge to destroy, harm, fight, etc. The actual human situation is a little more complicated, as sometimes a certain aspect of an object attracts us, whereas another aspect repels us, and if so, under certain conditions what is lovable will turn out to be repulsive. The kind of emotional ambivalence that exists between parents and children is a case in point. Then there are things that we consciously like but unconsciously detest.

In the ethico-psychological analysis of emotions that we find in Buddhism, there are a number of terms used to connote the existence and expression of anger and hatred: *dosa* (hate), *vyāpāda* (ill-will), *paṭigha* (aversion), *kodha* (anger), etc. Hatred is also related to the states such as *issā* (envy), *macchariya* (jealousy) and *hīna māna* (inferiority conceit).

Dosa (hate) is one of the basic roots of immoral action, along with greed and delusion. Sometimes in a particular situation all the roots of immoral action may be excited: a person is longing to obtain object X, but A stands in his way. Thus greed for X is followed by a hatred for A, and the desire for X is in turn nourished by the root delusion. The expression of hatred can take various forms, by way of thought (wishing the person dies), by way of harsh words, and by way of aggressive behaviour.

Due to certain forms of development that the human being has undergone, people often do not speak out their feelings but, by a process of repression and concealment, accumulate them. Accumulated anger of this sort can explode in very many subtle forms, as such anger exists at a subterranean level in the form of the *paṭighānusaya*. A baby who is angry with the mother will direct this on to a doll—this is called "displacement." If a person takes pleasure in beating a child, he will say it will do the child good—this is a form of rationalization. A person who unconsciously hates a person can be oversolicitous about his health—this is a reaction formation. If a person suspects that another person is harbouring a grievance against him without grounds, he is merely projecting his own hatred onto someone else.

We have elsewhere discussed this concept of self-deception, but it is relevant to the emotion of hatred for very good reason. Hatred is an emotion which has been generally condemned by the Buddha, so it is difficult to think of any positive forms it may take, such as "righteous indignation" or a "just war." Thus it expresses itself in many subtle forms. If a person starves himself to death because of a social grievance it may be a way of directing the accumulated hatred on to himself. While suicide has been condemned by the Buddha, no form of self-torture can be accepted according to the path of the Buddha. There is a classic case of the child who refused to take medicine, and finally through compulsion, drank it with a vengeance. It is in the understanding of the deceptive spell of the aggressive urges in man that the Buddha condemned the path of self-mortification (*attakilamathānuyoga*). It is a way of life that generates suffering (*dukkha*), annoyance (*upaghāta*), trouble (*upāyāsa*) and fret (*pariyāha*). The Buddha advocated a middle path that will dry up both the roots of greed and hatred, and delusion too.

It is in an era close to ours that Sigmund Freud remarked that the voice of aggression is sometimes subtle, invisible, and difficult to unravel. It is perhaps the subtle appreciation of these psychological mechanisms in Buddhism which made Rhys Davis remark that "compared with the ascetic excess of the times, the Buddhist standpoint was markedly hygienic."[26] Not merely does the Buddha grasp the subtle mechanism through which the aggressive urge manifests, but he has presented the finest antidote to the spring of hatred in man preaching the doctrine of the four sublime states. If the genius for both good and evil rests within ourselves the Buddha has given us a sense of optimism to deal with the turmoil around us.

---

26. Rhys Davids, "Sin," *Encyclopedia of Religion and Ethics* (New York, 1910-21), Vol. II p. 71.

Though the Buddha attempted to deal with the emergence of hatred both at the social and individual level, the inner transformation of the individual is the basis on which the urge to aggression can be tamed. Thus in working out the different levels of spiritual development, there are references to the forms of anger, hatred, and ill-will that obstruct man. Hatred in the form of *vyāpāda* is referred to as one of the hindrances (*nivāraṇa*), along with sensuality, sloth and torpor, restlessness and remorse, and doubt. *Vyāpāda* is one of the fetters that bind beings to the wheel of existence. *Vyāpāda* (ill-will), *kodha* (anger) and *upanāho* (malice), *issā* (envy) and *macchariya* are considered as defilements (*upakkilesa*) in a list of sixteen defilements. These defilements have to be eliminated for the development of insight. These states work in significant combinations; for instance, in contempt there is a combination of aversion and conceit, and denigration is a stronger form of this contempt.[27] Envy is fed by greed and aversion. If we succumb to the last defilement of negligence, then these defilements will form into a layer which is hard to break through, and has got hardened through habit. It is in this way that we can account for the emergence of certain personality types, and the type referred to as the *dosa-carita* will be the very embodiment of hatred.

There is a graphic description of the angry man in the Aṅguttara Nikāya, some of which we shall reproduce briefly:

When anger does possess a man;
He looks ugly; he lies in pain;
What benefit he may come by
He misconstrues as a mischance;
He loses property (through fines)
Because he has been working harm
Through acts of body and speech
By angry passion overwhelmed;
The wrath and rage that madden him
Gain him a name of ill-repute;
His fellows, relatives and kin
Will seek to shun him from afar;

---

27. Nyanaponika Thera, *Simile of the Cloth*, B.P.S. (Sri Lanka, 1957).

*And anger fathers misery:
This fury does so cloud the mind
Of man that he cannot discern
This fearful inner danger.
An angry man no meaning knows,
No angry man sees the Dhamma,
So wrapped in darkness, as if blind,
Is he whom anger dogs.
Someone a man in anger hurts;
But, when his anger is later spent
With difficulty or with ease,
He suffers as if seared by fire.
His look betrays the sulkiness
Of some dim smoky smouldering glow.
Whence may flare up an anger-blaze
That sets the world of men aflame.
He has no shame or conscience curb,
No kindly words come forth from him,
There is no island refuge for
The man whom anger dogs.
Such acts as will ensure remorse,
Such as are far from the true Dhamma:
It is of these that I would tell,
So harken to my words.
Anger makes man a parricide,
Anger makes him a matricide,
Anger can make him slay the saint
As he would kill the common man.
Nursed and reared by a mother's care,
He comes to look upon the world,
Yet the common man in anger kills
The being who gave him life.
No being but seeks his own self's good,
None dearer to him than himself,
Yet men in anger kill themselves,
Distraught for reasons manifold:
For crazed they stab themselves with daggers,
In desperation swallow poison,
Perish hanged by ropes, or fling*

Themselves over a precipice.
Yet how their life-destroying acts
Bring death unto themselves as well,
That they cannot discern, and that
Is the ruin anger breeds.
This secret place, with anger's aid,
Is where mortality sets the snare.
To blot it out with discipline,
With vision, strength, and understanding,
To blot each fault out one by one,
The wise man should apply himself,
Training likewise in the true Dhamma;
"Let smouldering be far from us."
 Then rid of wrath and free from anger,
And rid of lust and free from envy,
Tamed, and with anger left behind,
Taintless, they reach Nibbāna.

AN 7:60

On the therapeutic side there are many contexts where the Buddha offers advice to face situations, such that one's anger, wrath, and ill-will not be excited, and if one is agitated there are techniques to get rid of them. This is not a process of repression by which you push them into a lower level of consciousness, but a process by which understanding, insight, and mindfulness lead one to control and restraint. While the Buddhist analysis of genesis of emotional states helps one to understand their emergence, positive techniques are advocated to deal with them and this is done in the case of anger, fear, greed, jealousy, or any such unwholesome emotional state. The Vitakkasaṇṭhāna Sutta recommends five techniques to deal with such states.[28]

Grief and Sorrow

Grief is a universal phenomenon. It is basically a reaction to bereavement, but it is also consequent on other types of losses. If

---

28. Vitakkasaṇṭhāna Sutta, MN 20. Also see Piyatissa Thera, *The Elimination of Anger*, B.P.S. (Sri Lanka 1975).

there has been a close identification with the person or the thing lost, the person concerned feels as if a part of himself has been lost. The most significant observations on the nature of "mourning and melancholy" were made by Sigmund Freud.[29]

When an object is charged with a strong emotional cathexis, or in Buddhist terminology "clinging" (*upādāna*), a sudden loss or separation creates a disturbing vacuum. Feelings of guilt, depression, and self-pity may colour the emotion of grief in various situations. The *Atthasālinī* warns that sometimes people will not be able to distinguish between sorrow and compassion; while the distant enemy of compassion is cruelty, the close enemy is a kind of self-pity filled with worldly sorrow.[30] While a deep sense of compassion has a power to transform a person spiritually, worldly sorrow binds him more insidiously to the wheel of *saṃsāra*.

Sorrow, grief, and lamentation are all facets of *dukkha* and can be overcome only by grasping the philosophy of the "tragic" in Buddhism.[31] Mourning and weeping are not effective in dealing with the tragic. We should understand the causes and conditions of suffering and work out a therapy to remove the causes of suffering. The Buddhist attitude demands a sense of reality; this is different from either excessive mourning or the use of diversions to drown one's sorrow. Dukkha is a universal feature of saṃsāric existence along with impermanence and egolessness. The Buddha has said: "What is impermanent, that is suffering. What is suffering, that is void of an ego." To think that there is an ego where there is only a changing psycho-physical complex is to create the conditions that generate sorrow, grief and dejection.

The Buddhist philosophy of tragedy is contained in the four noble truths: the truth of suffering, the origin of suffering, the extinction of suffering, the eightfold path leading to the extinction of suffering. The nature of suffering is thus described by the Buddha: birth, decay, disease, death, sorrow, lamentation, pain, grief, and despair are suffering. To be joined with the unpleasant

---

29. See, Sigmund Freud, "Mourning and Melancholia," in *Complete Works of Sigmund Freud*, ed. Strachey, (London 1953). Vol. XIV.
30. *Atthasālinī*, 63.
31. Padmasiri de Silva, "Buddhism and the Tragic Sense of Life," *University of Ceylon Review* (April-October 1967).

and to be separated from the pleasant is suffering; the failure to get what one wants is suffering. In short, clinging to the five groups of mental and physical qualities that go to make up the individual constitutes suffering. It is the last part of the formula that gives a sense of depth to the meaning of tragedy in Buddhism.

If the nature of the Buddhist analysis of *dukkha* is understood, within that setting the confrontation with genuine tragic situations in life may have a positive role to play; it could break through the natural slumber and complacency and create the sense of urgency in the mind of the Buddhist. Authentic tragic experience (*saṃvega*) should be a spur to the religious life and strengthen one's faith in the doctrine.

The way in which the impact of genuine tragic situations may bring about a spiritual alertness without falling into the unwholesome extreme of morbidity is brought out clearly in the Aṅguttara Nikāya.[32] A certain person hears that in a village or town someone is afflicted or dead, and stirred in this way he realizes the truth; another beholds with his own eyes... and realizes the truth; the third person sees a kinsman afflicted and realizes the truth; and finally the person himself is stricken with pain and suffering and this situation stirs him to a realization of the truth of suffering. This is by analogy compared to a steed that is stirred when the stick is seen, one stirred when the stick touches the skin, a third when the flesh is pierced and a fourth when the very bone is pierced by a stick. There is an element of stirring (which the translator renders as agitation) which awakens a person to the tragic sense of life and the emergence of faith in the doctrine. Even if we call this a state of "agitation," it is different from a person whose fear, anger, or grief has been aroused. Even the sense of the tragic in life can turn out to be a creative emotional response.

The Four Sublime States

Not only does compassion form the basis for a wholesome dimension of emotional warmth and positive concern for others, but it is specifically advocated as a corrective to the elimination of hatred, fear, and allied states. But it has its own alluring disguises

---

32. AN 4:113.

and as stated earlier it must be saved from the near enemies of worldly sorrow and pseudo-love and superficial attachments.

The four sublime states (the Brahma Vihāras) are *mettā* (loving kindness), *karuṇā* (compassion), *muditā* (sympathetic joy) and *upekkhā* (equanimity). Their potentiality to deal with conflicts, jealousies, prejudice, and hatred are immense, and at the social level very significant. In the words of Ven. Nyanaponika: "They are the great removers of tension, the great peace-makers in social conflict, the great healers of wounds suffered in the struggle of existence: levellers of social barriers, builders of harmonious communities, awakeners of slumbering magnanimity long forgotten, revivers of joy and hope..."[33]

In the early part of the lecture it was mentioned that morality has a significant relation to the psychology of human emotions. In the context of the four sublime states, this observation has much relevance. Gunapala Dharmasiri has pointed out that one type of moral justification advocated by the Buddha was the appeal to sympathetic feelings.[34] "The simple fact that others are living beings is the reason why I should not harm and this is based on an inference from one's personal experience to that of others: as all people dislike punishment and are scared of death, one should not kill or harm others." In the context of the four sublime states, a kind of disinterestedness or neutrality is a safeguard against the emergence of sentimental attachments.

These states are considered as boundless, as they are not limited, narrowed down to a special person or persons. These are not merely principles of conduct, but subjects of methodical meditation, and these could only get rooted in a strong affinity with this unbounded outlook by the integration of the meditational level and the practical level of conduct. It is by meditative practice that they sink deeply into the heart and thus later become spontaneous attitudes.[35] In the four sublime states we see the finest base for a creative emotional response, and moreover a response related to the emotion of natural sympathy and concern for fellow beings.

---

33. Nyanaponika Thera, *The Four Sublime States*, B.P.S. (Sri Lanka, 1960).
34. Gunapala Dharmasiri, "Principles of Moral Justification in Buddhism and Schopenhauer," *Sonderdruck aus dem 53, Schopenhauer-Jahrbuch*, 1972.
35. *The Four Sublime States*.

The Aesthetic Dimension of the Emotions (an unfinished postscript)

Having dealt with the psychological and ethical aspects of the emotions in Buddhism, it would naturally fall in line with our discussion to say a few words on the aesthetic aspects too. These comments are made as an incentive to further reflection rather than in the form of a definitive statement.

In the course of our discussion it was observed that Buddhism upholds the cultivation of good emotions and the elimination of unwholesome emotions. Art and aesthetics is basically a medium of human communication. Is there a facet of the aesthetic that can enhance the education of the emotions? There are two sides to the question, one from the standpoint of art, the other from the standpoint of Buddhism.

Let us take the standpoint of art first. There are three views on the relationship between art and morality, out of which philosophers like R.W. Beardsmore favour the third.[36] The view called "Moralism" upholds that the aim of art is to teach morality; "Autonomism" is the belief that the art has nothing to do with morality. Both points are mistaken on Beardsmore's view; art does not crudely teach morality or deliberately eliminate it; rather, art can give an understanding which makes moral judgment sensitive and intelligent. In the recent development of what is called "Situational Ethics," examples from literature are used for the discussion of moral issues. By thus reflecting on the conflicts and dilemmas of the characters we can enrich our own sensibility. Without having undergone the experience ourselves, moral and religious problems can be viewed with a "sense of detachment." Thirdly, the uses of pure reason are sometimes limited, and the use of literary techniques are extremely effective on occasions; the fact is quite obviously seen in the importance of the Jātaka stories, the Thera- and Therī-gāthā verses, etc. Finally, philosophers like Aristotle discovered a certainly cathartic purpose in art. By the use of the sympathetic imagination, one tends to see the common human nature that exists behind the façade of divisive doctrines.[37]

---

36. R.W. Beardsmore, *Art and Morality* (London 1971).
37. John Hospes, "Philosophy of Art and Aesthetics," *Encyclopedia of Philosophy*.

Now can a Buddhist absorb the aims of art and aesthetics in this manner? As we have already mentioned, for the purpose of efficient communication a wide variety of techniques have been used by the Buddha: stories, fables, poetry, paradoxes, similes, etc. Some of these techniques are well developed—for instance, in Zen Buddhism. Drama and song are used today as media for depicting thematically a Buddhist idea. Sculpture and painting have developed over the years with a Buddhist inspiration.

But there are problems in this area. Though the five precepts do not directly prohibit artistic activity, the call to restrain the senses is important. Also in the more stringent code of morality (the ten precepts), and for monks, seeing dances and such forms of amusements is prohibited. The crucial question is how do we differentiate between the "sensuous" with its harmful effects and the "aesthetic"? O.H. de A. Wijesekera, discussing the relationship between "Buddhism and Art,"[38] says: "In the Sigāla homily we have one of the best abstracts of the Buddha's attitude as to what a lay disciple should do and not do. One will find that the Buddha there admonishes Sigāla not to fall into the error of developing a habitual liking for amusements, but he certainly does not ask Sigāla to cut himself off completely from all aesthetic pursuits, only that which is bad and demoralizing." Thus if we do not adopt a very limited notion of the "sensuous" to eliminate the aesthetic, education of the emotion through aesthetic media is possible.

Jothiya Dhirasekera says "... the Buddhist recognizes beauty where the senses can perceive it. But in the beauty he also sees its own change and destruction. He remembers what the Buddha said with regard to all components things, that they come in to being, undergo change and are destroyed."[39] It is because of the ability to look at life with equanimity that Buddhism provided a base for the development of a very rich nature poetry: the images of peace and tranquillity, of change and continuity—all these find graphic expression in Buddhist poetry.

---

38. O. H. de A. Wijesekera, "Buddhism and Art," *The Mahā-Bodhi Journal* May-August, 1945
39. Jothiya Dhirasekera, *Buddhism and Beauty*, B.P.S. (Sri Lanka).

There is also a devotional aspect of religion which finds fitting expression in aesthetic media, and within the concept of *saddhā*, art and aesthetic can stimulate faith and reverence for the Dhamma.

To conclude—in the depiction of human tragedy, the lure of power, the pitfalls of ambition, the roots of passion and the springs of compassion, the Jātakas have already provided a veritable gold mine for the education of the emotions. With the tranquillity and peace that one sees in the Samādhi statue or the beauty of the ancient cave paintings, we enter into a dimension which is predominantly Buddhist. These observations are offered to reactivate a facet of human nature (namely the affective side) that comes most naturally to man and harness this potential in the wake of a higher spiritual transformation.

Aṅguttara Nikāya

Discourses of the Buddha

An Anthology
Part III

Selected and translated from the Pali

by

**Nyanaponika Thera
and
Bhikkhu Bodhi**

WHEEL PUBLICATION NO. 238/239/240

Copyright © Kandy; Buddhist Publication Society, (1976, 1990)

IX. The Chapter of the Nines

128. Meghiya

On one occasion the Blessed One was dwelling at Cālikā, on the Cālikā hill. There the Venerable Meghiya, who was at that time the Blessed One's attendant,[1] approached the Blessed One, paid homage to him, and said to him while standing at one side:

"Lord, I wish to go to Jantugāma for alms."

"You may do as you think fit, Meghiya."

Then the Venerable Meghiya, dressing himself in the morning and taking robe and bowl, entered Jantugāma for alms. Having made the alms round and taken his meal, he went to the bank of the Kimikālā River.

There, while walking around to stretch his legs, he saw a pleasant and beautiful mango grove. Seeing it, he thought: "Pleasant, indeed, is this mango grove; it is beautiful. Truly, it is fit for a clansman who wishes to strive in meditation. If the Blessed One allows it, I shall return to this mango grove to strive in meditation."

Then the Venerable Meghiya approached the Blessed One ... and said to him: "Lord, after my alms round in Jantugāma, when I had taken my meal, I went to the bank of the Kimikālā River. While walking there I saw a pleasant and beautiful mango grove which I thought to be fit for a clansman who wishes to strive in meditation. If the Blessed One permits me, I shall go there and strive."

"Wait a while, Meghiya. We are now alone here. First let another monk come."

But the Venerable Meghiya repeated his request, saying: "Lord, for the Blessed One there is nothing further to achieve and no need to consolidate what he has achieved. But as for me, Lord, there is still more to achieve and the need to consolidate what I have achieved. If the Blessed One permits me, I shall go to that mango grove and strive."

Again the Blessed One asked him to wait and again the Venerable Meghiya made his request for a third time. (Then the Blessed One said:)

"As you speak of striving, Meghiya, what can we say? You may do now as you think fit."

The Venerable Meghiya then rose from his seat, saluted the Blessed One, and keeping him to his right, left for the mango grove. Having arrived, he went deeper into the grove and sat down under a tree to spend the day there. But while staying in that mango grove, three kinds of evil, unwholesome thoughts constantly assailed him: sensual thoughts, thoughts of ill will and thoughts of violence.

Then he thought: "Truly, it is strange, it is amazing! I have gone forth from home into the homeless life out of faith, and yet I am harassed by these three kinds of evil, unwholesome thoughts: sensual thoughts, thoughts of ill will, and thoughts of violence."[2]

Then the Venerable Meghiya went back to the Blessed One, and having saluted him, he told him what had occurred and exclaimed: "Truly it is strange, it is amazing! I have gone forth from home into the homeless life out of faith, and yet I am harassed by those three kinds of evil, unwholesome thoughts."

"If, Meghiya, the mind still lacks maturity for liberation, there are five conditions conducive to making it mature. What five?

"The first thing, Meghiya, for making the immature mind mature for liberation is to have a noble friend, a noble companion, a noble associate.[3]

"Further, Meghiya, a monk should be virtuous, restrained by the restraint of the Pātimokkha, perfect in conduct and resort, seeing danger in the slightest faults. Having undertaken the training rules, he should train himself in them. This is the second thing that makes the immature mind mature for liberation.

"Further, Meghiya, the talk in which a monk engages should befit an austere life and be helpful to mental clarity; that is to say, it should be talk on fewness of wishes, on contentment, on solitude, on seclusion, on application of energy, on virtue, concentration, wisdom, liberation, and on the knowledge and vision of liberation. If a monk finds opportunities for such talk easily and without difficulty, this is the third thing that makes the immature mind mature for liberation.

"Further, Meghiya, a monk lives with his energy set upon the abandoning of everything unwholesome and the acquiring of everything wholesome; he is steadfast and strong in his effort, not shirking his task in regard to wholesome qualities. This is the fourth thing that makes the immature mind mature for liberation.

"Further, Meghiya, a monk possesses wisdom; he is equipped with that wisdom which sees into the rise and fall of phenomena, which is noble and penetrative, leading to the complete destruction of suffering. This is the fifth thing that makes the immature mind mature for liberation.

"When, Meghiya, a monk has a noble friend, a noble companion and associate, it can be expected the he will be virtuous ... that he will engage in talk befitting the austere life and helpful to mental clarity ... that his energy will be set upon the abandoning of everything unwholesome and the acquiring of everything wholesome ... that he will be equipped with the wisdom that leads to the complete destruction of suffering.

"Then, Meghiya, when the monk is firmly grounded in these five things, he should cultivate four other things: he should cultivate the meditation on the foulness (of the body) for abandoning lust; he should cultivate loving-kindness for abandoning ill will; he should cultivate mindfulness of breathing for cutting off distracting thoughts; he should cultivate the perception of impermanence for eliminating the conceit 'I am'. In one who perceives impermanence, the perception of non-self becomes firmly established; and one who perceives non-self achieves the elimination of the conceit 'I am' and attains Nibbāna in this very life."[4]

(9:3)

129. Freed of Fivefold Fear

"There are, O monks, four powers. What four? The power of wisdom, the power of energy, the power of an unblemished life and the power of beneficence.

"And what, monks, is the power of wisdom? As to those things which are unwholesome and are held to be unwholesome, those things which are wholesome and are held to be wholesome; blameless and blameworthy, and held to be so; dark and bright, and held to be so; fit or unfit to be practised, and held to be so; worthy and unworthy of noble ones, and held to be so—to see all these things clearly and to consider them well, this is called the power of wisdom.

"And what, monks, is the power of energy? As to those things that are unwholesome, blameworthy, dark, unfit to be practised, unworthy of noble ones, and which are held to be so—to generate desire, to make an effort and stir up one's energy for abandoning all these things; and as to those things that are wholesome, blameless, bright, fit to be practised, worthy of noble ones, and which are held to be so—to generate desire, to make an effort and stir up one's energy for gaining all these things, this is called the power of energy.

"And what, monks, is the power of an unblemished life? Here, monks, a noble disciple is unblemished in his deeds, unblemished in his words, unblemished in his thoughts. This is called the power of an unblemished life.

"And what, monks, is the power of beneficence? There are four bases of beneficence:[5] by gifts, by friendly speech, by helpful acts and by bestowal of equity. This is the best of gifts: the gift of Dhamma. And this is the best of friendly speech: to teach the Dhamma again and again to those who wish for it and who listen attentively. And this is the best of helpful acts: to arouse, instil and strengthen faith in the unbeliever; to arouse, instil, and strengthen virtue in the immoral; to arouse, instil and strengthen generosity in the miser; to arouse, instil, and strengthen wisdom in the ignorant. And this is the best bestowal of equity: if a stream-enterer becomes equal to a stream-enterer; a once-returner equal to a once-returner; a non-returner equal to a non-returner; and an *arahant* equal to an *arahant*. This, monks, is called the power of beneficence.

"And this concludes the four powers.

"Now, monks, a noble disciple endowed with these four powers has left behind five fears: the fear for his livelihood, the fear of disrepute, the fear of embarrassment in assemblies, the fear of death and the fear of an unhappy future destiny.

"A noble disciple thus endowed will think: 'No fear do I have for my livelihood. Why should I have fear about it? Have I not the four powers of wisdom, energy, unblemished life and beneficence? It is one who is foolish and lazy, of blameworthy conduct in deeds, words, and thoughts, and who has no beneficence—such a one might have fear for his livelihood.

'No fear do I have about disrepute or about embarrassment in assemblies; nor have I fear of death or of an unhappy future destiny. Why should I have these fears? Have I not the four powers of wisdom, energy, unblemished life, and beneficence? It is one who is foolish and lazy, of blameworthy conduct in deeds, words, and thoughts, and who has no beneficence—such a one might have all these fears.'

"Thus it should be understood, monks, that a noble disciple endowed with the four powers has left behind five fears."

(9:5)

130. Sāriputta's Lion's Roar

On one occasion the Blessed One was dwelling at Sāvatthī in Jeta's Grove, Anāthapiṇḍika's monastery. At that time the Venerable Sāriputta approached the Blessed One. Having paid homage to the Blessed One, he sat down to one side and said to him:

"Lord, I have now completed the rains retreat at Sāvatthī and wish to leave for a country journey."

"Sāriputta, you may go whenever you are ready." The Venerable Sāriputta rose from his seat, saluted the Blessed One, and keeping him to his right, departed.

Soon after the Venerable Sāriputtā had left, one monk said to the Blessed One: "The Venerable Sāriputta has hit me and has left on his journey without an apology."[6]

Then the Blessed One called another monk and said: "Go, monk, and call the Venerable Sāriputta, saying, 'The Master calls you, Sāriputta.'"[7] The monk did as he was bidden, and the Venerable Sāriputta responded, saying, "Yes, friend."

Then the Venerable Mahāmoggallāna and the Venerable Ānanda, taking the keys, went around the monks' lodgings and said: "Come, revered sirs, come! For today the Venerable Sāriputta will utter his lion's roar in the presence of the Blessed One."

The Venerable Sāriputta approached the Blessed One, and after saluting him, sat down to one side. When he was seated, the Blessed One said: "One of your fellow monks here has complained that you hit him and left on your journey without an apology."

"Lord, one in whom mindfulness directed to the body[8] is not present in regard to the body may well hit a fellow monk and leave without an apology.

"Just as, Lord, people throw upon the earth things clean and unclean, dung, urine, spittle, pus and blood, yet for all that the earth has no revulsion, loathing or disgust towards it;[9] even so, Lord, do I dwell with a heart that is like the earth, vast, exalted and measureless, without hostility, and without ill will. However, one in whom mindfulness directed on the body in regard to the body is not present may well hit a fellow monk and leave without an apology.

"Just as, Lord, people use water to wash things clean and unclean, things soiled with dung, urine, spittle, pus and blood, yet for all that the water has no revulsion, loathing or disgust towards it; even so, Lord, do I dwell with a heart that is like water, vast, exalted and measureless, without hostility, and without ill will. However, one in whom … and leave without an apology

"Just as, Lord, fire burns things clean and unclean, things soiled with dung, urine, spittle, pus and blood, yet for all that the fire has no revulsion, loathing or disgust towards it; even so, Lord, do I dwell with a heart that is like fire, vast, exalted and measureless, without hostility, and without ill will. However, he in whom … and leave without an apology.

"Just as, Lord, the wind blows over things clean and unclean, over dung, urine, spittle, pus and blood, yet for all that the wind has no revulsion, loathing or disgust towards it; even so, Lord, do I dwell with a heart that is like the wind, vast, exalted and measureless, without hostility, and without ill will. However, he in whom … and leave without an apology.

"Lord, just as a duster wipes over things clean and unclean, things soiled with dung, urine, spittle, pus and blood, yet for all that the duster has no revulsion, loathing or disgust towards it; even so, Lord, do I dwell with a heart that is like a duster, vast, exalted and measureless, without hostility, and without ill will. However, he in whom … and leave without an apology.

"Lord, just as an outcast boy or girl, begging-vessel in hand and clad in rags, enters a village or town with a humble heart; even so, Lord, do I dwell with a heart like that of an outcast youth, a heart that is vast, exalted and measureless, without hostility, and without ill will. However, he in whom … and leave without an apology.

"Lord, just as a bull with his horns cut, gentle, well tamed and well trained, when roaming from street to street, from square to square, will not hurt anyone with feet or horns; even so, Lord, do I dwell like a bull with horns cut, with a heart that is vast, exalted and measureless, without hostility, and without ill will. However, he in whom ... and leave without an apology.

"Lord, just as a woman or a man, young, youthful and fond of ornaments, who has just washed the head, would be filled with revulsion, loathing and disgust if the carcass of a snake, a dog or a man were to be slung around the neck; even so, Lord, am I filled with revulsion, loathing and disgust for this foul body of mine. However, one in whom mindfulness directed to the body in regard to the body is not present may well hit a fellow monk and leave without an apology.

"Lord, just as one were to carry around a bowl of liquid fat that is full of holes and crevices, oozing and dripping; even so, Lord, do I carry around this body that is full of holes and crevices, oozing and dripping. However, one in whom mindfulness directed on the body in regard to the body is not present may well hit a fellow monk and leave without an apology."

Then that accusing monk rose from his seat, arranged his upper robe over one shoulder, and with his head on the ground bowed at the feet of the Blessed One, saying: "Lord, I committed an offence when I was so foolish, stupid and unskilful that I accused the Venerable Sāriputta falsely, wrongly and untruthfully. Let the Blessed One accept my admission of the offence and pardon me, and I shall practise restraint in the future."

"Truly, monk, you committed an offence when you were so foolish, stupid and unskilful that you accused Sāriputta falsely, wrongly and untruthfully. But as you have recognized your offence as such and make amends for it according to the rule, we pardon you. For it is a sign of growth in the Discipline of the Noble One that one recognizes one's offence, makes amends for it according to the rule, and in future practises restraint."

The Blessed One then turned to the Venerable Sāriputta and said: "Forgive this foolish man, Sāriputta, before his head splits into seven pieces on this very spot."

"I shall forgive him, Lord, if this revered monk asks for my pardon. And he, too, may forgive me."

(9:11)

131. Samiddhi

(Once the Venerable Samiddhi went to see the Venerable Sāriputta and the latter questioned him as follows:)

"What, Samiddhi, is the conditioning basis of the purposive thoughts that arise in a person?"—"Name-and-form, venerable sir."[10]
"From what does their variety derive? —"From the elements."
"What is their origin?" —"Contact."
"On what do they converge?"—"Feeling."
"What is their head?"—"Concentration."
"What is their master?"—"Mindfulness."
"What is their climax?"—"Wisdom."
"What is their essence?"—"Liberation."
"Where do they merge?"—"In the Deathless."[11]

(In the original text, the Venerable Sāriputta repeats these questions and answers, and concludes:)

"Well spoken, Samiddhi, well spoken! You have answered well the various questions put to you. But do not be proud of yourself on that account!"

(9:14)

132. Rooted in Craving

Monks, I shall teach you nine things rooted in craving. Listen and attend carefully, I shall speak.

What are the nine things rooted in craving? Because of craving there is pursuit; because of pursuit, there is acquisition; because of acquisition, there is decision; because of decision there is desire and lust; because of desire and lust there is selfish tenacity; because of selfish tenacity there is possessiveness; because of possessiveness there is avarice; because of avarice there is concern for protection; and for the sake of protection there is the seizing of cudgels and weapons, and various evil, unwholesome things such as quarrels, strife, dissension and offensive talk, slander and lies.[12]

These are the nine things rooted in craving.

(9:23)

X. The Chapter of the Tens

133. The Benefits of Virtue

On one occasion the Blessed One was dwelling at Sāvatthī in Jeta's Grove, Anāthapiṇḍika's monastery. At that time the Venerable Ānanda approached the Blessed One, paid homage to him, and asked:[1]

"What, Lord, is the benefit of virtuous ways of conduct, what is their reward?"

"Non-remorse, Ānanda, is the benefit and reward of virtuous ways of conduct."

"And what, Lord, is the benefit and reward of non-remorse?"
"Gladness, Ānanda."

"And what, Lord, is the benefit and reward of gladness?"
"Joy."

"And what, Lord, is the benefit and reward of joy?"
"Serenity."

"And what, Lord, is the benefit and reward of serenity?"
"Happiness."

"And what, Lord, is the benefit and reward of happiness?"
"Concentration of the mind."

"And what, Lord, is the benefit and reward of concentration?"
"Knowledge and vision of things as they really are."

"And what, Lord, is the benefit and reward of knowledge and vision of things as they really are?"
"Revulsion and dispassion."

"And what, Lord, is the benefit and reward of revulsion and dispassion?"
"The knowledge and vision of liberation.

"Hence, Ānanda, virtuous ways of conduct have non-remorse as their benefit and reward; non-remorse has gladness as its benefit and reward; gladness has joy as its benefit and reward; joy has serenity as its benefit and reward; serenity has happiness as its benefit and reward; happiness has concentration as its benefit and reward; concentration has knowledge and vision of things as they really are as its benefit and reward; knowledge and vision of things as they really are has revulsion and dispassion as its benefit and reward; revulsion and dispassion have the knowledge and vision of liberation as their benefit and reward. In this way, Ānanda, virtuous ways of conduct lead step by step to the highest."

(10:1)

134. Lawfulness of Progress

For one who is virtuous and endowed with virtue, there is no need for an act of will: "May non-remorse arise in me!" It is a natural law, monks, that non-remorse will arise in one who is virtuous.

For one free of remorse, there is no need for an act of will: "May gladness arise in me!" It is a natural law that gladness will arise in one who is free from remorse.

For one who is glad at heart, there is no need for an act of will: "May joy arise in me!" It is a natural law that joy will arise in one who is glad at heart.

For one who is joyful, there is no need for an act of will: "May my body be serene!" It is a natural law that the body will be serene for one who is joyful.

For one of serene body, there is no need for an act of will: "May I feel happiness!" It is a natural law that one who is serene will feel happiness.

For one who is happy, there is no need for an act of will: "May my mind be concentrated!" It is a natural law for one who is happy that the mind will be concentrated.

For one who is concentrated, there is no need for an act of will: "May I know and see things as they really are!" It is a natural law for one with a concentrated mind to know and see things as they really are.

For one who knows and see things as they really are, there is no need for an act of will: "May I experience revulsion and dispassion!" It is a natural law for one who knows and sees things as they really are to experience revulsion and dispassion.

For one who experiences revulsion and dispassion, there is no need for an act of will: "May I realize the knowledge and vision of liberation!" It is a natural law for one who experiences revulsion and dispassion to realize the knowledge and vision of liberation.

Thus, monks, revulsion and dispassion have knowledge and vision of liberation as their benefit and reward … (continued in conformity with the above, back to) ... virtuous ways of conduct have non-remorse as their benefit and reward.

Thus, monks, the preceding qualities flow into the succeeding qualities; the succeeding qualities bring the preceding qualities to perfection, for going from the near shore to the far shore.[2]

(10:2)

135. The Meditative Experience of Nibbāna–I

Once the Venerable Ānanda approached the Blessed One and asked:

"Can it be, Lord, that a monk attains to such a concentration of mind that in earth he is not percipient of earth, nor in water is he percipient of water, nor in fire ... air ... the base of the infinity of space ... the base of the infinity of consciousness ... the base of nothingness ... the base of neither-perception-nor-non-perception is he percipient of all these; nor is he percipient of this world or a world beyond—but yet he is percipient?"[3]

"Yes, Ānanda, there can be such a concentration of mind that in earth he is not percipient of earth ... nor is he percipient of this world or a world beyond—but yet he is percipient."

"But how, Lord, can a monk attain to such a concentration of mind?"

"Here, Ānanda, the monk is percipient thus: 'This is the peaceful, this is the sublime, namely, the stilling of all formations, the relinquishment of all acquisitions, the destruction of craving, dispassion, cessation, Nibbāna.' It is in this way, Ānanda, that a monk may attain to such a concentration of mind."[4]

(10:6)

136. The Meditative Experience of Nibbāna–II

Once the Venerable Ānanda approached the Venerable Sāriputta and asked:

"Can it be, friend Sāriputta, that a monk attains to such a concentration of mind that in earth he is not percipient of earth ... (as above) ... nor is he percipient of this world or a world beyond—but yet he is percipient?"

"Yes, friend Ānanda, he can attain to such a concentration of mind."

"But how, friend Sāriputta, can a monk attain to such a concentration of mind?"

"Once, friend Ānanda, I lived here in Sāvatthī, in the Dark Forest. There I attained to such a concentration of mind that in earth I was not percipient of earth … (as above) … nor was I percipient of this world or a world beyond—and yet I was percipient."

"But what was the Venerable Sāriputta percipient of on that occasion?"

"'Nibbāna is cessation of becoming, Nibbāna is cessation of becoming'[5]—one such perception arose in me and another such perception ceased. Just as, friend Ānanda, from a fire of faggots one flame arises and another flame ceases, even so, 'Nibbāna is cessation of becoming, Nibbāna is cessation of becoming'—one such perception arose in me and another such perception ceased. On that occasion, friend, I perceived that Nibbāna is the cessation of becoming."

(10:7)

137. The Buddha's Lion's Roar

Monks, the lion, the king of beasts, comes forth from his lair in the evening. Then he stretches himself, surveys the four directions all around, and roars three times his lion's roar.[6] And why? (He does so with the thought:) "May I not cause the death of small creatures that have gone astray!"

"The lion"—this, monks, is a name for the *Tathāgata*, the Arahant, the Fully Enlightened One. When, monks, the *Tathāgata* expounds the Dhamma in an assembly, that is his lion's roar.

There are, monks, these ten *Tathāgata* powers[7] of a *Tathāgata*, endowed with which the *Tathāgata* claims the foremost rank, utters his lion's roar in the assemblies and sets rolling the supreme Wheel of the Dhamma.[8] What are these ten *Tathāgata* powers?

(1) Here, the *Tathāgata* understands, as it really is, cause as cause and non-cause as non-cause.[9] This is a *Tathāgata* power of the *Tathāgata*, by reason of which he claims the foremost rank, utters his lion's roar in the assemblies and sets rolling the supreme Wheel of the Dhamma.

(2) Again, the *Tathāgata* understands, as it really is, by way of cause and root condition,[10] the result of past, future, and present actions that are performed. This too is a *Tathāgata* power of the *Tathāgata*....

(3) Again, the *Tathāgata* understands, as it really is, the way leading to all destinies.[11] This too is a *Tathāgata* power of the *Tathāgata* ....

(4) Again, the *Tathāgata* understands, as it really is, the world with its many and different elements.[12] This too is a *Tathāgata* power of the *Tathāgata*....

(5) Again, the *Tathāgata* understands, as it really is, the different dispositions of beings.[13] This too is a *Tathāgata* power of the *Tathāgata*....

(6) Again, the *Tathāgata* understands, as it really is, the inferior and superior condition of the faculties of other beings, of other persons.[14] This too is a *Tathāgata* power of the *Tathāgata*....

(7) Again, the *Tathāgata* understands, as it really is, with regard to the *jhānas*, the liberations, the concentrations and the meditative attainments, their defects and purity and the emergence from them.[15] This too is a *Tathāgata* power of the *Tathāgata*....

(8) Again, the *Tathāgata* recollects his manifold past lives, that is to say, one birth, two births, three births, four births, five births, ten births, twenty births, thirty births, forty births, fifty births, a hundred births, a thousand births, a hundred thousand births, many aeons of world-contraction, many aeons of world-expansion, many aeons of world-contraction and expansion ... (as in Text 34) ... Thus with their aspects and particulars he recollects his manifold past lives. This too is a *Tathāgata* power of the *Tathāgata*....

(9) Again, with the divine eye, which is purified and surpasses the human, the *Tathāgata* sees beings passing away and reappearing, inferior and superior, fair and ugly, of good or bad destination. He understands beings as faring according to their deeds ... (as in Text 34) ...This too is a *Tathāgata* power of the *Tathāgata*....

(10) Again, the *Tathāgata*, by the destruction of the taints, in this very life enters and dwells in the taintless liberation of mind, liberation by wisdom, having realized it for himself by direct knowledge. This too is a *Tathāgata* power of the *Tathāgata*, by reason of which he claims the foremost rank, roars his lion's roar in the assemblies and sets rolling the supreme Wheel of the Dhamma.

These, monks, are the ten *Tathāgata* powers of the *Tathāgata*, endowed with which the *Tathāgata* claims the foremost rank, roars his lion's roar in the assemblies and sets rolling the supreme Wheel of the Dhamma.

(10:21)

138. Doctrinal Terms

Once the Venerable Ānanda approached the Blessed One and, after paying homage to him, sat down to one side. The Blessed One then addressed the Venerable Ānanda thus:

"Here, Ānanda, I am confident about those things that lead to the realization by direct knowledge of the various doctrinal terms,[16] and I claim to teach the Dhamma about these matters in such a way that a person who acts accordingly will know the real as being real and the unreal as being unreal; he will know the inferior as being inferior and the excellent as being excellent; he will know what can be surpassed as being surpassable and the unsurpassable as being unsurpassable; and there is the possibility that he will know, understand and realize it just as it ought to be known, understood and realized.

"But that, Ānanda, is the highest knowledge, namely, the knowledge of these things as they really are. And I say, Ānanda, there is no knowledge higher and more excellent than this."

(Here follows a full repetition of the text on the ten *Tathāgata* powers, as in the preceding sutta).

(10:22; extract)

139. Universal Impermanence

(1) Monks, as far as there are Kāsi[17] and Kosala people, as far as the realm of King Pasenadi of Kosala extends, King Pasenadi of Kosala ranks as the highest. But even for King Pasenadi change[18] takes place, transformation takes place. When seeing this, monks, an instructed noble disciple is repelled by it; being repelled, he becomes dispassionate towards the highest,[19] not to speak of what is low.

(2) Monks, as far as sun and moon revolve and illuminate all directions by their radiance, so far does the thousandfold world

system extend. And in that thousandfold world system there are a thousand moons, a thousand suns, a thousand Mount Sinerus the king of mountains, a thousand Jambudīpa continents, a thousand Western Goyana continents, a thousand Northern Kuru continents, a thousand Eastern Videha continents, a thousand four great oceans, a thousand Four Divine Kings and their heavens, a thousand each of the heavens of the Tāvatiṃsa devas, of the Yāma devas, of the Tusita devas, of the Nimmāṇarati devas, of the Paranimmitavasavattī devas, and there are a thousand Brahma-worlds. As far, monks, as this thousandfold world system extends, Mahābrahmā ranks there as the highest. But even for Mahābrahmā change takes place, transformation takes place. When seeing this, monks, an instructed noble disciple is repelled by it; being repelled, he becomes dispassionate towards the highest, not to speak of what is low.

(3) There will be a time, monks, when this world comes to an end. And at that time, beings are generally reborn among the devas of Streaming Radiance.[20] There they live, made of mind, feeding on joy, radiating light from themselves, traversing the skies, living in glory, and thus they remain for a very long time. When the world comes to an end, monks, these devas of Streaming Radiance rank as the highest. But even for these devas change takes place, transformation takes place. When seeing this, monks, an instructed noble disciple is repelled by it; being repelled, he becomes dispassionate towards the highest, not to speak of what is low.

(4) Monks, there are the ten *kasiṇa* devices.[21] What are the ten? Someone perceives the earth *kasiṇa*, above, below, on all sides, undivided, unbounded; another person perceives the water *kasiṇa* ... the fire *kasiṇa* ... the wind *kasiṇa* ... the blue ... yellow ... red ... white *kasiṇa* ... the space *kasiṇa* ... the consciousness *kasiṇa*, above, below, on all sides, undivided, unbounded. These are the ten *kasiṇa* devices. Among these ten, this is the highest: when one perceives the consciousness *kasiṇa* above, below, on all sides, undivided, unbounded. There are indeed, monks, persons who perceive in such a way. But even for them change takes place, transformation takes place. When seeing this, monks, an instructed noble disciple is repelled by it; being repelled, he becomes dispassionate towards the highest, not to speak of what is low.

(5) Monks, there are eight stages of mastery.[22] What are the eight?

(i) Perceiving forms internally, one sees forms externally, small ones, beautiful or ugly; and in mastering them, one understands: "I know, I see!" This is the first stage of mastery....
(viii) Not perceiving forms internally, one sees forms externally, white forms, of white colour, white appearance, white lustre, and mastering these, one understands: "I know, I see!" This is the eighth stage of mastery.

Among these eight, the last is the highest. There are indeed, monks, persons who perceive in such a way. But even for them change takes place, transformation takes place. When seeing this, monks, an instructed noble disciple is repelled by it; being repelled, he becomes dispassionate towards the highest, not to speak of what is low.

(6) Monks, there are four modes of progress: the mode of progress that is painful, with sluggish direct knowledge; the mode of progress that is painful, with quick direct knowledge; the mode of progress that is pleasant, with sluggish direct knowledge; and the mode of progress that is pleasant, with quick direct knowledge.[23] Among these four, the highest is the mode of progress that is pleasant, with quick direct knowledge. There are indeed, monks those who make progress in such a way. But even for them change takes place, transformation takes place. When seeing this, monks, an instructed noble disciple is repelled by it; being repelled, he becomes dispassionate towards the highest, not to speak of what is low.

(7) Monks, there are four modes of perception: one person perceives what is limited; another perceives what is exalted; another perceives what is measureless; and still another, aware that "There is nothing," perceives the base of nothingness.[24]

Among these four modes of perception, the highest is when, aware that "There is nothing," one perceives the base of nothingness. There are indeed, monks, those who perceive in such a way. But even for them change takes place, transformation takes place. When seeing this, monks, an instructed noble disciple is repelled by it; being repelled, he becomes dispassionate towards the highest, not to speak of what is low.

(8) Monks, among the views of outsiders, this is the highest: "I might not be and it might not be mine; I shall not be and it will not be mine."[25]

For one, monks, who has such a view, it can be expected that he will not feel attracted to becoming and will have no aversion against the cessation of becoming.[26] There are indeed, monks, those who have such a view. But even for them change takes place, transformation takes place. When seeing this, monks, an instructed noble disciple is repelled by it; being repelled, he becomes dispassionate towards the highest, not to speak of what is low.

(9) Monks, there are some ascetics and brahmins who teach an "ultimate purification."[27] Those who teach an "ultimate purification" regard it as the highest if, after transcending the base of nothingness, one enters into and dwells in the base of neither-perception-nor-non-perception. They teach their doctrine for the direct knowledge and realization of that. There are indeed, monks, those who teach thus. But even for them change takes place, transformation takes place. When seeing this, monks, an instructed noble disciple is repelled by it; being repelled, he becomes dispassionate towards the highest, not to speak of what is low.

(10) Monks, there are some ascetics and brahmins who teach the supreme Nibbāna in this very life.[28] To those who teach the supreme Nibbāna in this very life, the highest is the liberation-without-clinging attained after seeing the six bases of contact as they really are, namely, their arising and passing away, the gratification and danger in them, and the escape from them.

And though I teach and proclaim thus, some ascetics and brahmins wrongly, baselessly, falsely and incorrectly misrepresent me thus: "The ascetic Gotama does not teach the full understanding of sensual pleasures, nor of forms, nor of feelings." But, monks, I do teach the full understanding of sensual pleasures, and of forms, and of feelings.[29] And being stilled, quenched and cooled even in this very life, I proclaim the supreme Nibbāna that is free from clinging.[30]

(10:29)

140. King Pasenadi's Homage to the Buddha

On one occasion the Blessed One was dwelling at Sāvatthī in Jeta's Grove, Anāthapiṇḍika's monastery. At that time King Pasenadi of Kosala had returned from a sham battle,[31] having been victorious and having achieved his purpose. The king then set out in the direction of the monastery. He rode by chariot as far as the road went; then he alighted from his chariot and entered the monastery on foot.

At that time, a number of monks were walking up and down in the open. The king approached them and asked: "Where, venerable sirs, is the Blessed One staying now?"

"He is staying in the lodging there, great king, where the door is shut. You may go there quietly and without haste. Then enter the verandah, clear your throat, and knock with the door bar. The Blessed One will open the door for you."

The king did as he was told and the Blessed One opened the door for the king. Having entered the dwelling, King Pasenadi bent low before the Blessed One with his head on the ground and kissed the Blessed One's feet, embracing them with his hands. Then he announced his name: "I am Pasenadi, Lord, the king of Kosala. I am Pasenadi, Lord, the king of Kosala."

"But, great king, what reason do you see for showing to this body such profound humility and for offering it such loving devotion?"

"To express my grateful thanks, Lord; for that reason do I show to the Blessed One such profound humility and offer him my loving devotion.

"The Blessed One, Lord, lives for the welfare of the multitude, for the happiness of the multitude, he has established many people in the noble way, in good and wholesome principles. It is for this reason, Lord, that I show to the Blessed One such profound humility and offer him my loving devotion.

"Again, Lord, the Blessed One is virtuous, of mature virtue, of noble virtue, of wholesome virtue; he is endowed with wholesome virtue. It is for this reason ….

"Again, Lord, the Blessed One has been a forest dweller for a long time; he resorts to remote forest lands, to secluded dwellings. It is for this reason ….

"Again, Lord, the Blessed One is content with whatever robes, alms-food, lodging, and medicinal requisites he receives. It is for this reason ....

"Again, Lord, the Blessed One is worthy of gifts, worthy of hospitality, worthy of offerings, worthy of reverential salutation, being the unsurpassed field of merit for the world. It is for this reason ....

"Again, Lord, the Blessed One obtains at will, without trouble or difficulty, (the opportunity for) talk that befits an austere life and is helpful to mental clarity; that is to say, talk on fewness of wishes, on contentment, on solitude, on seclusion, on application of energy, on virtue, concentration, wisdom, liberation and the knowledge and vision of liberation. It is for this reason ....

"Again, Lord, the Blessed One attains at will, without trouble or difficulty, the four jhānas, which pertain to the higher mind and are pleasant dwellings in this very life. It is for this reason ....

"Again, Lord, the Blessed One recollects his manifold past lives, that is to say, one birth ... (as in Text 137) ... It is for this reason ....

"Again, Lord, with the divine eye, which is purified and surpasses the human, the Blessed One sees beings passing away and reappearing ... (as in Text 137) ... It is for this reason ....

"And again, Lord, the Blessed One, by the destruction of the taints, in this very life enters and dwells in the taintless liberation of mind, liberation by wisdom, having realized it for himself by direct knowledge. It is for this reason, Lord, that I show to the Blessed One such profound humility and offer him my loving devotion.

"But now, Lord, we must go. We have much work and many duties."

"Do as you think fit, great king."

And King Pasenadi of Kosala rose from his seat, paid homage to the Blessed One, and respectfully and keeping him to his right, he departed.

(10:30)

141. Self-Examination

If, O monks, a monk is not skilled in knowing the ways of others' minds, he should resolve, "I must become skilled in knowing the ways of my own mind." Thus, monks, should you train yourselves.

And how is a monk skilled in knowing the ways of his own mind? It is just as if a woman or a man, young, youthful and fond of ornaments, would look at their face in a clean, bright mirror or in a bowl of clear water. If they then see any dust or dirt, they will make all effort to remove it. But if no dust or dirt is seen, they will be glad about it, and their wish satisfied, they will think, "How good! I am clean!"

Similarly, monks, for a monk self-examination is very helpful for the growth of wholesome qualities: "Am I often covetous or often not covetous? Do I often have ill will in my heart or am I often free of it? Am I often immersed in sloth and torpor or am I often free of it? Am I excited or often free of excitement? Am I often in doubt or often free of doubt? Am I often angry or often free of anger? Is my mind often defiled by unwholesome thoughts or often free of defilements? Is my body often restless or often free of restlessness? Am I often lazy or often energetic? Am I often unconcentrated or often concentrated?"

When, by such self-examination, a monk finds that he is often covetous, full of ill will, slothful, excited, doubtful, angry, mentally defiled, bodily restless, lazy and unconcentrated, then he should apply his utmost zeal and energy, effort and exertion, as well as unremitting mindfulness and clear comprehension, to the abandoning of all those evil, unwholesome qualities.

Just as a man whose clothes or turban are on fire would apply his utmost zeal and energy, effort and exertion, as well as mindfulness and clear comprehension, so that he may extinguish the fire; even so, the monk should apply his utmost zeal and energy ... for the abandoning of those evil, unwholesome qualities.

But if, on examining himself, that monk finds that he is more often without covetousness and ill will, more often free from sloth and torpor, free from excitement and doubt; more often free from anger; and finds that his mind is more often undefiled and his body free of restlessness; that he is more often energetic and well concentrated—then grounding himself firmly in all these wholesome qualities, he should make a further effort for the destruction of the taints.

(10:51)

142. Do Not Stagnate!

I do not approve, monks, of stagnation in things wholesome, not to speak of a decline. It is growth in things wholesome that I praise, and not stagnation, not decline in them.

(10:53, extract)

143. The Roots of Everything

It may be, O monks, that wandering ascetics of another persuasion might ask you:[32] "In what are all things rooted? How do they come to actual existence? Where do they arise? Where do they converge? What is the foremost in all things? What is their master? What is the highest of all things? What is the essence in all things? Where do all things merge? Where do they end?"

If you are thus questioned, monks, you should reply as follows: "All things are rooted in desire.[33] They come to actual existence through attention,[34] originate from contact, and converge on feelings. The foremost of all things is concentration. All things are mastered by mindfulness. Their peak is wisdom, their essence liberation. All things merge in the Deathless, and Nibbāna is their culmination."[35]

(10:58)

144. The Spirit of Monkhood

O monks, you should train yourselves thus: "In the spirit of our going forth should our mind be strengthened![36] No evil, unwholesome thoughts should persist obsessing our minds! In the perception of impermanence shall our mind be strengthened! In the perception of non-self shall our mind be strengthened! In the perception of foulness shall our mind be strengthened! In the perception of danger shall our mind be strengthened! In knowing the even and uneven ways of the world shall our mind be strengthened! In knowing growth and decline in the world shall our mind be strengthened![37] In knowing the origination and the passing away of the world shall our mind be strengthened![38] In the perception of abandoning shall our mind be strengthened! In the perception of dispassion shall our mind be strengthened! In the perception of cessation shall our mind be strengthened!"[39] In such a way, monks, should you train yourselves.

When a monk's mind is strengthened in all these ways, one of two fruits may be expected: either final knowledge in this present life, or else, if there is a residue of clinging, the stage of non-returning.

(10:59)

145. Ignorance and Craving

(AN 10:61) A first beginning of ignorance, O monks, cannot be discerned,[40] of which it can be said, "Before that, there was no ignorance and it came to be after that." Though this is so, monks, yet a specific condition of ignorance is discerned. Ignorance, too, has its nutriment, I declare; and it is not without a nutriment. And what is the nutriment of ignorance? "The five hindrances" should be the answer.[41]

(AN 10:62) A first beginning of the craving for becoming, O monks, cannot be discerned, of which it can be said, "Before that, there was no craving for becoming and it came to be after that." Though this is so, monks, yet a specific condition for the craving for becoming is discerned. The craving for becoming, too, has its nutriment, I declare; and it is not without a nutriment. And what is the nutriment of the craving for becoming? "Ignorance" should be the answer. But ignorance, too, has its nutriment; it is not without a nutriment. And what is the nutriment of ignorance? "The five hindrances" should be the answer.

(AN 10:61 & 62) But the five hindrances, too, have their nutriment, monks; they are not without a nutriment. And what is the nutriment of the five hindrances? "The three ways of wrong conduct" should be the answer.[42]

The three ways of wrong conduct, too, have their nutriment; they are not without a nutriment. And what is their nutriment? "Lack of sense restraint" should be the answer.

Lack of sense restraint, too, has its nutriment; it is not without a nutriment. And what is its nutriment? "Lack of mindfulness and clear comprehension" should be the answer.

Lack of mindfulness and clear comprehension, too, has its nutriment; it is not without a nutriment. And what is the nutriment of the lack of mindfulness and clear comprehension? "Improper attention" should be the answer.

Improper attention, too, has its nutriment; it is not without a nutriment. And what is the nutriment of improper attention? "Lack of faith" should be the answer.

Lack of faith, too, has its nutriment; it is not without a nutriment. And what is the nutriment of the lack of faith? "Listening to wrong teachings" should be the answer.

Listening to wrong teachings, too, has its nutriment; it is not without a nutriment. And what is the nutriment of listening to wrong teachings? "Association with bad people" should be the answer.

Hence, when association with bad people prevails, listening to wrong teachings will prevail.[43] When listening to wrong teachings prevails, it will make lack of faith prevail. When lack of faith prevails, it will make improper attention prevail. When improper attention prevails, it will make lack of mindfulness and clear comprehension prevail. When lack of mindfulness and clear comprehension prevails, it will make lack of sense restraint prevail. When lack of sense restraint prevails, it will make the three ways of wrong conduct prevail. When the three ways of wrong conduct prevail, they will make the five hindrances prevail. When the five hindrances prevail, they will make ignorance prevail. (AN 10:62 adds: When ignorance prevails, it will make the craving for becoming prevail.) Such is the nutriment of that ignorance (AN 10:62: of that craving for becoming), and so it prevails.

Just as, when there is heavy rain high up in the mountains and the sky is rumbling, the water, flowing downwards, will fill up the clefts, crevices and fissures in the mountains, and when these are full, they will fill up the little pools; the full little pools will fill up the lakes; the full lakes will fill up the small rivers; the full small rivers will fill up the big rivers; and the full big rivers will fill up the great ocean. Such is the nutriment of the great ocean, and so it becomes full.

In the same way, monks, when association with bad people prevails, listening to wrong teachings will prevail ... when the five hindrances prevail, ignorance (and the craving for becoming) will prevail. Such is the nutriment of ignorance (and of the craving for becoming), and so it prevails.

Liberation by supreme knowledge too, O monks, has its nutriment, I declare; it is not without a nutriment. And what is the nutriment of liberation by supreme knowledge? "The seven factors of enlightenment" should be the answer.

The seven factors of enlightenment, too, have their nutriment, I declare; they are not without a nutriment? And what is the nutriment of the seven factors of enlightenment? "The four foundations of mindfulness" should be the answer.

The four foundation of mindfulness, too, have their nutriment; they are not without a nutriment. And what is the nutriment of the four foundations of mindfulness? "The three ways of good conduct" should be the answer.

The three ways of good conduct, too, have their nutriment; they are not without a nutriment. And what is the nutriment of the three ways of good conduct? "Restraint of the senses" should be the answer.

Restraint of the senses, too, has its nutriment; it is not without a nutriment. And what is the nutriment of restraint of the senses? "Mindfulness and clear comprehension" should be the answer.

Mindfulness and clear comprehension, too, have their nutriment; they are not without a nutriment. And what is the nutriment of mindfulness and clear comprehension? "Proper attention" should be the answer.

Proper attention, too, has its nutriment; it is not without a nutriment. And what is the nutriment of proper attention? "Faith" should be the answer.

Faith, too, has its nutriment; it is not without a nutriment. And what is the nutriment of faith? "Listening to the true Dhamma" should be the answer.

Listening to the true Dhamma, too, has its nutriment; it is not without a nutriment. And what is the nutriment of listening to the true Dhamma? "Association with superior people" should be the answer.

Hence, when association with superior people prevails, it will make prevail the listening to the true Dhamma ... When the seven factors of enlightenment prevail, they will make prevail liberation by supreme knowledge. Such is the nutriment of that liberation by supreme knowledge, and so it prevails.

Just as, when there is heavy rain high up in the mountains and the sky is rumbling, the water, flowing downwards, will fill up the clefts, crevices and fissures in the mountains, and when these are full, they will fill up the little pools; the full little pools will fill up the lakes; the full lakes will fill up the small rivers; the full small rivers will fill up the big rivers; and the full big rivers will fill up the great ocean. Such is the nutriment of the great ocean, and so it becomes full.

In the same way, monks, when association with superior people prevails, listening to the true Dhamma will prevail. When listening to the true Dhamma prevails, faith will prevail. When faith prevails, proper attention will prevail. When proper attention prevails, mindfulness and clear comprehension will prevail. When mindfulness and clear comprehension prevail, restraint of the senses will prevail. When restraint of the senses prevails, the three ways of good conduct will prevail. When the three ways of good conduct prevail, the four foundations of mindfulness will prevail. When the four foundations of mindfulness prevail, the seven factors of enlightenment will prevail. When the seven factors of enlightenment prevail, liberation by supreme knowledge will prevail. Such is the nutriment of that liberation by supreme knowledge, and so it prevails.

(10:61 & 62; combined)

146. Happiness and Suffering

On one occasion the Venerable Sāriputta was dwelling in Magadha, in the village Nālaka.[44] On that occasion, Sāmaṇḍakāni, a wandering ascetic, approached him and asked:

"What, friend Sāriputta, is happiness, and what is suffering?"

"To be reborn, friend, is suffering; not to be reborn is happiness."

(10:65; extract)

147. Birth, Old Age, and Death

If, O monks, three things were not to be found in the world, the *Tathāgata*, the Arahant, the Fully Enlightened One, would not appear in the world, nor would the Dhamma and Discipline proclaimed by him shed its light over the world. What are these three things? Birth, old age, and death. But since these three things are to be found in the world, the *Tathāgata* appears in the world, the Arahant, the Fully Enlightened One, and the Dhamma and Discipline proclaimed by him sheds its light over the world.

Without abandoning three things, one is unable to abandon birth, old age, and death. What are these three? Greed, hatred, and delusion: without abandoning these three things one is unable to abandon birth, old age, and death.

Without abandoning three things, one is unable to abandon greed, hatred, and delusion. They are: personality view, sceptical doubt, and clinging to rules and vows.[45]

Without abandoning three things, one is unable to abandon personality view, sceptical doubt, and clinging to rules and vows. They are: improper attention, pursuing wrong ways, and mental lassitude.

Without abandoning three things, one is unable to abandon improper attention, the pursuing of wrong ways and mental lassitude. They are: unmindfulness, lack of clear comprehension, and mental distraction.

Without abandoning three things, one is unable to abandon unmindfulness, lack of clear comprehension and mental distraction. They are: disinterest in seeing noble ones, disinterest in listening to their teachings, and a fault-finding mentality.

Without abandoning three things, one is unable to abandon lack of interest in seeing noble ones, disinterest in listening to their teachings, and a fault-finding mentality. They are: restlessness, lack of restraint, and immorality.

Without abandoning three things, one is unable to abandon restlessness, lack of self-control, and immorality. They are: lack of faith, unfriendliness, and laziness.

Without abandoning three things, one is unable to abandon lack of faith, unfriendliness, and laziness. They are: disrespect, stubbornness, and bad friendships.

Without abandoning three things, one is unable to abandon disrespect, stubbornness, and bad friendships. They are: shamelessness, lack of moral dread and negligence.

There is a person, monks, who is shameless, morally reckless, and negligent. Being negligent, he cannot abandon disrespect, stubbornness, and bad friendships. Having bad friends, he cannot abandon lack of faith, unfriendliness, and laziness. Being lazy, he cannot abandon restlessness, lack of restraint and immorality. Being immoral, he cannot abandon disinterest in seeing noble ones, disinterest in listening to their teachings, and a fault-finding mentality. Being a fault-finder, he cannot abandon unmindfulness, lack of clear comprehension, and mental distraction. Having a distracted mind, he cannot abandon improper attention, the pursuit of wrong ways and mental lassitude. With mental lassitude, he cannot abandon personality view, sceptical doubt, and clinging to rules and vows. Troubled by sceptical doubt, he cannot abandon greed, hatred, and delusion. And without giving up greed, hatred, and delusion, he cannot abandon birth, old age, and death.

But by abandoning three things, one is able to abandon birth, old age, and death. What are these three? They are: greed, hatred, and delusion. By abandoning them, one is able to abandon birth, old age, and death.

By abandoning three things, one is able to abandon greed, hatred, and delusion. They are: personality view, sceptical doubt, and clinging to rules and vows.

(To be continued with the same sequence of terms as above, up to:)

By abandoning three things, one is able to abandon disrespect, stubbornness, and bad friendships. They are: shamelessness, lack of moral dread, and negligence.

There is a person, monks, who is conscientious, scrupulous, and diligent. Being diligent, he can abandon disrespect, stubbornness, and bad friendships. Having noble friends, he can abandon lack of faith, unfriendliness, and laziness. Being energetic, he can abandon restlessness, lack of restraint, and immorality. Being virtuous, he can abandon disinterest in seeing noble ones, disinterest in listening to their teachings, and a fault-finding mentality. Not being a fault-finder, he can abandon unmindfulness, lack of clear comprehension, and mental distraction. Having an undistracted mind, he can abandon improper attention, pursuit of wrong ways, and mental lassitude. Being without mental lassitude, he can abandon personality view, sceptical doubt, and clinging to rules and vows. Being free from doubt, he can abandon greed, hatred, and delusion. Having abandoned greed, hatred, and delusion, he can abandon birth, old age, and death.

(10:76)

148. A Discriminative Teaching

On one occasion the Blessed One was dwelling near Campā, on the bank of the Gaggarā lotus pond.

One day the householder Vajjiyamāhita left Campā at an early hour in order to see the Blessed One.[46] Then he thought: "It is not the right time to visit the Blessed One, who will now be in seclusion. Nor is it the proper time to visit the venerable monks; they, too, will be in seclusion. Let me now go to the park where the wandering ascetics of another persuasion stay."

When Vajjiyamāhita the householder arrived at the park, those wanderers were gathered there in company and were sitting together shouting and speaking loudly, engaged in diverse kinds of low talk. But when they saw Vajjiyamāhita the householder approaching in the distance, they admonished each other to be quiet, saying: "Make less noise, your reverences, and be quiet! Here the householder Vajjiyamāhita is coming, a disciple of the ascetic Gotama. He is one of the white-clad lay disciples of the ascetic Gotama who stays now at Campā. These worthy ones do not like much noise, they are used to being noiseless and they praise noiselessness. Perhaps if Vajjiyamāhita sees our group to be quiet, he may think of coming here."

These wandering ascetics now kept silent. When the householder Vajjiyamāhita arrived there, he exchanged polite greetings and cordial talk with them and sat down at one side. When he was seated, the wanderers asked him:

"Is it true, householder, what they say—that the ascetic Gotama blames all asceticism and that he unreservedly condemns and reproves all ascetics who live a harsh and austere life?"

"No, venerable sirs, the Blessed One does not blame all asceticism, nor does he unreservedly condemn and reprove all ascetics living a harsh and austere life. What is blameworthy, the Blessed One blames; what is praiseworthy, he praises. By blaming what is blameworthy and praising what is praiseworthy, the Blessed One teaches with discrimination, he does not teach here in a one-sided way."[47]

At these words, a certain wanderer said this to the householder Vajjiyamāhita: "Wait a moment, householder! That ascetic Gotama, whom you praise so much, is a nihilist, and he is one who refrains from making any definite declarations."[48]

"About that, too, venerable sir, I shall speak to your reverences according to the Dhamma. The Blessed One, venerable sir, declares that some things are wholesome and other things unwholesome. The Blessed One, having thus declared what is wholesome and what is unwholesome, is in fact one who makes definite declarations. He is not a nihilist, nor one who refrains from making definite declarations."

At these words the wanderers kept silent, embarrassed, sitting there with slumping shoulders and heads lowered, brooding and unable to utter a word. When Vajjiyamāhita saw them in that condition, he rose from his seat and left to see the Blessed One. Having arrived, after saluting the Blessed One, he told him of his conversation with these wanderers of another persuasion. And the Blessed One said:

"Good, householder, good! In that way, householder, should such foolish persons, when occasion offers, be well refuted by you according to the Dhamma.

"I do not say, householder, that all asceticism should be practised; nor do I say of all asceticism that it should not be practised. I do not say that all undertakings should be performed; nor do I say of all undertakings that they should not be performed. I do not say that every spiritual effort should be done or every act of renunciation be carried out; nor do I say of every spiritual effort that it should not be done nor of every act of renunciation that it should not be carried out. I do not say that one should free oneself by every kind of freedom; nor do I say of every kind of freedom that one should not free oneself by it.

"What I declare, householder, is that such an asceticism should not be practised which makes unwholesome states grow and wholesome states wane. But, I declare, an asceticism which makes unwholesome states wane and wholesome states grow should be practised.

"If in performing undertakings, making spiritual efforts, carrying out acts of renunciation, freeing oneself by certain kinds of freedom, unwholesome states grow, then, I declare, all these practices should not be carried out."

"But if in performing undertakings, making spiritual efforts, carrying out acts of renunciation, freeing oneself by certain kinds of freedom, unwholesome states wane and wholesome states grow, then, I declare, all these practices should be carried out."

Then Vajjiyamāhita the householder, thus instructed by the Blessed One's Dhamma talk, roused by it, inspired and gladdened, rose from his seat, saluted the Blessed One respectfully, and keeping him to his right, departed.

Soon after he had left, the Blessed One addressed the monks thus: "Monks, even a monk who has had for a long time clear vision as to this Dhamma and Discipline would well refute those wanderers of another persuasion in the very same way that the householder Vajjiyamāhita has done."

(10:94)

149. Will All Beings Attain Liberation?

On one occasion a wandering ascetic named Uttiya approached the Blessed One. After exchanging greetings and cordial talk, he sat down to one side and asked the Blessed One:

"How is it, Master Gotama: is the world eternal—is only this true and everything else false?"

"This, Uttiya, I have not declared: that the world is eternal; and that only this is true and everything else false."

"How then, Master Gotama: is the world non-eternal—is only this true and everything else false?"

"That, too, Uttiya, I have not declared: that the world is non-eternal; and that only this is true and everything else false."

"How is it, Master Gotama: is the world finite or infinite? Are the life principle and the body the same or different? Does the *Tathāgata* exist after death or does he not exist after death? Does he exist as well as not exist or neither exist nor not exist after death? Is any one of these statements the only one that is true and everything else false?"

"All that, Uttiya, I have not declared: that the world is finite ... that the *Tathāgata* neither exists nor does not exist after death; nor do I declare that any one of these statements is the only true one and everything else false."

"But how is it, Master Gotama? To all my questions you have replied that you have not so declared. What, after all, does Master Gotama actually declare?"

"Having directly known it, Uttiya, I have taught the Dhamma to my disciples for the purification of beings, for getting beyond sorrow and lamentation, for the ending of pain and grief, for attaining to the method of liberation and for realizing Nibbāna."

"But if Master Gotama, from direct knowledge, teaches the Dhamma to his disciples for the purification of beings, for getting beyond sorrow and lamentation, for the ending of pain and grief, for attaining to the method of liberation and for realizing Nibbāna, will the whole world thereby be emancipated,[49] or half of it or a third part of it?"

At these words, the Blessed One kept silent.[50]

Then this thought occurred to the Venerable Ānanda: "May Uttiya the wanderer not conceive a harmful opinion, by thinking, 'When I asked the ascetic Gotama a question on an ultimate issue, he foundered and did not reply. Probably he was unable to do so.' For such a view would bring harm and suffering to Uttiya for a long time."

Then the Venerable Ānanda turned to Uttiya, saying: "I shall give you a simile, friend Uttiya, for with the help of a simile intelligent people may come to understand the meaning of what was said.

"Suppose, friend Uttiya, there is a king's border town, with strong ramparts and turrets on sound foundations, and with a single gate. There is also a gatekeeper, intelligent, experienced and prudent, who keeps out people unknown and admits only those who are known. That gatekeeper walks along the path that girdles the town all round, and while doing so he does not notice in the ramparts any hole or opening, not even one big enough for a cat to slip through. Though he does not have the knowledge of how many creatures enter the town or leave it, yet he does know this:

'Any larger creatures that enter or leave this town can do so only by this gate.'

"Similarly, friend Uttiya, the *Tathāgata* is not concerned with whether the entire world will be emancipated by his teaching or half of it or a third part. But the *Tathāgata* is aware that whosoever has been emancipated, is now emancipated or will be emancipated from the world, all these will do so by removing the five hindrances that defile the mind and weaken understanding, by firmly establishing their minds in the four foundations of mindfulness, and by cultivating the seven factors of enlightenment in their true nature. That same question, friend Uttiya, which you had asked the Blessed One before, you have asked him again in another way."[51]

(10:95)

150. Not Outside the Buddha's Discipline

Ten things, monks, do not have purity and clarity outside the Discipline of the Sublime Master. What are the ten?

(AN 10:123) Right view, right intention, right speech, right action, right livelihood, right effort, right mindfulness, right concentration, right knowledge, and right liberation.[52]

(AN 10:124) And if these ten things have not arisen, they will not arise outside the Discipline of the Sublime Master.

(AN 10:125) Outside the Discipline of the Sublime Master, these ten things will not be of great fruit and benefit.

(AN 10:126) Outside the Discipline of the Sublime Master, these ten things will not end in the elimination of greed, hatred, and delusion.

(AN 10:127) Outside the Discipline of the Sublime Master, these ten things will not conduce to complete disenchantment, dispassion, cessation, peace, direct knowledge, enlightenment, and Nibbāna.

(10:123–27)

151. The Concatenation of Kamma

The destruction of life, monks, I declare to be threefold: as caused by greed, caused by hatred, caused by delusion. So too, taking what is not given, sexual misconduct, false speech, divisive speech, harsh speech, frivolous chatter, covetousness, ill will and wrong view, I declare to be threefold: as caused by greed, caused by hatred and caused by delusion.[53]

Hence, monks, greed is a producer of kammic concatenation, hatred is a producer of kammic concatenation, delusion is a producer of kammic concatenation. But by the destruction of greed, hatred, and delusion, there is the exhaustion of kammic concatenation.

(10:174)

152. The Extinction of Kamma

I declare, monks, that actions willed, performed and accumulated will not become extinct as long as their results have not been experienced, be it in this life, in the next life or in subsequent future lives. And as long as these results of actions willed, performed, and accumulated have not been experienced, there will be no making an end to suffering, I declare.[54]

There are, monks, tainted failures in living caused by unwholesome volition, issuing in suffering, resulting in suffering. These tainted failures are threefold in bodily acts, fourfold in verbal acts and threefold in mental acts.

How are these tainted failures in living caused by unwholesome volition threefold in bodily acts?

There is a person who destroys life; he is cruel and his hands are blood-stained; he is bent on slaying and murdering, having no compassion for any living being.

He takes what is not given to him, appropriates with thievish intent the property of others, be it in the village or the forest.

He conducts himself wrongly in matters of sex: he has intercourse with those under the protection of father, mother, brother, sister, relatives, or clan, or of their religious community; or with those promised to a husband, protected by law, and even with those betrothed with a garland.[55]

In this way tainted failure in living is threefold in bodily acts.

And how is tainted failure in living fourfold in verbal acts?

There is one who is a liar. When he is in the council of his community or in another assembly, or among his relatives, his guild, in the royal court, or when he has been summoned as a witness and is asked to tell what he knows, then, though he does not know, he will say, "I know"; though he does know, he will say, "I do not know"; though he has not seen, he will say, "I have seen"; and though he has seen, he will say, "I have not seen." In that way he utters deliberate lies, be it for his own sake, for the sake of others, or for some material advantage.

He utters divisive speech: what he hears here he reports elsewhere to foment conflict there; and what he hears elsewhere he reports here to foment conflict here. Thus he creates discord among those united, and he incites still more those who are in discord. He is fond of dissension, he delights and rejoices in it, and he utters words that cause dissension.

He speaks harshly, using speech that is coarse, rough, bitter, and abusive, that makes others angry and causes distraction of mind. It is such speech that he utters.

He indulges in frivolous chatter: he speaks what is untimely, unreasonable, and unbeneficial, having no connection with the Dhamma or the Discipline. His talk is not worth treasuring, it is inopportune, inadvisable, unrestrained, and harmful.

In this way, tainted failure in living is fourfold in verbal acts.

And how is tainted failure in living threefold in mental acts?

There is a person who is covetous; he covets the wealth and property of others, thinking: "Oh, that what he owns might belong to me!"

There is also one who has ill will in his heart. He has depraved thoughts, such as these: "Let these beings be slain! Let them be killed and destroyed! May they perish and cease to exist!"

He has wrong views and perverted ideas, such as these: "There is no moral value in a gift, offering or sacrifice; there is no fruit or recompense from deeds good or evil; there is neither this world nor another world;[56] there are no duties towards mother and father; there are no spontaneously reborn beings; and there are no ascetics and brahmins in this world, living and conducting themselves rightly, who can explain this world and the world beyond, having realized them by their own direct knowledge."

In this way tainted failure in living, which is caused by unwholesome volition, issuing in suffering and resulting in suffering, is threefold in mental acts.

As to that tainted failure in living, which is threefold in bodily acts, fourfold in verbal acts and threefold in mental acts, and which, having been caused by unwholesome volition, issues in suffering, results in suffering—it is due to that very failure in living that with the breakup of the body, after death, beings are reborn in the plane of misery, in a bad destination, in the lower world, in hell.

Just as a perfect throw of dice, when thrown upwards, will come to rest firmly wherever it falls, similarly, due to those tainted failures in living caused by unwholesome volition, beings will be reborn in the plane of misery ... in hell.

I declare, monks, that actions willed, performed and accumulated will not become extinct as long as their results have not been experienced, be it in this life, in the next life or in subsequent future lives. And as long as these results of actions willed, performed, and accumulated have not been experienced, there will be no end to suffering, I declare.

There are, monks, successes in living caused by wholesome volition, issuing in happiness, resulting in happiness. They are threefold in bodily acts, fourfold in verbal acts and threefold in mental acts.

How are these successes in living caused by wholesome volition threefold in bodily acts?

There is a person who abstains from the destruction life; with the rod and weapon laid aside, he is conscientious and kindly and dwells compassionate towards all living beings.

He does not take what is not given to him and does not appropriate with thievish intention the property of others, be it in the village or the forest.

He gives up sexual misconduct and abstains from it. He does not have intercourse with those under the protection of father, mother ... nor with those betrothed with a garland.

In this way, success in living is threefold in bodily acts.

And how is success in living fourfold in verbal acts?

There is a person who has given up false speech and abstains from it. When he is in the council of his community or in another assembly, or among his relatives, his guild, in the royal court, or has been summoned as a witness and is asked to tell what he knows, then, when he knows, he will say, "I know"; and when he does not know he will say, "I do not know"; when he has seen, he will say, "I have seen"; and when he has not seen, he will say, "I have not seen." He will not utter any deliberate lie, be it for his own sake, for the sake of others or for some material advantage.

He has given up divisive speech and abstains from it. What he has heard here he will not report elsewhere to foment conflict there; and what he has heard elsewhere he will not report here to foment conflict here. In that way he unites those who are divided and encourages those who are in harmony. Concord gladdens him, he delights and rejoices in concord, and he utters words that foster concord.

He has given up harsh speech and abstains from it. His words are gentle, pleasant to hear, endearing, heart-warming, courteous, agreeable to many folk, pleasing to many folk.

He has given up vain talk and abstains from it. He speaks at the right time, in accordance with facts and of matters that are beneficial. He speaks on the Dhamma and the Discipline and talks in a way that is worth treasuring. His talk is opportune, helpful, moderate, and meaningful.

In this way success in living is fourfold in verbal acts.

And how is success in living threefold in mental acts?

Here a person is free from covetousness; he does not covet the wealth and property of others, thinking, "Oh, that what he owns might belong to me!"

He has no ill will in his heart. He has pure thoughts and intentions, such as these: "May these beings be free from enmity, free from anxiety! May they be untroubled and live happily!"

He has right view and a correct perspective, such as this: "There is moral value in gifts, offerings and sacrifice; there is fruit and recompense from deeds good or evil; there is both this world and another world; there are duties towards mother and father; there exist beings who have been spontaneously reborn; and there exist in this world ascetics and brahmins living and conducting themselves rightly, who can explain this world and the world beyond, having realized them by their own direct knowledge."

In this way, success in living, which is caused by wholesome volition, is threefold in mental acts.

As to that success in living which is threefold in bodily acts, fourfold in verbal acts and threefold in mental acts, and which, having been caused by wholesome volition, issues in happiness, results in happiness—it is due to that very success in living that with the breakup of the body, after death, beings are reborn in a good destination, in a heavenly world.

Just as a perfect throw of dice, when thrown upwards, will come to rest firmly wherever it falls, similarly, due to success in living caused by wholesome volition, beings will be reborn in a good destination, in a heavenly world.

I declare, monks, that actions willed, performed, and accumulated will not become extinct as long as their results have not been experienced, be it in this life, in the next life or in subsequent future lives. And as long as these results of actions willed, performed, and accumulated have not been experienced, there will be no making an end to suffering, I declare.

(10:206)

153. The Four Boundless States

"I declare, monks, that actions willed ... (*as at the end of the preceding text*).

"But a noble disciple—devoid of covetousness, devoid of ill will, unconfused, clearly comprehending, ever mindful—dwells pervading one quarter with a mind imbued with loving-kindness, likewise the second quarter, the third and the fourth. Thus above, below, across and everywhere, and to all as to himself, he dwells pervading the entire world with a mind imbued with loving-kindness, vast, exalted, measureless, without hostility, and without ill will.

"He knows: 'Formerly my mind was narrow and undeveloped; but now my mind is measureless and well developed. No measurable *kamma* will remain in it, none will persist there.'[57]

"What do you think, monks: if a young man, from his boyhood onwards, were to develop the liberation of the mind by loving-kindness, would he then do an evil deed?"

"He would not, Lord."

"And not doing any evil deed, will suffering afflict him?"[58]

"It will not, Lord. How could suffering afflict one who does no evil deeds?"

"Indeed, monks, the liberation of the mind by loving-kindness should be developed by a man or a woman. A man or a woman cannot take their body with them and depart; mortals have consciousness as the connecting link.[59]

"But the noble disciple knows: 'Whatever evil deeds I did before with this physical body, their results will be experienced here and they will not follow me along.'[60]

"Loving-kindness, if developed in such a way, will lead to the state of non-returning, in the case of a monk who is established in the wisdom found here in this teaching, but who has not penetrated to a higher liberation.[61]

"He dwells pervading one quarter with a mind imbued with compassion ... with altruistic joy ... with equanimity, likewise the second quarter, the third, and the fourth. Thus above, below, across and everywhere, and to all as to himself, he dwells pervading the entire world with a mind imbued with compassion, altruistic joy, and equanimity, vast, exalted, measureless, without hostility, and without ill will.

"He knows: 'Formerly my mind was narrow and undeveloped; but now my mind is measureless and well developed. No measurable *kamma* will remain in it, none will persist there.'

"What do you think, monks: if a young man, from his boyhood onwards, were to develop compassion, altruistic joy, and equanimity, would he then do an evil deed?"

"He would not, Lord."

"And not doing any evil deed, will suffering afflict him?"

"It will not, Lord. How could suffering afflict one who does no evil deeds?"

"Indeed, monks, the liberation of the mind by compassion ... by altruistic joy ... by equanimity should be developed by a man or a woman. A man or a woman cannot take their body with them and depart; mortals have consciousness as the connecting link.

"But the noble disciple knows: 'Whatever evil deeds I did before with this physical body, their results will be experienced here and they will not follow me along.'

"Compassion, altruistic joy, and equanimity, if developed in such a way, will lead to the state of non-returning, in the case of a monk who is established in the wisdom found here in this teaching, but who has not penetrated to a higher liberation."

(10:208)

XI. The Chapter of the Elevens

154. The Blessings of Loving-Kindness

If, O monks, the liberation of the mind by loving-kindness is developed and cultivated, frequently practised, made one's vehicle and foundation, firmly established, consolidated, and properly undertaken, eleven blessings may be expected. What eleven?

One sleeps peacefully; one awakens peacefully; one sees no bad dreams; one is dear to human beings; one is dear to non-human beings; one will be protected by devas; fire, poison and weapons cannot injure one; one's mind becomes easily concentrated; one's facial complexion will be serene; one will die unconfused; and if one does not penetrate higher, one will be reborn in the Brahma-world.[1]

(11:16)

Notes

IX. The Chapter of the Nines

1. During the first twenty years of his ministry the Buddha did not have a regular attendant but would select different monks for this task, not all of whom proved satisfactory. After twenty years, when he was fifty-five, he appointed the Venerable Ānanda as his permanent attendant. Ānanda served in this post diligently for the next twenty-five years until the Master's *parinibbāna*.

2. See Ch. III, n.61. A-a gives a quaint explanation why these thoughts assailed him so suddenly and forcefully: "In 500 successive rebirths, Meghiya had been a king. When he went out into the royal park for sport and amusement together with dancing girls of three age groups, he used to sit down at that very spot, called 'the auspicious slab'. Therefore, at the very moment when Meghiya sat down at that place, he felt as if his monkhood had left him and he was a king surrounded by beautiful dancers. And when, as a king, he was enjoying that splendour, a thought of sensuality arose in him. At that very time it happened that his great warriors brought to him two bandits whom they had arrested, and Meghiya saw them as distinctly as if they were standing in front of him. Now when (as a king) he was ordering the execution of one bandit, a thought of ill will arose in him; and when he was ordering the manacling and imprisonment of the other, a thought of violence arose in him. So even now, as Meghiya, he became entangled in these unwholesome thoughts like a tree in a net of creepers or like a honey-gatherer in a swarm of honey bees."

3. The Buddha repeatedly emphasized the importance of noble friendship in the living of the holy life. Elsewhere he calls a noble friend the chief external support for the cultivation of the Noble Eightfold Path (proper attention being the chief internal support; SN 45:49, 55) and on several occasions he even declared the whole of the holy life to be noble friendship (SN 45:2-3).

4. This text occurs also in Ud 4.1 with an additional concluding stanza.

5. *Saṅgaha-vatthu*. These are means of propitiating others.

6. A-a explains that this monk had felt neglected by Sāriputta and, conceiving a grudge against him, he thought: "I shall put an obstacle to his journey." When leaving, Sāriputta had passed a group of monks and a whiff of wind had blown the edge of his robe against the monk's face. This was used by the monk as a pretext for the complaint. The story is also found,

with some elaboration, in Dhp Comy (to v.95); see Burlingame, *Buddhist Legends*, 2:203–5.

7. According to A-a, the Buddha knew well that Sāriputta was quite incapable of hurting anyone, but to exclude the reproach of partiality he summoned him.

8. *Kāye kāyagatāsati*. See Text 8.

9. The similes of the four elements also occur at MN 62, though there they are developed somewhat differently.

10. Here *ārammaṇa* does not have its familiar meaning of "object," but its original literal meaning of "hold" or "support." A-a glosses it as condition (*paccaya*). "Name-and-form" (*nāma-rūpa*) is explained by A-a as the four mental aggregates (= "name") and the four material elements with their material derivatives (= "form"); these are the conditions for the arising of purposive thoughts.

11. An explanation derived from A-a is as follows: the elements (*dhātu*) are the six sense objects, forms, sounds, etc.; for thought about forms is one, thought about sounds another, etc. "Contact" is the contact associated with such thoughts. They converge on feeling (*vedanā-samosaraṇā*) because feeling, the affective value of an experience (as pleasant, unpleasant or neutral), holds the various aspects of a conscious moment together. Concentration is "the head" (*samādhi-pamukhā*) in the sense of playing the key role in bringing the mind to its highest intensity. Mindfulness is said to be the "master" (*satādhipateyyā*) to emphasize its dominant role in mastery of the mind. Wisdom is "the climax" (*paññuttarā*) because it is wisdom that issues in the attainment of the supramundane path. Liberation is the "essence" or core (*vimutti-sārā*), the goal in which the path culminates; according to A-a, the essence or core is the fruition stage of emancipation (*phala-vimutti*). All these thoughts are said to "merge in the Deathless" (*amatogadha*) because they "merge with" Nibbāna by taking it as object (in the path and fruit) and because they are established upon it.

12. "Decision" (*vinicchaya*) refers to thoughts of deciding on the utilization or value of what has been acquired; whether it should be used or stored, etc. "Desire and lust" (*chanda-rāga*), according to A-a, signifies a weaker degree of desire caused by unwholesome thoughts arising from the object; this weaker desire is intensified at the next stage, "selfish tenacity" (*ajjhosāna*), the strong insistence on "I" and "mine." The nine are also mentioned in the Mahānidāna Sutta (DN 15.9–18).

X. The Chapter of the Tens

1. This sutta partly replicates Text 96. See Ch. VI, n.16 for explanation of the technical terms.

2. A-a: "From 'the near shore' of the three realms of becoming to the 'far shore', Nibbāna."

3. A-a: "He is not percipient through perception that arises taking earth as object." The perceptions of the four elements correspond with the jhānas, which sometimes take the elements as object (see Text 139). The next four perceptions clearly refer to the formless meditations. The last two perceptions are intended to be all-inclusive, to show that he has transcended all mundane perceptions. See AN 11:10, which adds an eleventh item.

4. The word "percipient" (saññī) rules out the identification of this state with the cessation of perception and feeling (saññāvedayita-nirodha). A-a identifies this concentration with the concentration of fruition attainment (of arahantship): "If he applies his mind to the peaceful (aspect of Nibbāna), he may, while seated, continue with that thought 'peaceful' even for a full day. And so with the other (aspects of Nibbāna). All this refers to the concentration of fruition attainment (phala-samāpatti-samādhi)."

5. Bhavanirodho nibbānaṃ. The common rendering of the term bhava by "existence" might suggest the cessation of the objective reality, which would not be appropriate. What is meant is the cessation of re-becoming, the stopping of rebirth, in the case of an arahant.

6. See Text 47.

7. Dasa Tathāgata-balāni. A-a: "They are the powers of a Tathāgata only, as he does not have them in common with others." Though disciples may have them in part, only the Buddhas possess them completely, perfect in every respect. The ten Tathāgata powers also occur at MN 12, and are treated in detail at Vibh 335–44 (§§809–31) and its commentary.

8. Brahma-cakkaṃ. A-a: "Brahma has here the meaning of best, highest, superior. Brahma-cakka is the dhamma-cakka, the Wheel of Truth. And this is twofold, consisting in the knowledge of penetration (paṭivedha-ñāṇa) and the knowledge of teaching (desanā-ñāṇa). The knowledge of penetration is produced by wisdom and brought the Tathāgata to his own attainment of noble fruition (ariyaphala); the knowledge of teaching is produced by compassion and enables the Tathāgata to lead others to the attainment of noble fruition. The former is supramundane (lokuttara), the latter mundane (lokiya). Both kinds of knowledge, however, are not held in common with others; they are the Enlightened One's very own kinds of knowledge."

9. *Ṭhānañ ca ṭhānato aṭṭhānañ ca aṭṭhānato*. A-a: "Those phenomena, which are the cause and condition (*hetu-paccaya*) for the arising of other phenomena, are 'cause' (*ṭhāna*); and those phenomena which are not cause and condition for their arising—these are 'non-cause' (*aṭṭhāna*)." At Vibh 335–38 (§809), as examples of cause and non-cause, the possibilities and impossibilities mentioned at AN 1:15 (= MN 115) are given, a few of which are translated in Text 7.

10. *Ṭhānaso hetuso*. A-a explains *ṭhāna* here as those conditions (*paccaya*) which can modify results of *kamma*; while *hetu* (root condition) denotes *kamma*. At Vibh 338 (§810) it is said: "The *Tathāgata* comprehends thus: There are some evil actions performed which, prevented by fortunate rebirth (*gati*) ... by fortunate body (*upadhi*) ... by fortunate time (*kāla*) ... by fortunate effort (*payoga*), do not mature; there are some evil actions performed which, because of unfortunate rebirth ... unfortunate body ... unfortunate time ... unfortunate effort, do mature." The modifications in the results of good *kamma* are similarly treated.

11. *Sabbatthagāmini-paṭipadā*. A-a: "Among many people who have each killed just one living being, the kammic volition of one will lead him to hell, and that of another to rebirth in the animal world. In that way, the Blessed One knows unfailingly the nature of the action, i.e. the wholesome or unwholesome volitions which arise in the same situations (but may lead to different destinies)."

12. A-a: "'Many elements', as for instance the eye element, etc., the sensuality element, etc.; 'different' refers to the variegated characteristics of those elements. The world: the world of the aggregates, sense bases, elements."

13. *Adhimutti*. Vibh 339 (§813): "There are beings with inferior dispositions and beings with superior dispositions. Those with inferior dispositions associate with, approach, and frequent beings of (likewise) inferior dispositions. Those of superior dispositions associate with, approach, and frequent beings of (likewise) superior dispositions. And so has it been in the past and will be in the future."

14. *Indriya-paropariyattaṃ*. Vibh 340 (§814): "The *Tathāgata* understands their inclinations (*āsaya*), underlying tendencies (*anusaya*), habits (*caritta*) and dispositions (*adhimutti*); he understands beings with little dust in their eyes and with much dust; with keen spiritual faculties (faith, etc.) and with weak faculties; of good and bad qualities; those easy or hard to instruct; capable and incapable ones."

15. *Jhāna-vimokkha-samādhi-samāpatti*. The four jhānas are at Text 33, etc.; for the eight liberations, see Nyanatiloka Thera, *Buddhist Dictionary*, s.v. *vimokkha*. The concentrations are: with thought (*vitakka*) and examination

(*vicāra*), without thought but with examination, and without either. The nine meditative attainments are the four jhānas, the four formless attainments, and the cessation of perception and feeling.

This knowledge pertains, e.g. to the progress or otherwise on the part of certain types of "*jhāna*-attainers" mentioned in Vibh 342–43 (§828): those who, having attained, believe that they have failed; those who, having failed, believe that they have attained, etc.; those who attain quickly or slowly, emerge quickly or slowly, both attain and emerge quickly or slowly, those who possess or lack skill either in concentrating or in maintaining the concentration, those who possess or lack skill in both.

16. A-a says "these things" are the ten *Tathāgata* powers (see preceding text). Doctrinal terms (*abhivuttipadāni*) are explained in A-a and A-ṭ as views (*diṭṭhi*) and concepts (*paññatti*). As concepts, these "doctrinal terms" are said to be the teachings on the aggregates, sense bases and elements, which are common to all Buddhas of the past and the future as well, since they are the main topics for a philosophical exposition of the teaching.

17. Kāsi is another name for Benares.

18. *Vipariṇāma*, that is, death (A-a).

19. *Agge virajjati*: the highest in worldly power and achievement.

20. See Ch. VII, n.9

21. "*Kasiṇa* devices" are discs or similar objects used as supports for the practice of tranquillity meditation; see Vism, Chs. IV and V. The space *kasiṇa* and the consciousness *kasiṇa* are, respectively, the objective supports of the first and second formless meditations, the base of the infinity of space and the base of the infinity of consciousness.

22. *Abhibhāyatana*: modes of mastering the *kasiṇa* meditations. We have abridged the text here, as the intermediate stages merely describe variations in the objective forms over which the meditator achieves mastery.

23. For analysis, see AN 4:162.

24. A-a: "Limited (*paritta*) perception is that of the sense sphere, exalted (*mahaggata*) perception is that of the form sphere, measureless (*appamāṇa*) perception is supramundane perception (of the four paths and fruits), and the fourth is perception of the base of nothingness (the third immaterial *jhāna*)." So A-a, but it seems improbable that the Buddha would declare a mundane perception superior to supramundane perception. More likely, the "measureless" perception refers to the perception of measureless forms, or to the divine abodes (wherein loving-kindness, etc., are extended to measureless beings), or to the first two formless attainments (which take infinities as objects).

25. *No c'assaṃ no ca me siyā; na bhavissāmi, na me bhavissati.* This terse, cryptic, mantra-like saying is found in the Suttas in two forms. In the form recorded here it is expressive of the creed of the annihilationists (*uccheda-diṭṭhi*), as is explicitly confirmed by SN 22:81; the exact meaning remains a matter of conjecture. The Buddha incorporated this saying, with slight alterations in phrasing, into his own system and commended it to the monks as a theme of meditation that could lead to non-returning and even to arahantship. As adopted by the Buddha the saying reads: *No c'assa no ca me siyā; na bhavissati na me bhavissati*, which might be translated: "It might not be and it might not be mine; it will not be (and) it will not be mine." A-a explains: "If there were no defilements and *kamma* in the past, there would not be for me at present the five aggregates; I so determine that at present there will be no defilements and *kamma*, and thus in the future there will be for me no renewal of the five aggregates." At MN 106 the Buddha's version of the formula occurs as one of the reflections of a noble disciple, which, on the path of tranquillity, may lead to the base of nothingness; or, if used as a theme for insight, may culminate in arahantship. At SN 22:55, the Buddha recommends meditation on the formula as a way to cut off the five lower fetters (i.e. to reach the stage of non-returning). At AN 7:52, the formula is mentioned in connection with five types of non-returner and the attainment of arahantship.

26. *Bhave appaṭikkulyatā ... na bhavissati*: lit.: there will not be non-disgust towards existence. *Bhavanirodhe paṭikkulyatā ... na bhavissati*: lit.: there will not be disgust towards cessation of existence. As annihilationism arises from a repulsion towards existence, the annihilationist welcomes the cessation of existence, though he generally "goes too far" in misinterpreting such cessation as the annihilation of a real self, an existent person (see It 49).

27. *Paramattha-visuddhi*. A-a: This is a designation for the base of neither-perception-nor-non-perception. For the base of nothingness is highest as the foundation for insight, but the base of neither-perception-nor-non-perception is highest in terms of long lifespan.

28. *Parama-diṭṭhadhamma-nibbānaṃ*. The Brahmajāla Sutta (DN 1) mentions five varieties of this view as held by non-Buddhist ascetics: the first identifies sensual enjoyment as the supreme Nibbāna in this life, the other four identify the four jhānas with supreme Nibbāna. See *All Embracing Net of Views*, BPS.

29. A-a glosses "full understanding" (*pariññā*) here with transcending (*samatikkama*). The full understanding (or transcending) of sensual pleasures comes about by the first *jhāna*; of forms, by the formless meditative attainments; and of feelings, by the attainment of Nibbāna, wherein all modes of feeling have been abandoned.

30. *Anupādā-parinibbānaṃ*. A-a: This is final Nibbāna which is free from any conditioning (*appaccaya*). A-a explains that the Buddha spoke this sutta to dispel the discontent of 500 bhikkhus who were feeling oppressed by the celibate life. On hearing it they overcame their discontent and attained stream-entry. On a later occasion, after developing insight further, they attained arahantship.

31. *Uyyodhikā*. This was probably an army manoeuvre in which the king had actively joined one of the competing sides, which was victorious. A-a, however, perhaps influenced by the term "victorious," takes it to refer to an actual battle with King Ajātasattu. King Pasenadi performs a similar act of homage to the Buddha at MN 89, though the reasons he gives there differ from those offered in the present sutta.

32. Cp. Text 131. While in the latter the questions refer throughout to "purposive thoughts," here they are applied to "all (conditioned) things." See the explanations in Ch. IX, n.11. Some of the renderings used here are derived from Bhikkhu Ñāṇananda's translation of this text in *The Magic of the Mind*, BPS.

33. *Chandamūlakā sabbe dhammā*. The sense seems to be that the five aggregates ("all things") come to be through the craving of the previous life, which brought about the present existence.

34. *Manasikārasambhavā sabbe dhammā*. The world of objects becomes present to consciousness only through attention (*manasikāra*).

35. Since the Deathless and Nibbāna are synonymous, to justify the distinction between them here, A-a identifies "the Deathless" with the Nibbāna-element with a residue left, and "Nibbāna" with the Nibbāna-element with no residue left. See Ch.IV, n.10.

36. *Yathā-pabbajjā-paricitaṃ*: that is, in conformity with the purpose and aim of ordination, i.e. the attainment of arahantship.

37. *Bhavañ ca vibhavañ ca*: The translation follows A-a, which explains these words by *vuddhi-vināsa* (growth and decline) and *sampatti-vipatti* (success and failure).

38. This refers to the arising and dissolution of the five aggregates.

39. The perceptions of impermanence, non-self, foulness, danger, abandoning, dispassion and cessation are analysed in AN 10:60 just below.

40. Ignorance (*avijjā*) is the first link in the chain of dependent origination. By showing that ignorance is itself conditioned, our text excludes the misconception that it is a metaphysical First Cause; the same holds true of craving which, according to the second noble truth, is the origin of suffering, but likewise not an uncaused cause. Hence the same statements about ignorance

are made about craving in the next paragraph. Ignorance and craving, though very powerful root conditions of *saṃsāra*, are themselves mere conditioned phenomena and therefore can be eliminated; otherwise deliverance would be impossible. See Vism XVII, 36–39.

41. "Nutriment" (*āhāra*) is used here in the sense of a strong supporting condition. An example of how the five hindrances condition ignorance is found in AN 5:193, where they are said to prevent one from knowing one's own good and the good of others. In MN 9, the taints (*āsava*) are stated to be the conditioning factors for ignorance, and in Text 99 ignorance is said to be the condition for the taints. See Ch. VI, n.29.

42. Wrong conduct by way of deeds, words, and thoughts.

43. Lit.: "When association with unworthy people becomes full, it will fill up the listening to wrong teachings." So also in the following. The expression "becomes full" links up with the simile in the following paragraph.

44. The village of Nālaka was the place of the Venerable Sāriputta's birth and death. Since, after his ordination, he had visited his birthplace only once, in order to expire there, this dialogue must have taken place then.

45. These are the first three fetters, which are abandoned by the path of stream-entry.

46. Vajjiyamāhita is one of those lay disciples of whom it is said at AN 6:131: "He has come to certainty regarding the Blessed One, has seen the Deathless, and dwells having realized the Deathless." According to A-a, this refers to the stage of a trainee (*sekha*), not an *arahant*, as several interpreters of that passage have assumed.

47. *Vibhajjavādī bhagavā, na so bhagavā ettha ekaṃsavādī*. In later times the Buddha's Teaching, as documented in the Pāli Tipiṭaka and handed down by the Theravāda school, was called Vibhajjavāda, i.e. a discriminative, differentiating doctrine, in contrast to a generalizing and one-sided (*ekaṃsa*) doctrine. The expression may have been derived from the present sutta.

48. The word *venayiko*, here rendered "nihilist," means literally "one who leads astray"; it seems to have been used by the brahmins to stigmatize the Buddha because he rejected the authority of the Vedas, the validity of caste distinctions and the idea of a permanent self. A-a gives, in explanation of *apaññattiko*, "not making definite declarations": "(The accusation is that) the Buddha makes declarations about an unknowable (*apaccakkha*) Nibbāna, but cannot declare anything (definite) about (the world being) self-created (or created by another), etc." See in this connection Text 149.

49. *Nīyati*: lit.: "will be led out," i.e. from *saṃsāra*, the world of suffering.

50. A-a: "The Blessed One remained silent because the question was an inadmissable one, being based upon the wrong view of a self."

51. Uttiya's earlier questions about the eternity of the world, etc., as well as his later question about the salvation of the entire world, both belong to the class of questions that are "to be put aside" (*thapanīya*), because they presuppose non-existent substantial entities, be it the generalized concept of "the world" or the notion of an abiding self.

52. These are the eight factors of the Noble Eightfold Path, augmented by their fruits, right knowledge and right liberation. The "Sublime Master" (*sugata*) is the Buddha. This series of suttas should dispense with the notion that traditional Buddhist tolerance means that Buddhism regards all religions as being equally viable means to deliverance. According to the Buddha, other spiritual systems might teach wholesome practices conducive to a good rebirth, but the path to final liberation—Nibbāna, release from the whole round of rebirths—is available only through his Teaching.

53. The ten items are the ten courses of unwholesome action (*akusala-kammapatha*), explained in detail in Text 152. While the present text states that these can be motivated by any of the three unwholesome roots, the commentaries align particular unwholesome actions with particular unwholesome roots, e.g. hatred with the destruction of life and harsh speech, greed with stealing and sexual misconduct, etc.

54. On the threefold ripening of *kamma*, see Text 20 and Ch. III, n.13. The Buddha's statement—that there is no making an end to suffering without experiencing the results of all actions performed—must be understood with the reservation (which A-a makes explicit in connection with "*kamma* ripening in future lives") that reference is to "*kamma* that is actually capable of yielding a kammic result" (*vipākāraha-kamma*). But under certain circumstances *kamma* can be annulled by a counteractive or destructive *kamma*, and the *arahant*, by terminating the conditions for rebirth, extinguishes the potential for ripening of all his past *kamma*. The statement in our text must also be understood in the light of the following sutta passage: "If one says that in whatever way a person performs a kammic action, in that very same way he will experience the result—in that case there will be no (possibility for) the holy life, and no opportunity would appear for making a complete end to suffering. But if one says that a person who performs a kammic action (with a result) that is variably experiencable, will reap its result accordingly—in that case there will be (a possibility for) the holy life, and an opportunity would appear for making a complete end to suffering" (AN 3:110).

55. The last four refer respectively to: (i) a woman protected by her co-religionists; (ii) one promised to a husband at birth or in childhood; (iii) one

with whom sexual relations entail punishment by the authorities (perhaps female convicts?); and (iv) a girl whom a man has garlanded as a sign of betrothal.

56. A-a to MN 41: "For those living in this world, there is no other world (to go to after death); and for those living in another world, there is no this world (to come to after death)." Perhaps, however, the intention is that there is no rebirth either back into this world or into some other world. On either interpretation the view maintains that beings are annihilated at death.

57. *Pamāṇakataṃ kammaṃ*: A-a: = *kamma* belonging to the sense-sphere (*kāmāvacara-kamma*). The point is that if a person attains and masters the "liberation of the mind by loving-kindness" at the level of *jhāna*, the kammic potential of this *jhāna* attainment will take precedence over sense-sphere *kamma* and will generate rebirth into the form realm.

58. That is, suffering resulting from previous unwholesome *kamma*.

59. *Cittantaro*. A-a gives two explanations: (1) by taking *antara* in its meaning of cause, "With (kammic) consciousness as cause, one will be a deity or a hellish being"; (2) by taking *antara* in the sense of in-between, intermediate, "In immediate sequence to death-consciousness, at the second moment, i.e. the rebirth-consciousness, one will become a deity, a hell being or an animal."

60. A-a: "It will be a *kamma* ripening in this existence (*diṭṭha-dhamma-vedanīya-kamma*). They will not follow one along to the next existence, because the ripening in the next existence (*upapajja-vedanīya*) has been cut off through the practice of loving-kindness. This passage has to be understood as a reflection made by a stream-enterer or a once-returner."

61. "Non-returning" (*anāgāmitā*), according to A-a, refers to an attainment of non-returning based on a *jhāna* obtained through meditation on loving-kindness. So also in the cases of the other *brahma-vihāras*.

A-a explains *idha-paññassa bhikkhuno* (lit. "a here-wisdom monk") as a monk with the wisdom found here, in this teaching (*imasmiṃ sāsane*), which a noble disciple possesses who is established in the noble wisdom of a life that is in conformity with the teaching but "who has not penetrated to a higher liberation," that is, to arahantship.

XI. The Chapter of the Elevens

1. These benefits are explained at Vism IX, 59–76.

The Worn-out Skin

Reflections on the Uraga Sutta

by
Nyanaponika Thera

WHEEL PUBLICATION NO. 241/242

Copyright © Kandy; Buddhist Publication Society, (1977, 1990)

Introduction

The Suttanipāta, in its oldest and most characteristic parts, is a deeply stirring Song of Freedom. The verses of this ancient book are a challenging call to us to leave behind the narrow confines of our imprisoned existence with its ever-growing walls of accumulated habits of life and thought. They beckon us to free ourselves from the enslavement to our passions and to our thousand little whims and wishes.

A call to freedom is always timely because in our lives we constantly bind ourselves to this and that, or let ourselves be bound in various ways by others and by circumstances. To some extent, normal life cannot entirely escape from such a situation. In fact, "binding" oneself to a worthy task and duty or to an ennobling human relationship is an indispensable antidote to the opposite tendency: the dissipation of our energies. The physical act of walking consists not only in the "freeing" action of lifting and stretching the foot, but also in the "binding" function of lowering it and placing it firmly on the ground. Analogously, in mental movement, there is the same need for support as well as for uplift and forward advancement.

But, having the comfort of a "secure footing" in life, we too easily forget to walk on. Instead, we prefer to "strengthen our position," to improve and embellish the little cage we build for ourselves out of habits, ideas and beliefs. Once we have settled down in our habitual ways of living and thinking, we feel less and less inclined to give them up for the sake of risky ventures into a freedom of life and thought full of dangers and uncertainties. True freedom places on us the uncomfortable burden of ever-fresh responsible decisions, which have to be guided by mindfulness, wisdom and human sympathy. Few are willing to accept the full weight of such a burden. Instead, they prefer to be led and bound by the rules given by others, and by habits mainly dominated by self-interest and social conventions. With the habituation to a life of inner and outer bondage, there grows what Erich Fromm calls a "fear of freedom." Such fear, if allowed to persist and take root, inevitably leads to a stagnation of our inner growth and creativeness as well as to a stagnant society and culture. In a state of stagnation, toxic elements will endanger mankind's healthy progress—physical and mental, social and spiritual. Then William Blake's words will prove true: "Expect poison from stagnant water."

Those too who say "Yes" to life and wish to protect mankind from decline by its self-produced toxins—biological and psychological—will also have to shed that "fear of freedom" and enter freedom's arduous way. It is an arduous way because it demands of us that we break the self-forged fetters of our lusts and hates, our prejudices and dogmas—fetters we foolishly cherish as ornaments. But once we see them for what they really are, obstacles to true freedom, the hard task of discarding them will become at the same time a joyous experience.

The Suttanipāta, however, warns repeatedly of false ideas of freedom. He is not truly free who only follows his self-willed whims and desires (*chandagū*, v. 913), who is carried along by them (*chandānunīto*, v. 731). Nor can true freedom be found by those who only seek to exchange one bondage for another.

> *Leaving the old through craving for the new—*
> *Pursuit of longings never from bondage frees;*
> *It is but letting go to grasp afresh*
> *As monkeys reach from branch to branch of trees.*

v. 791

Mankind is always in need of both lawgivers and liberators. It is for echoing the voice of that great liberator, the Buddha, that the following pages have been written as a humble tribute.

What follows are free musings on the first poem of the Suttanipāta, the Uraga Sutta, interspersed with gleanings from the Buddhist texts, which may help to illuminate the verses.

The Serpent

1. He who can curb his wrath
   as soon as it arises,
   as a timely antidote will check
   snake's venom that so quickly spreads,
   —such a monk gives up the here and the beyond,
   just as a serpent sheds its worn-out skin.

2. He who entirely cuts off his lust
   as entering a pond one uproots lotus plants,
   —such a monk gives up the here and the beyond,
   just as a serpent sheds its worn-out skin.

3. He who entirely cuts off his craving
   by drying up its fierce and rapid flow,
   —such a monk gives up the here and the beyond,
   just as a serpent sheds its worn-out skin.

4. He who entirely blots out conceit
   as the flood demolishes a fragile bamboo bridge,
   —such a monk gives up the here and the beyond,
   just as a serpent sheds its worn-out skin.

5. He who does not find core or substance
   in any of the realms of being,
   like flowers that are vainly sought
   in fig trees that bear none,
   —such a monk gives up the here and the beyond,
   just as a serpent sheds its worn-out skin.

6. He who bears no grudges in his heart,
   transcending all this "thus" and "otherwise,"
   —such a monk gives up the here and the beyond,
   just as a serpent sheds its worn-out skin.

7. He who has burned out his evil thoughts,
   entirely cut them off within his heart,
   —such a monk gives up the here and the beyond,
   just as the serpent sheds its worn-out skin.

8. He who neither goes too far nor lags behind,
   entirely transcending the diffuseness of the world,
   —such a monk gives up the here and the beyond,
   just as a serpent sheds its worn-out skin.

9. He who neither goes too far nor lags behind
   and knows about the world: "This is all unreal,"
   —such a monk gives up the here and the beyond,
   just as a serpent sheds its worn-out skin.

10. He who neither goes too far nor lags behind,
    greedless he knows: "This is all unreal,"
    —such a monk gives up the here and the beyond,
    just as a serpent sheds its worn-out skin.

11. He who neither goes too far nor lags behind,
    lust-free he knows: "This is all unreal,"
    —such a monk gives up the here and the beyond,
    just as a serpent sheds its worn-out skin.

12. He who neither goes too far nor lags behind,
    hate-free he knows: "This is all unreal,"
    —such a monk gives up the here and the beyond,
    just as a serpent sheds its worn-out skin.

13. He who neither goes too far nor lags behind,
    delusion-free he knows: "This is all unreal,"
    —such a monk gives up the here and the beyond,
    just as a serpent sheds its worn-out skin.

14. He who has no dormant tendencies whatever,
    whose unwholesome roots have been expunged,
    —such a monk gives up the here and the beyond,
    just as a serpent sheds its worn-out skin.

15. States born of anxiety he harbours none
    which may condition his return to earth,
    —such a monk gives up the here and the beyond,
    just as a serpent sheds its worn-out skin.

16. States born of attachment he harbours none
    which cause his bondage to existence,

—such a monk gives up the here and the beyond,
just as a serpent sheds its worn-out skin.

17. He who has the five hindrances discarded,
doubt-free and serene, and free of inner barbs,
—such a monk gives up the here and the beyond,
just as a serpent sheds its worn-out skin.

I Reflections on the Refrain

The Refrain:

1. Such a monk gives up the here and the beyond,
   just as a serpent sheds its worn-out skin.

The Simile of the Serpent

The ancient masters of the Theravada Buddhist tradition explain the simile of the serpent's worn-out skin, occurring in the last line of each of the poem's verses, as follows:

The shedding of the serpent's old skin is done in four ways:

1. in following the law of its own species,
2. through disgust,
3. with the help of a support, and
4. with effort.

1. "Its own species" is that of those long-bodied animals, the snakes. Snakes do not transgress these five characteristics of their species: in regard to their birth, their death, their surrendering to (a long and deep) sleep, their mating with their own kind only, and the shedding of the old, worn-out skin. Hence, in shedding the skin, a snake follows the law of its own kind.

2. But in doing so, it sheds the old skin out of disgust. When only half of the body has been freed of the old skin and the other half is still attached, the snake will feel disgust.

3. In such disgust, the snake will support its body on a piece of wood, a root or a stone, and

4. making an effort, using all its strength, it will wind its tail around the supporting object, exhale forcefully and expand its hood, and shed the old skin fully. Then it will go freely wherever it likes.

It is similar with a monk. The "law of his own species" is virtue (*sīla*). Standing firm in his own law of virtue, and seeing the misery involved, he becomes disgusted with the "old worn-out skin" of the "here and the beyond," comprising (such pairs of opposites) as his own and others' personalized existence, etc., which are productive of suffering. Thus he becomes disgusted and, seeking the support of a noble friend (a wise teacher and meditation master), he summons his utmost strength by way of the path factor, right effort. Dividing day and night into six periods, during daytime, while walking up and down or sitting, he purifies his mind from obstructive things; doing so also in the first and the last watch of the night, he lies down for rest only in the night's middle watch. Thus he strives and struggles. Just as the serpent bends its tail, so he bends his legs to a crosslegged posture. As the serpent exhales forcefully, so the monk musters all his unremitting strength. As the serpent expands its hood, so the monk works for an expansion of his insight. And just as the serpent sheds its old skin, so the monk abandons the here and the beyond, and being now freed of the burden, he goes forth to the Nibbāna-element that is without a residue of the groups of existence (*anupādisesa-nibbānadhātu*).

Commentary to the Suttanipāta

Conforming to the "law of its own species," the serpent discards what has become only a burden. It is worn-out, outgrown skin which the snake gladly sheds. And thus it will finally be with him who earnestly walks the path to the freedom from all burdens (*yogakkhema*). Daily practice of alienation from what has been understood to be actually alien will wear thin the bondage to "self" and the world, loosen more and more clinging's tight grip, until, like the serpent's worn-out skin, it falls away almost effortlessly. Just as, according to similes given by the Buddha, the handle of a hatchet is wasted away by constant use; just as the strongest ship-ropes will become brittle by constant exposure to wind, sun and rain and finally fall asunder—so will constant acts of giving up, of letting go, wear thin and fragile the once so stout and unbreakable fetters of craving and ignorance, until one day they drop off completely.

By such an act of "shedding the old skin," no "violence against nature" is done; it is a lawful process of growing, of *out*growing that which is no longer an object of attachment—just as the old skin is no longer attached to the snake's body. Only in such a way can a person vanquish those passionate urges and deceptive notions of his, which are so powerful and so deeply rooted. In the act of ultimate liberation, nothing is violently broken which was not already detached from the living tissues of mind and body or only quite loosely joined with them. Only a last effort of the powerful muscles will be needed to shake off the empty sheath—this hollow concept of an imaginary self which had hidden for so long the true nature of body and mind.

Here it lies before the meditator's feet—like the serpent's worn-out skin—a lifeless heap of thin and wrinkled thought tissue. Once it had seemed to be so full of alluring beauty—this proud and deceptive idea of "I" and "mine." Now this illusion is no more, and a new "conceptual skin" has grown which, though likewise made of imperfect words, has no longer the deceptive colourings of conceit, craving and false ideas. Mind-and-body are now seen as they truly are. Now one no longer misconceives them for what they are *not* and no longer expects of them what they cannot give: lasting happiness. How big a burden of anxiety, fear, frustration and insatiate craving will have been discarded! How light and free the heart can become if one sheds attachment to what is not one's own!

What actually has to be shed is this attachment rooted in the ego-illusion. But until discarded entirely, this ego-illusion will still cling to mind-and-body by the force of three powerful strands which are also its feeders: conceit, craving and false ideas. Even if false ideas about a self have been given up intellectually, the other two "feeders," conceit and craving, are strong enough to cause an identification of mind-and-body (or of some of their features) with the imaginary self.

This identification has to be dissolved on all three levels until mind-and-body are seen to be as alien as those dry leaves of the Jeta Grove which the Buddha once picked up, asking the monks whether these leaves are their self or their self's property. And the monks replied: "They are surely not our self or anything belonging to our self." Then the Master said: "Therefore, monks, give up what is not yours! Give up all clinging to body, feelings, perceptions, volitions and consciousness."[1] (MN 22)

---

1. These are the "five aggregates" (*pañcakkhandhā*) into which the Buddha analyzes the individual personality.

It is certainly not difficult to give up what is so obviously foreign to us, and worthless, too, like those dry leaves or any other insignificant trifles we encounter in our lives. It is harder to give up a cherished material object or a beloved human being. It is hardest, however, to detach ourselves from the body and its pleasures, from our likes and dislikes, from the intellectual enjoyment of our thoughts, from deep-rooted tendencies and habits; in short, from all that we instinctively and without question identify with as "ourselves." All these constituents of our supposed "self" are visibly changing, sometimes rapidly and radically; sometimes the changes of our likes and dislikes, habits and ideas, turn them into their very opposite. Yet we still continue to identify ourselves whole-heartedly with those new states of mind as if they were the old ego. So tenacious is the ego-illusion and therefore so hard to break.

Yet it is to that hardest task that the Master summons us: "Give up what is not yours! And what is not yours? The body is not yours: give it up! Giving it up will be for your weal and happiness. Feelings, perceptions, volitions and consciousness are not yours: give them up! Giving them up will be for your weal and happiness."

We must recall here that it is *attachment* to these five aggregates that has to be given up and that this is a gradual process. We must not expect our habitual likes and dislikes, our intellectual enjoyments and our desires to vanish all at once; nor can or should they be broken by force. This seemingly compact and identifiable personality has been gradually built up by the intake of physical and mental nourishment. Again and again, thousands of times during a single day, we have approached and absorbed the physical and mental objects of our desire. One after the other we have made them "our own" and believed them to be our own. This continuous process of accumulating attachments and self-identifications must now be reversed by a gradual process of detachment achieved by dissolving or stopping the false identifications. The Buddha's teaching chiefly consists of aids assisting us in that task of gradual detachment—aids to right living and to right thinking. The simile of the snake's worn-out skin is one of these aids, and if seen as such it has much to teach. These are some of the ways in which contemplation can be helpful:

1. We look at our skin encasing the body: it is now firm and taut, healthily alive, our warm blood pulsating beneath it. Imagine it now lying before you, empty and limp, like a snake's discarded slough. In such a manner you may visualize the feature *skin* among the thirty-two parts of the body, a meditation recommended by the Buddha.[2] When thus brought vividly to life, it will help you to alienate and detach yourself from the body.

2. Just as the serpent does not hesitate to fulfil the biological "law of its kind" in shedding its old skin, so right renunciation will not waver or shrink from those acts of giving up which right understanding of reality demands. Just as the serpent does not mourn over the loss of its worn-out slough, so right renunciation has no regrets when it discards what has been seen as void of value and substance and replaces it by something new and more beautiful: the happiness of letting go, the exhilaration of the freedom won, the serenity of insight and the radiance of a mind purified and calmed. It is the growing strength of this new experience which will gradually clear the road to final emancipation.

3. According to the commentary quoted by us, the snake feels disgust towards its old skin when the sloughing is not yet complete and parts of the old skin still adhere to its body. Similarly, the disgust felt towards residual attachments and defilements will give to the disciple an additional urgency in his struggle for final liberation. Such disgust is a symptom of his growing detachment. It is strengthened by an increasing awareness of the perils inherent in the uneliminated defilements—perils to oneself and to others. On seeing these perils, the whole misery of man's situation, the saṃsāric predicament, will gain for him increasing poignancy; and the more he progresses in mental training and moral refinement, the stronger his distaste will become for what is still unamenable in him to that training and refinement. Therefore the Buddha advised his son Rāhula: "Make disgust strong in you" (Sn v. 340).

This disgust (*nibbidā*) is often mentioned in the Buddhist scriptures as an aid as well as a phase on the road to full detachment.

---

2. In this method of meditation, mentioned in the Satipaṭṭhāna Sutta and explained at length in the *Visuddhimagga* (Chap. VIII), the body is contemplated by way of its constituent parts, such as skin, muscles, sinews, bones, the internal organs, secretions and excretions.

Thus among the eight insight knowledges the contemplation of disgust (*nibbidānupassanā*) follows upon the awareness of the peril and misery in *saṃsāra*, when formations of existence have become tasteless and insipid to the meditator. And in innumerable *sutta* passages the Buddha says that when the disciple sees the constituents of body and mind as impermanent, suffering and not self, he becomes disgusted with them; through his disgust he becomes dispassionate, and through dispassion he is liberated. The Noble Eightfold Path itself is extolled because it leads to complete disgust with worldliness, to dispassion, cessation, peace, direct knowledge, enlightenment and Nibbāna.[3]

When insight is deepened and strengthened, what has been called here "disgust" (in rendering the Pali *nibbidā*) loses the strong emotional tinge of aversion and revulsion. It manifests itself instead as a withdrawal, estrangement and turning away from worldliness and from the residue of one's own defilements.

4. Just as the snake, in its effort to throw off its old skin, uses as support a stone or the root of a tree, similarly, the teachers of old say that the striving disciple should make full use of the support of noble friendship in his efforts towards full liberation. A friend's watchful concern, his wise counsel and his inspiring example may well be of decisive help in the arduous work of freeing oneself from the burdensome encumbrance of passions, frailties and tenacious habits.

Often and emphatically, the Buddha praised the value of noble friendship. Once the venerable Ānanda, who was so deeply devoted to the Master, spoke of noble friendship as being "half of the holy life," believing he had duly praised its worth. The Buddha replied: "Do not say so, Ānanda, do not say so: it is the entire holy life to have noble friends, noble companions, noble associates" (Saṃyutta Nikāya). If this holds true for the spiritual life of a monk, there are additional reasons for cherishing noble friendship within the common life of the world with all its harshness and perils, struggles and temptations, and its almost unavoidable contact with fools and rogues. Noble friendship, so rare and precious, is indeed one of the

---

3. See *Visuddhimagga*, XXI, 43; discourse on The Not-self Characteristic and The Fire Sermon (in *Three Cardinal Discourses of the Buddha*, trans. by Bhikkhu Ñāṇamoli, Wheel No. 17); Majjhima Nikāya 83.

few solaces which this world can offer. But this world of ours would be truly "disconsolate" if, besides the solace of friendship, it did not harbour the still greater solace of the Buddha's compassionate message of an open way to final deliverance from suffering.

The Meaning of "Monk"

The word monk (*bhikkhu*) has to be taken here in the same sense as explained in the old commentary on the Satipaṭṭhāna Sutta:

> *Monk* is a term to indicate a person who earnestly endeavours to accomplish the practice of the teaching. Though there are others, gods and men, who earnestly strive to accomplish the practice of the teaching, yet because of the excellence of the state of a monk ... by way of practice, the Master spoke here of a monk ... Verily, one who follows the teaching, be it a deity or a human being, is called a monk.

The Here and the Beyond (*ora-pāraṃ*)

Now what is it that should be given up finally and without regret? Our text calls it "the here and the beyond," using Pali words that originally signified the two banks of a river. The "here" is this world of our present life experience as human beings; the "beyond" is any world beyond the present one to which our willed actions (*kamma*) may lead us in our future existences in *saṃsāra*, the round of rebirths. It may be a world of heavenly bliss, or one of hell-like suffering, or a world which our imagination creates and our heart desires; for life in any world beyond the present one belongs as much to the totality of existence as life on earth, Nibbāna alone being the "beyond of existence."

The phrase "the here and the beyond" also applies to all those various discriminations, dichotomies and pairs of opposites in which our minds habitually move: the lower and the higher, the inner and the outer, the (life-affirming) good and the bad, acceptance and rejection. In brief, it signifies the ever-recurring play of opposites, and as this play maintains the game of life with its unresolvable dissatisfactions, disappointment and suffering, the Buddha calls on us to give it up.

The overcoming of the opposites, the detachment from "both sides," is one of the recurrent themes of the Suttanipāta. Among the various pairs of opposites structuring our thoughts, attitudes and feelings, the most prominent is that of "the lower and the higher." All the numerous religious, ethical, social and political doctrines devised by man employ this dichotomy, and though their definitions of these two terms may differ enormously, they are unanimous in demanding that we give up the low and attach ourselves, firmly and exclusively, to whatever they praise as "high," "higher" or "highest."

> *Espousing among views his own as highest,*
> *Whatever he regards as "best,"*
> *All else he will as "low" condemn;*
> *Thus one will never get beyond disputes.*

(Sn 796)

However, in any area of human concern, secular or religious, clinging to discriminations of "high and low" is bound to result in suffering. When we are attached to anything as "high," if the object changes, we will meet with sorrow; if our attitudes change, we will find ourselves feeling flustered and discontent.

But despite their repeated experience of transiency, and despite all their prior disappointments, men still foster the vain hope that what they cherish and cling to will remain with them forever. Only those few "with little or no dust in their eyes" understand that this play of opposites, on its own level, is interminable; and only one, the Buddha, has shown us how to step out of it. He, the Great Liberator, showed that the way to genuine freedom lies in relinquishing both sides of the dichotomy, even insisting that his own teaching is only a raft built for crossing over and not for holding on to:

> "You, O monks who understand the Teaching's similitude to a raft, you should let go even of good teachings, how much more the false ones."

(MN 22)

> "Do you see, my disciples, any fetter, coarse or fine, which I have not asked you to discard?"

(MN 66)

One should, however, know well and constantly bear in mind that the relinquishing of both sides, the transcending of the opposites, is the final goal—a goal which comes at the end of a long journey. Because this journey unavoidably leads through the ups and downs of *saṃsāra*, the traveller will repeatedly encounter the play of opposites, within which he will have to make his choices and select his values. He must never attempt to soar above the realm of opposites while ill-equipped with feeble wings or else his fate, like that of Icarus, will be a crash landing. For a time, to the best of his knowledge and strength, he must firmly choose the side of the "higher" against the "lower," following what is beneficial from the standpoint of the Dhamma and avoiding what is harmful. But he should regard his choices and values as a raft, not clinging to them for their own sake, always ready to leave them behind to embark on the next phase of the journey. While still on the mundane plane, he must never forget or belittle the presence within himself of the "lower," the dark side of his nature, and he must learn to deal with this wisely, with caution as well as firmness.

To cross the ocean of life and reach "the other shore" safely, skill is needed in navigating its currents and cross-currents. In adapting oneself to those inner and outer currents, however, one must always be watchful. The currents can be powerful at times and one must know when it is necessary to resist them. Sometimes right effort has to be applied to avoid or overcome what is evil and to produce and preserve what is good. At other times it is wise to restrain excessive and impatient zeal and revert to a receptive attitude, allowing the processes of inner growth to mature at their own rate. By wisely directed adaptation we can learn to give full weight to both sides of every situation—to the duality in our own nature and in the objective circumstances we face. Only by confronting and understanding the two sides within one's own experience can one master and finally transcend them.

An increasingly refined response to the play of opposites will teach one how to balance, harmonize and strengthen one's spiritual faculties (*indriya*) by reducing excess and making up deficiencies. When it concerns two equally positive qualities— such as the faculties of energy and calm—one will naturally prefer to strengthen the weaker side instead of reducing the stronger, thus re-establishing the balance of faculties on a higher level. Only by a harmonious balance of highly developed faculties can one move on to the next phase of progress: the "transcending of both sides," the final comprehension and mastery of merely apparent opposites, such as firmness and gentleness, which appear opposed only when isolated or unbalanced.

This harmony, which is dynamic and not static, gains perfection in the equipoise and equanimity of the Arahant, the Liberated One, an equanimity far wider, deeper and stronger than any the ordinary man can even envision.

On the *emotional* level, the Arahant's equanimity is marked by perfect and unshakable equipoise in the midst of the vicissitudes of life and in the face of all the problems and conflicts that may come within the range of his experience. This equanimity is not indifferent aloofness but a balanced response to any situation—a response motivated and directed by wisdom and compassion.

On the *volitional and active* level, the Arahant's equanimity appears as freedom from partiality; as a thoughtful choice between action and non-action, again motivated by wisdom and compassion; and as perfect equipoise when the choice has been made.

On the *cognitive and intellectual* level, his equanimity shows up in a balanced judgement of any situation or idea, based on a mindful and realistic appraisal; it is the equipoise of insight that avoids the pitfalls of extreme conceptual viewpoints.

This is the triple aspect of the Arahant's equanimity as an embodiment of the middle path rising above the extremes and opposites.

The Structure of the Verses

In each verse of the poem, the giving up of "the here and the beyond" mentioned in the refrain is connected with the abandonment of certain mental defilements (*kilesa*), basic distortions of attitude and understanding, mentioned in the first lines of the verse (always two in the original Pali). The purport behind this connection is that only if the mental defilements mentioned in the first lines are eliminated entirely (*asesaṃ*, "without remainder")—as stated expressly in verses 2, 3 and 4—can one rise above the opposites involved in those defilements. Only by entire elimination are the defilements eradicated in their lower and higher, coarse and subtle forms, in their manifest and latent states. If even a minute residue of them is left, it will suffice to revive the full play of the opposites and a recurrence of the extremes. No member of a pair of opposites can exclude the influence of its counterpart and remain stationary within the same degree of strength or weakness. There is a constant fluctuation between "high" and "low" as to degree of the defilements, as to evaluation of mental qualities, and as to forms of existence to which the defilements may lead.

It is the *complete* uprooting of the defilements alone which will make an end of rebirth—of the here and the beyond, the high and the low, which remain in constant fluctuation as long as the defilements persist. When such an uprooting is made, the here and the beyond will be transcended, left behind as something empty, coreless and alien—"just as a serpent sheds its worn-out skin."

II Reflections on the Verses

Wrath

1. *He who can curb his wrath*
   as soon as it arises,
   as a timely antidote will check
   snake's venom that so quickly spreads,
   —such a monk gives up the here and the beyond,
   just as a serpent sheds its worn-out skin.

This first verse compares wrath, which is vehement anger or rage, to a snake's poison that rapidly spreads in the body of the person bitten; for snakes, or at least some of the species, have always been regarded as irascible animals of venomous ire. Wrath is an outcome of hate, one of the three powerful roots of all evil and suffering.[4] The term "hate" (*dosa*) comprises all degrees of antipathy, from the weakest dislike to the strongest fury. In fact, the Pali word *kodha*, used in this verse and rendered here by "wrath," actually extends to the whole scale of antagonistic emotions. We have, however, singled out its extreme form, "wrath," because of the simile and in view of the fact that its less vehement forms will find their place under the heading of "grudge," in verse 6.

Of the evil root hate in its entire range the Buddha says, "It is a great evil but (relatively) easy to overcome" (AN 3:68). It was perhaps for both these reasons that wrath is mentioned here first, preceding the other defilements which appear in the following verses. Hate is a great evil because of its consequences. Its presence poses a much greater danger of a straight fall into the lowest depths of inhuman conduct and into the lowest forms of existence than, for instance, greed or lust, another of the three evil roots. On the other hand, hate is relatively easy to overcome, for it produces an unhappy state of mind which goes counter to the common human desire for happiness. But hate will be "easy to overcome" only for those who also know of the need to purify their own hearts and are willing to make that effort. For those, however, who identify themselves fully with their aversions or even try to justify

---

4. See *Hate as Unwholesome Root* by Irene Quittner, Bodhi Leaves No. A 16.

their outbursts of temper—for them hate, too, is very difficult to overcome and may well harden into a character trait of irritability.

Just as a snakebite needs prompt treatment to prevent the venom from spreading rapidly and widely through the body, so also any uprising of wrath should be curbed at once to prevent it from erupting into violent words and deeds of possibly grave consequence.

The true curative antidote for hate in all its forms is loving kindness (*mettā*), assisted by patience, forbearance and compassion. But unless the mind is well trained, when vehement wrath flares up, it will rarely be possible to replace it immediately by thoughts of loving kindness. Nevertheless, a mental brake should be applied at once and the thoughts of anger curbed[5] without delay; for if this is not done, the situation may be aggravated by continual outbursts of anger to the point where it gets completely out of control. This temporary curbing of wrath accords with the fifth method of removing undesirable thoughts as mentioned in the 20th Discourse of the Middle Length Sayings (Majjhima Nikāya),[6] namely, by vigorously restraining them. By such an act of firm restraint, time will be won to compose the mind for dealing with the situation thoughtfully and calmly. But if the anger thus suppressed is left smouldering under the ashes, it may well flare up on a future occasion with greater vehemence. Hence, in a quiet hour on the very same day, one should try to dissolve that anger fully, in a way appropriate to the situation. The Dhamma can offer many aids for doing so.

Hate can bind beings to each other as strongly as lust does, so that they drag each other along through repeated life situations of revenge and counter-revenge. This may first happen in the "here," that is, within one life, or in continued human rebirths. But persistent hate harbours the constant danger of dragging the hater down into a subhuman world of misery, "beyond the human pale"; or the hater's fate might be a rebirth among the Asuras,

---

5. The words *he can curb* in verse 1 are a rendering of the Pali word *vineti*, which, among other connotations, may have the two nuances of "restraining" and "removing."
6. See *The Removal of Distracting Thoughts*, trans. by Soma Thera (Wheel No. 21).

the demonic titans of militant pride and aggressive power-urge, some of whom, in turn, seem to have taken human birth as great conquerors and rulers.

Whipped up by hate and wrath, towering waves of violence and fierce tempests of aggression have swept again and again through human history, leaving behind a wake of destruction. Though issuing from the one root of evil, hate, these upheavals have taken a multitude of forms: as racial, national, religious and class hatred as well as other varieties of factional and political fanaticism. Those who crave for leadership among men have always known that it is so much easier to unite people under the banner of a common hate than by a shared love. And all too often these leaders have made unscrupulous use of their knowledge to serve the ends of their burning ambition and power urge, even using millions of people as tools or victims of their own unquenchable hate for others or themselves. Untold misery has been wrought thus and is still being wrought today, as history books and the daily newspapers amply testify. Now mankind is faced by the mortal danger posed by tools of violence and aggression made utterly destructive through modern technology, and by a climate of hate made more infectious through modern mass media and subtle mind manipulation.

So there are, indeed, reasons enough for curbing wrath individually and for helping to reduce it socially. An appeal for the reduction of hate and violence in the world of today can no longer be dismissed as unrealistic moralizing. For the individual and for mankind, it has now become a question of survival, physically and spiritually.

He, however, who "sees danger in the slightest fault," and knows that even slight but persistent resentments may grow into passionate hate and violence, will earnestly strive for the final eradication of the deepest roots of any aversion. This is achieved on the third stage of the path to liberation, called the stage of non-return (*anāgāmitā*). At that stage, no return to the "here" of existence in the sense sphere can any longer come about, while the end of the "beyond," that is, the existence in the fine-material and immaterial spheres, will also be assured.[7]

---

7. Buddhist cosmology recognizes three spheres of existence—the sense sphere, the fine-material sphere and the immaterial sphere. Human existence

You must slay wrath if you would happily live;
You must slay wrath if you would weep no more.
The slaughter of anger with its poisoned source
And fevered climax, murderously sweet—
That is the slaughter noble persons praise;
That you must slay in order to weep no more.

(SN 11:21)

Lust

2. *He who entirely cuts off his lust*
As entering a pond one uproots lotus plants,
—such a monk gives up the here and the beyond,
just as a serpent sheds its worn-out skin.

Lust (*rāga*) is here compared to the lotus flower as a symbol of beauty. Because of its loveliness one too easily forgets that the enchanting blossoms of sense enjoyment will soon wilt and lose their beauty and attraction. But the mere awareness of that impermanence is not enough, for it may even add to the enchantment and whet the desire to pluck the flowers of lust again and again as long as strength lasts. But desire often lasts longer than the strength to seek or obtain its fulfilment—and this is just one of the ways in which lust brings suffering and frustration.

In a single moment the roots of lust can sink deeply into a man's heart; its fine hair-roots of subtle attachments are as difficult to remove as the great passions, or even more so. Thus the Buddha says that "greed is hard to overcome"; but in the same text he also says that greed "is a lesser evil" (or, literally rendered, "less blameworthy").[8] This statement may appear strange in view of the fact that greed is one of the evil roots and also a form of craving, the fundamental cause of suffering. Yet greed is "less blameworthy" than hate in all those cases where the gratification of lust does not violate basic morality and is not harmful to others; for instance,

---

belongs to the sense sphere. Non-returners, after death, are reborn in the fine-material sphere and attain liberation there.
8. Aṅguttara Nikāya, 3:68.

in the enjoyment of delicious food, sexual gratification within the bounds of the third precept, and so forth.

Nevertheless, all forms of lust, be they inside or outside the moral norms, are still *unwholesome* (*akusala*), as they chain man to kammic bondage and necessarily result in suffering. Therefore, for one who aspires to perfect purity and final liberation, all forms of lust, coarse or refined, are obstructions.

"All lust wants eternity" (Friedrich Nietzsche)—but cannot obtain it. For, though lust itself may well go on eternally without ever being quenched, its objects are all inevitably evanescent. When the objects of lust perish, as they must, or are unattainable, as they often are, suffering results for the lusting person; and when his desire for a loved person fades and changes, suffering will result for the beloved.

Lust receives its full dimension of depth as an expression of craving, an unexhaustible neediness, the state of ever being in want. This craving is the subject of the next verse.

Lust is "entirely cut off" at the stage of Arahantship, when desire even for the worlds of refined material form or the immaterial has vanished forever. With the elimination of lust, its unavoidable concomitants also disappear: the frustration, torment or despair of non-gratification and the listlessness, boredom or revulsion of surfeit. He who frees himself of lust is also free of its "both sides," attraction and repulsion, like and dislike. He too has given up the here and the beyond.

Craving

3. *He who entirely cuts off his craving*
   by drying up its fierce and rapid flow,
   —such a monk gives up the here and the beyond,
   just as a serpent sheds its worn-out skin.

Craving (*taṇhā*) is the mighty stream of desire that flows through all existence, from the lowest microbes up to those sublime spheres free from coarse materiality. Craving is threefold: craving for sensuality, for continued existence, and for annihilation or destruction.

Sensuous craving (*kāma-taṇhā*), within that mighty river of which our verse speaks, is a powerful whirlpool dragging everything into its depth. The infinity of all craving appears here as the bottomless abyss which vainly longs for fullness and fulfilment. But though it ceaselessly sucks into itself the objects of desire, it can never find safety and peace. For like the hunger for food, this perpetual hunger of the senses daily craves afresh for gratification: "The senses are greedy eaters." The habit of daily sense gratification produces in us a *horror vacui*. We fear being left empty of sense experience, and this fear, an expression of the fear of death, stands dark and threatening behind each sensual craving as an additional driving force. We see starkly the partnership of fear and desire in the pathological avarice, the hectic grasping and clinging, of those old people so masterly described by Moliere and Balzac.

Driven by the burning sensation of a void within, by a feeling of constant lack and neediness, we try to suppress that painful sensation by swelling our ego. We strive to absorb into our ego what is non-ego or "alien"; we chase hectically and insatiably after sense enjoyment, possessions or power; we yearn to be loved, envied or feared. In short, we try to build up our "personality"—a *persona*, a hollow mask. But such attempts to satisfy sensual craving must fail. If the supposed ego expands its imagined boundaries, then, by the extension of its periphery, its points of contact with a hostile or tempting world also grow, inevitably bringing along a growth of both irritation and neediness.

One believes that by the mere gratification of lust what has been "appropriated" from the outside world of objects or persons becomes a part of the ego or its property, becomes "I" and "mine." But what the ego thus appropriates from outside it can never fully assimilate. There remains an undissolved alien residue which accumulates and slowly but deeply alters the structure of body and mind. This process will finally end in the disruption of the organism—in death. To some extent, this is normal, an ever-present process as it is also a formula for the intake and assimilation of food.[9] But if sensory craving grows excessive and becomes an uncontested or only weakly contested master, it may well happen that "the food devours the eater": that the craving and search for sensual nourishment becomes so dominant that it weakens other functions of the human mind, and just those which are most refined and distinctively human.

---

9. See below, "The Four Nutriments of Life."

Unrestrained sensual craving makes a personality "featureless" and "impersonal"; it reduces human individuation and thus brings us into dangerous proximity to the animal level which is bare or poor of individuation. Specific sensual enjoyment may easily become habit-forming and even compulsive, again pulling us down to the animal level of instinctive behaviour at the cost of conscious control. A life dominated by sensual craving may turn into a monotonous automaton of sense-stimulus, craving, and sense gratification. Uninhibited sensuality reduces our relative freedom of choice and may drag us, by way of rebirth, into subhuman realms of existence. We say this, not to moralize but to emphasize the psychological effects of sensual craving and to show its implications for our progress towards true human freedom, that is, towards an increase of our mindfully responsible moral choices.

In the threatening effacement of individuation, in the rapturous submergence of individuality at moments of highest passion—in these features sensual craving approaches its apparent opposite, the craving for annihilation (*vibhava-taṇhā*). It is ancient knowledge: the affinity of Eros and Thanatos, of passionate love and death.

Craving for annihilation, for non-being, may be likened to the flooding of the river of individualized life. The waters revolt against the banks, the restricting boundaries of individuality. Suffering under their frustrating limitations, they seek to burst through all dams in quest of the great ocean, longing to be one with it, to submerge painful separateness in an imagined Oneness. It is the enticing melody of "Unbewusst—hoechste Lust!" ("To be unconscious—oh highest lust!", Richard Wagner), the "descent to the mother goddess," the cult of the night.

On a simpler level, the craving for annihilation is the outcome of sheer despair, the reverse of worldly enchantment. Worn out by the vicissitudes of life, one longs for a sleep without awakening, to obliterate oneself as a protest against a world that does not grant one's wishes. As an irrational revenge, one wants to destroy oneself or others. In some cases, fanatical creeds of violence and destruction stem from this very source.[10]

---

10. On these necrophilic, "death-loving" tendencies, see Erich Fromm, *The Heart of Man* (New York: Harper and Row, 1964), pp. 37ff.

Finally, in its rationalized form, this craving appears as the view or theory of annihilation (*uccheda-diṭṭhi*), expressed in various types of materialist philosophies throughout the history of human thought.

Craving for continued existence (*bhava-taṇhā*) is the unceasing, restless flow of the river of life towards goals hoped for, but never attained. It is fed by our persistent hope that happiness will come tomorrow, or in a heaven or golden age of our belief. Even when all our toil gives little or no present satisfaction and happiness, we console ourselves with the thought that we work for our children or our nation or mankind; and each generation repeats that deferred hope.

As a longing for life eternal, desired and imagined in many forms, this craving for existence appears in many religions and philosophies. In Buddhist texts, it is called "the eternalist view" (*sassata-diṭṭhi*).

Craving for existence is the driving force that keeps the Wheel of Life in rotation. If viewed by an unclouded eye, this wheel is seen as a treadmill kept in motion by those who have condemned themselves to that servitude. It is a contraption "where you are perpetually climbing, but can never rise an inch" (Walter Scott). The beings who rotate in it are again and again victimized by their illusion that the stepping-board before their eyes is the cherished goal, the desired end of their toil. They do not know that within a turning wheel there is no final goal or destination; and that the end of the world with its suffering cannot be reached by walking on a treadmill. It can be attained only by stopping the driving forces within us—craving and ignorance. Yet those beings who have committed themselves to that wheel still believe that, within this truly vicious circle, they do "get on in life," and hopefully speak of progress and evolution.

This is the sober and sobering view of existence and the craving for its continuation. But if there were not also a tempting aspect, beings would not cling to life and crave for it to go on. We need not dwell here on those tempting aspects high or low, as there have been, and still are, many eulogists of life and its beauties. Hence we shall speak here only of some of the more subtle forms of allurement which the craving for existence takes.

Among its numerous forms, craving for existence may appear as a longing for variety. This longing frequently makes people seek for happiness somewhere else than in the here and now, and in some form other than the one they actually possess. The mirage of a "happiness elsewhere" becomes a bait that moves further away the closer it is approached, ever eluding the hand that tries to grasp it. It is like the fate of Tantalus to which man has become so habituated that he even finds it pleasant, saying that "it adds spice to life."

There are others who thirst after ever-widening horizons of life, seeking new sensory or mental experiences for their own sake; some who are enamoured with their own prowess in confronting life; and some who enjoy their own creativeness. The latter includes many geniuses in diverse fields who may well be reborn as those deities of the Buddhist tradition who "delight in their own creations" (*nimmānarati-deva*). Characteristic of this mentality is Gotthold Ephraim Lessing's preference for the search for truth over the attainment of it; or Napoleon's words that he loved power just as a musician loves his instrument: for the sake of the music he produces on it. Those who enjoy life for its own sake proudly aver that they are willing to pay the price for it in life's coinage of suffering and pain, defeat and frustration. Often, however, this is just an heroic pose that hides feelings of frustration and pride. But even when that avowal is honest and stands firm against pain and failure, it will finally break down when body and mind lose their strength, or when satiety and boredom set in.

It is one of the most subtle and effective ruses of the "will to live" to lure man on and on, dangling before him hope, novelty or the gratification of pride. The allurement of "far horizons," the search for the unknown, has tempted many imaginative and adventurous minds; and those of an heroic mould it has urged to meet the vicissitudes of life as a challenge, appealing to their pride to rise above them. Only in the Arahant, the liberated one, will such detachment in face of adversity be genuine and unshakable. Only he can truly say of himself that he has risen above the vicissitudes of existence; that his "mind is unshaken by the eight worldly events" (Mahā-Maṅgala Sutta): gain and loss, repute and disrepute, praise and blame, joy and woe. Being free from all three cravings, he is free of "both sides": the longing for life and the longing for death, the fear of life and the fear of death. He who has conquered craving has conquered all the worlds, the "here and the beyond." For craving is the triune Lord of all the Worlds, their creator, sustainer and destroyer; and he who is craving's conqueror is also the true world conqueror.

Conceit

4. *He who entirely blots out conceit*
   as the flood demolishes a fragile bamboo bridge,
   —such a monk gives up the here and the beyond,
   just as a serpent sheds its worn-out skin.

Human conceit is here compared with a fragile bamboo bridge. In countries of the East, such bridges often consist of just two or three bamboo poles, sometimes with a railing of the same material. On such bridges one has to be quite sure of one's balance in order to safely cross a roaring mountain brook or a deep gorge. Human pride is just as fragile and shaky. It may easily be upset by a whiff of public opinion, hurt by any fool's snide remark, hurled down deep by defeat, failure or misfortune.

Conceit has its roots in ego-belief, which may be either intellectually articulated or habitually and tacitly assumed. In return, conceit gives a very powerful support to ego-belief. It does not tolerate any doubt or challenge of what it prides itself on so much: the existence and the supreme value of that precious self. Any attempt to question its existence and its worth is regarded with as much violent resentment as a powerful ruler would exhibit if he were to be subjected to a body search at the border of his country.

The noun *conceit* derives from the verb *conceiving*.[11] It is, indeed, a conceited conception to conceive oneself superior to others. But also to conceive oneself equal to another ("I am as good as you"), or as inferior (which often comes from frustrated pride)—these, too, are rooted in conceit, in an egocentric evaluation of oneself in relation to others. All three are modes of conceit:

---

11. Quite similarly, in the Pali language, *māna* (conceit) and *maññati* (conceiving).

the superiority complex, the equality claim, and the inferiority complex. This urge to compare oneself with others springs from an inner insecurity that deep within knows and fears the shakiness of the delusive ego image.

This triple conceit entirely vanishes only when even the most subtle ego reference disappears. This comes only with Arahantship, when the last vestige of the fetter of conceit (*māna-saṃyojana*) has been eliminated. The Arahant no longer needs the shaky bridge of ego conceit as he has given up "both sides," the discrimination of self and others, and has transcended both the here and the beyond of worldly existence.

The Search For Stability

5. *He who does not find core or substance*
   in any of the realms of being,
   like flowers that are vainly sought
   in fig-trees that bear none,
   —such a monk gives up the here and the beyond,
   just as a serpent sheds its worn-out skin.

Like ignorant people who want to pick flowers where none can be expected, since time immemorial men have sought in vain for an abiding core and substance within themselves and in the world they inhabit. Or they have hoped to find it beyond their own world, in celestial realms and in their gods. Man is driven to that unceasing but futile quest for something immortal by his longing for a state of security, living as he does in an entirely insecure world which he constantly sees crumbling around him and below his own feet. Not that the vast majority of men would care for the boredom of living forever in the immobility which any stable and secure condition implies. But they long for it as a temporary refuge to which they can resort, as children resort to the soothing arms of their mother after becoming sore and tired by their wild and reckless play.

Behind that longing for security, be it temporary or constant, there looms a still stronger driving force: the fear of death, the desire for self-preservation. This holds true for the coarsest as well as the subtlest form of that search for permanency, be it a wish for the perpetuation of sense enjoyment in a sensuous heaven, or the expression of a "metaphysical need," or the deep yearning for a *unio mystica*. This quest for permanency and security may also manifest itself as an urge for absolute power or for absolute self-surrender, for absolute knowledge or for absolute faith.

Since man's early days, as soon as he first started to reflect upon his life situation, he turned his glance everywhere in search of something stable in a world of instability. He looked for it in the personified forces of nature, in stellar bodies, in the four great elements of matter, believing one or another to be the ultimate matrix of life. But chiefly he sought it in those changing forms and symbols of the divine which he had created in the image of his own longings, within the scope of his own understanding, and for the furtherance of his own purposes, noble or low.

Firm belief in an Absolute, whether a god or a state, has appeared to man to be so absolutely necessary that he has used all subtleties of his intellect and all autosuggestive devices to persuade himself to accept this or that form of religious or political faith. He has also used every possible means, fair and foul, either to coax or to coerce others to recognize and worship his religious or political idols. Often not much coercion was needed, as there were always those who were only too glad to sacrifice their intellect and surrender their freedom at the altars of those idols, to win in return a feeling of security and doubt-free certainty.

Men have too easily believed, and made others believe, that when there is a word there must also be a "real thing" corresponding to it: hence an abiding core, an eternal substance, within or behind this transient world. It was the Buddha who urged men to desist from their vain search for the non-existent and see reality as it is:

Entirely coreless is the world.

(Sn 937)

He, the Awake, cleared the way to the open, leaving behind the towering edifices of ideologies and the debris in which they inevitably end. Showing up in their hollowness the claims of diverse Absolutes, he pointed out that only the hard way of critical examination, our precarious and limited freedom of choice, and the road of morally responsible thought and action can lead us to freedom from suffering. And only a world that is entirely changeable can give us hope for final liberation. Anything permanent found in the world would necessarily bind us to it forever, making liberation impossible.

But one who is instructed by the Buddha, "the Knower of the Worlds," will not find any core of permanency in any form of existence high or low, nor a core of lasting happiness or of an abiding personality. Such a one will not cling to the *here* nor yearn for a *beyond*; he will remain unattached to *either side.* Seeing world and self as void of an abiding core, he wins the unclouded vision of reality and, finally, Nibbāna's peace.

Grudge

6. *He who bears no grudges in his heart,*
transcending all this "thus" and "otherwise,"
—such a monk gives up the here and the beyond,
just as a serpent sheds its worn-out skin.

Grudge is felt towards people by whom one has been wronged or offended, or towards those who act against one's interests, even if in fair competition. Grudge may also have an impersonal character, as a resentful bitterness about one's life, if one feels that one has been treated unfairly in life by too long a chain of misfortunes. Such grudge and resentment may show up outwardly as angry words and deeds, or may rankle deep in the heart as a gnawing bitterness spreading a dark mood over all that one feels, thinks and speaks. With some temperaments it can foster vengeful and aggressive behaviour, with others an ever dissatisfied or melancholic and pessimistic mood. Habitual grudge and resentment can drain much joy from one's life. When growing into enmity, a deep personal grudge—just as strong attachment—may persist and grow from rebirth to rebirth, from the here to the beyond, repeatedly bringing dire misery to those linked in such an unhappy relationship. Also the impersonal grudge one bears against one's unhappy experiences may well reappear in a young child as an innate mood of resentment and discontent. All these are certainly more than sufficiently harmful consequences for spurring us on to banish grudge from our hearts as soon as it arises.

Personal grudge arises from an unwise reaction to conflicts in human relationships. It is avoided and abandoned by forgiveness, forbearance, and understanding of the fact that people are heirs of their *kamma*.

Impersonal grudge is caused by an unwise reaction to the unavoidable vicissitudes of life—the "thus" and "otherwise" of our text. It is prevented and abandoned by understanding and accepting the impermanent nature of existence, and again by an understanding of *kamma*.

Fertile soil for the arising of a deep-seated grudge is political fanaticism, and national, racial, religious and class prejudices. Such grudges can have a personal or impersonal character, or both. For the elimination of this type of grudge the aid of both intellectual and ethical faculties is required: impartial examination of facts, together with tolerance and a feeling for the common human nature shared with others in spite of differences.

Grudge—like all other forms and degrees of aversion—is entirely discarded, like the snake's worn-out skin, at the stage of the non-returner. Then it loses forever its power to germinate in lives beyond—though even at the earlier stages of the stream-enterer and the once-returner, it will have been greatly weakened. There is what may be called a "higher" form of grudge, appearing as "righteous indignation" and a resentful or even hostile attitude towards evil and evil-doers. But even this *"higher"* form of grudge, as well as its very common *lower* form, will be transcended in a mind that has grown mature in compassion and understanding.

Evil Thoughts

7. *He who has burned out his evil thoughts,*
   entirely cut them off within his heart,
   —such a monk gives up the here and the beyond,
   just as a serpent sheds its worn-out skin.

Our verse speaks only of "thoughts" (*vitakka*), without further qualification; but there is no doubt that only undesirable, unwholesome and evil thoughts are meant. Skilful and noble thoughts, particularly those aiming at liberation, should not be "burned out" from the heart. The commentary to our verse speaks of the threefold wrong thoughts of sensuality, ill will and cruelty, as opposed to the threefold right thought (*sammā-saṅkappa*) of the Noble Eightfold Path. The commentary further mentions thoughts of gain, position and fame; concern for personal immortality; excessive attachment to home and country, to one's family or to other persons. These latter types of thought apply chiefly to monks, since, according to Buddhist lay ethics, concern for home and family, and even a moderate concern for gain and position, are not discouraged when they contribute toward the fulfilment of a layman's duties. Yet all these attachments are fetters binding us to the here and the beyond, and one day they have to be discarded if the heart's freedom is to be won.

But the root thoughts of everything harmful and evil are those of greed, hatred and delusion, which are expressly mentioned in the "Discourse on the Quelling of Thoughts" (Vitakka-Saṇṭhāna Sutta).[12]

In that discourse, the Buddha sets forth five methods of removing such harmful thoughts from one's mind, given in a graded sequence from subtler methods of removal to increasingly coarser approaches.

The first method is that of immediately replacing undesirable, evil thoughts by their desirable and beneficial opposites: greedy thoughts should be superceded by thoughts of renunciation and selflessness; hate by thoughts of friendliness, love and compassion; delusion and confusion by wise comprehension and clarity of thought. The discourse gives here the simile of driving out a coarse peg with a fine one, as carpenters do. This method will work best when there is a strong natural tendency to turn away quickly from any inner defilement or outer temptation, and to replace these thoughts immediately by their antidote. When this spontaneity of moral reaction is weak or absent, this method of replacement may still be workable, if one has a fair degree of mind control, aided by alert mindfulness and firm determination. These latter qualities, however, can be gradually acquired or strengthened by mental training, until they ripen into spontaneous advertence to the good.

The second method makes use of the mental impact of strong *repugnance* against evil, by impressing on the mind the ugliness,

---

12. Majjhima Nikāya 20. See note 6 above.

depravity, danger and unworthiness of evil thoughts. This may serve as a transition to, or preparation for, the first method. The simile in the discourse is here that of a carcass thrown over the neck of a handsome young man or woman who will then feel "horrified, humiliated and disgusted" by it and will do the utmost to discard it.

Third, when these methods fail and undesirable thoughts still perturb the mind, one should deny them attention. One should not think about them or dwell on them in any way, but divert one's attention to any other thoughts or activity suitable to bind one's interest. This is the method of *diverting* the mind by non-attention. Here the simile is that of closing one's eyes before a disagreeable sight or turning the glance in another direction. This approach, too, can prepare the mind for the application of the first method.

The fourth method is to go back to the thought-source from which those undesirable thoughts started and to remove them from one's mind. This might be easier than to cope directly with the resulting undesirable thought. Such tracing back to the cause will also help to divert the mind and thus reduce the strength of the undesirable thoughts. In view of the latter fact, the simile in the discourse speaks of reducing coarser movements of the body by calmer ones: a man who is running asks himself, "Why should I run?", and he now goes slowly. He then continues the process of calming, by successively standing still, sitting and lying down. The commentary explains this method as referring to a tracing *of the cause*, or of the starting point of the undesirable thoughts.[13] The simile, however, seems to admit an interpretation of this method as one of *sublimation* or gradual refinement.

The fifth and last method is vigorous suppression, the last resort when undesirable thoughts, e.g., extremely passionate ones, threaten to become unmanageable. This method, likened to a strong man pressing or forcing down a weaker person, shows the realistic and undogmatic approach of the Buddha, which does

---

13. In the discourse, the relevant Pali term is *vitakka-saṅkhāra-saṇṭhāna*, and the commentary explains here *saṅkhāra* by condition (*paccaya*), cause (*kāraṇa*), and root or source (*mūla*). This phrase, however, could also be rendered by "stilling the thought formations (or processes)."

not exclude a method of suppression where the situation demands it, lest a serious worsening of that situation or a deterioration of one's character may occur.

By applying these methods, says the discourse, one may become a "master of the paths taken by one's thought processes. The thought he then wants to think, that he will think; and the thought he does not want to think, that he will not think. Thus, having cut down craving, removed the fetter (binding to existence), and fully mastered pride, he has made an end to suffering."

Hence the perfect mastery of defiled thoughts—their entire burning out, as our verse calls it—is identical with perfect holiness (*arahatta*), in which all the here and beyond has been transcended.

Transcending Diffuseness

8. *He who neither goes too far nor lags behind,*
   entirely transcending the diffuseness of the world,
   —such a monk gives up the here and the beyond,
   just as a serpent sheds its worn-out skin.

The first line of this stanza recurs five more times in the following verses 9–13. This sixfold repetition indicates the importance given to these few words by the creator of this poem, the Buddha, who "sees the deep meaning" (*nipuṇatthadassī*, Suttanipāta, v. 377) and "clads it in beautiful speech" (*vaggu-vādo*, v. 955).

The first two lines of the stanza, if viewed closely, are variations of the last two lines which speak of the transcending of "both sides"—taking the meaning of the Pali words *ora-pāraṃ* in their wider sense as explained above.

The range of meaning of these first few words is as wide as the "world entire," the world of diffuseness or plurality (*papañca*). In this context, it is significant that the Pali word *papañca* has also the connotation of "lagging behind" or "procrastination."[14]

---

14. Another important connotation of the term *papañca*, i.e., "conceptual proliferation," has been emphasized and ably explained by Bhikkhu Ñāṇananda in his book *Concept and Reality* (BPS, 1971), which mainly deals with that term. But we feel that this meaning chiefly applies to a psychological context and not, as the author thinks (ibid., p.26), also to our present text

Its over-active partner within that pair, providing the extreme of excessive movement, is craving, which tends to go far beyond what the retarding force of objectified *saṃsāra*, or *papañca*, will allow. Craving produces again and again the disillusioning experience of its own futility; and yet again and again it seeks "ever-new enjoyment, now here, now there" (*tatra tatr'ābhinandinī*). The failure to which craving is necessarily doomed is caused not only by its own inherent illusions, but also, on the objective side, by the unfathomable diffuseness of the world—that intricate saṃsāric net of interactions in which the frantic flutterings of craving are invariably caught, be it here or in a beyond, now or later.

The very same ideas as those of our verse are conveyed in the first text of the Saṃyutta Nikāya (Kindred Sayings). There we read:

"How, Lord, did you cross the flood (of *saṃsāra*)?"

"Without tarrying,[15] friend, and without struggling did I cross the flood."

"But how could you do so, O Lord?"

"When tarrying, friend, I sank, and when struggling I was swept away. So, friend, it is by not tarrying and not struggling that I have crossed the flood."[16]

What in our verse is called "going too far" is here spoken of as "struggling,"[17] which has the attendant danger of being "swept away" all over the wide expanse of the saṃsāric flood. The "lagging behind" is here expressed by "tarrying," which leads to "sinking" or declining—possibly to the lowest depth.

There is a similar metaphor in the verses 938-939 of the Suttanipāta:

---

where the range of reference is wider than the topic of delusive concepts. The first line of the verse, for instance, refers to extremes of conduct and not only to those of conceptual thought. The concluding two lines, too, point to a wider significance.

15. *Appatiṭṭhaṃ*, "without standing still" or "without seeking a hold."
16. See the translation of this text with notes by Bhikkhu Ñāṇananda in *Saṃyutta Nikāya Anthology, Part II* (Wheel No. 183/185).
17. The Pali word *āyūhana* also means "accumulation" of rebirth-producing actions (*kamma*), and thereby, of new lives.

I saw what is so hard to see,
the dart embedded in the heart—
the dart by which afflicted we
in all directions hurry on.
If once this dart has been removed,
one will not hurry, will not sink.

These two extremes—going too far (struggling) and lagging behind (tarrying)—point also to basic tendencies of life and mind, manifesting themselves in various ways: as motory impulses and inertia; the phases of "opening," developing, evolving, and of "closing," shrinking, receding;[18] dispersal and contraction; dilution and hardening; distraction and concentration; hypertension and laxity; the flights of imagination and the confinement by habit and routine; the will to conquer and the desire for self-preservation; the wish for independence and for security ("freedom and bread"); an imperturbable will to believe, and unappeasable scepticism, and so on.

The sets of paired terms given in the canonical texts considered here, that is:

going too far—lagging behind (Suttanipāta)
struggling—tarrying (Saṃyutta Nikāya)
being swept away—sinking (Saṃyutta Nikāya),

have been explained by the Buddhist commentators by corresponding dual concepts taken from the terminology of the Dhamma. A selection of these explanations follows. Where it serves greater clarity, the separate commentarial statements on the two texts have been combined, paraphrased and amplified by additional comments.

By *clinging* to the defiling passions, tarrying and seeking a hold in them, beings will sink into a low and unhappy existence in the course of future rebirths; and in this life, their moral and mental standard will sink and deteriorate; or at least they will "lag behind," stagnate, in whatever higher aims they have in their life.

Struggling for life's varied aims, for what is really a mere accumulation of kammic bondage, beings are liable to "go too far"

---

18. Here one may think too of the cosmic periods of evolving and shrinking (*vivaṭṭa-saṃvaṭṭa*) within one world-cycle (*kappa*).

by aiming at unattainable goals; be it the gratification of insatiable desires, the pursuit of insatiable ambitions, or the fulfilment of unrealizable ideals. In that vain effort, beings are swept away, carried along in all directions of the saṃsāric ocean.

Driven by *craving for continued existence*, longing after the bliss of a theistic heaven or for any other form of a happy rebirth, one "goes too far" by following one's wishful thinking or one's desire for self-perpetuation; and when turning to self-mortification of body or mind to achieve these aims, one likewise goes to excess. When adopting a materialist creed, *the view of annihilationism*, one struggles for an earthly paradise, fights fanatically against any religious teaching, and may even go so far as to deny dogmatically all moral and spiritual values.

In performing *evil actions* one lags behind, falls short of the basic human postulates; and deteriorating, one will finally sink and be submerged by the saṃsāric floods. In struggling for the performance of *worldly good actions*, with all their inherent limitations and attachments, illusions and frustrations, one will be carried away endlessly into the ever-receding horizon of the unattainable.

In *yearning after the past*, one strays too far from the present and even struggles to bring back the past, as for instance, when one tries to "appear young," or, in a more serious way, to impose one's romantic notions of the past upon the present. By doing so, one is carried far away from a realistic grasp of the present. In *hoping for the future*, for a heavenly beyond, a golden or messianic age to come, or even merely for "better luck tomorrow," one neglects present effort, lags behind in meeting the demands of present situations, and sinks into a multitude of fears, hopes and vain worries.

Given to lassitude, one will lag behind, fall short in one's achievements, and be submerged in sloth and torpor. In the *excitement and restlessness* of struggling, one will be inclined to go too far and be carried away to extremes.[19]

But he who, avoiding all these extremes, walks the middle path and harmonizes the five spiritual faculties (the balancing of faith with wisdom, and energy with calm, while mindfulness

---

19. This relates our paired terms to two of the five hindrances (*nīvaraṇa*). See verse 17 and commentary.

watches over this process of harmonizing)—he is one "who neither goes too far nor lags behind."

* * *

After these specific illustrations, a few general observations may be made on what may be called the structural or functional nature of these pairs of opposites.

"Going too far" is the extreme development of one single aspect of many-sided actuality. But the desire for dominance and ever-continued expansion on the part of that one single aspect has also an activating effect on its counterpart. In the neglected or suppressed function, it will rouse the will to self-preservation and assertion. But apart from such opposition, any unrestrained one-sided expansion will finally weaken that "extremist" factor itself. When "going too far abroad," the distance from its original source of strength will grow, and there will be a loss of concentrated energy. The initial recklessly self-assertive factor that set out on a journey of conquest in order to impose itself on the world, will gradually be thinned out and diluted in the process. Through those thousand things which it absorbs in its conquering career, it will imperceptibly become alienated from its original nature; and those thousand influences, wrongly believed to have been mastered in the "struggle," will carry their former master still further away into unrecognized and perilous self-alienation. This is a case of "the eater being devoured by what he eats." All these characteristics of "going too far" hold good for external activities (political, social, etc.) as well as for the interplay of the inner forces of the mind.

In "lagging behind," there is a preponderance of heaviness or inertia, a lack of self-impelling force, of powerful, springy tension, and even an aversion against it. As far as there is movement in that tarrying tendency, it is of a recoiling, centripetal nature. It is the cramped or contracted mind (*saṅkhitta-citta*) spoken of in the Satipaṭṭhāna Sutta. This centripetal and recoiling tendency is characteristic of an extremely introverted type of mind. Though an introvert type sometimes "goes too far" in certain psychological and ideological attitudes, generally it is shy and timid, or resentful and contemptuous. Recoil from too close a social contact places him on the side of "lagging behind." An extreme introvert type tries to resist even those slight shiftings of its inner centre of gravity called for by the human or psychological environment.

All manifestations of "lagging behind" show a lack of reciprocity and of exchange with the outside world. We may even call it "weak mental metabolism," since mental activity is also a process of nutrition. While the opposite tendency towards excessive expansion may run the risk of being invaded by an excess of "foreign bodies," there is here a deficiency of them; and this will make for poor adaptability and lack of stimulation for new developments. This may finally lead to such a degree of isolation and inbreeding that here, too, the neglected counterpart will rise in self-defence. If its counter-move succeeds, it may produce a harmonious balance of character, unless it starts on a one-sided development of its own. But if such a corrective is absent or remains unsuccessful, that particular life-process, by seriously "lagging behind," will "sink," that is, deteriorate, and may reach a point of complete stagnation.

Thus the strands of life's texture meet crosswise in their upward and downward path. In that way they weave the intricate net of the world's diffuseness (*papañca*), to which the interplay of these paired opposites adds uncountable meshes.

It is through balanced view and balanced effort that one can transcend all these extremes. If one has thus found the harmonizing centre in one's life and thought—the Noble Eightfold Path, the *Middle Way*—then the outer manifestations of the inner opposites and conflicts will also fall away, like the worn-out skin of the snake, never to be renewed again. Then there will be rebirth no more, neither in the lower nor in the higher realms, neither here nor beyond: both sides have been left behind. For the Liberated One, world migration, world creation, have utterly ceased.

Knowing the World

9. *He who neither goes too far nor lags behind and knows about the world: "This is all unreal,"*

10. *greedless he knows: "This is all unreal,"*

11. *lust-free he knows: "This is all unreal,"*

12. *hate-free he knows: "This is all unreal,"*

13. *delusion-free he knows: "This is all unreal,"*
   —such a monk gives up the here and the beyond, just as a serpent sheds its worn-out skin.

The world is unreal in the sense of presenting a deceptive appearance, being quite different in actuality from the way it appears to a greedy, lustful, hating and ignorant mind. The Pali word *vitatha*, here rendered by "unreal," has both in Pali and Sanskrit the meaning of "untrue" or "false." These verses, however, are not meant to convey the idea that the world is mere illusion, a play of the imagination. What underlies its deceptive appearance, the flux of mental and physical processes, is real enough in the sense that it is effect-producing. The unreality lies in what we attribute to the world, and not in the world itself.

What, now, is this "world" (*loka*) and this "all" (*sabba*), which should be seen as unreal, in the sense of being deceptive? When the Enlightened One was questioned about these two words, he gave the same answer for both:

1. "One speaks of 'the world,' Lord. In how far is there a world or the designation 'world'?"

   "When there is the eye and visible forms, visual consciousness and things cognizable by visual consciousness; when there is the ear and sounds ... ; nose and smells ... ; tongue and flavours ... ; body and tangibles ... ; mind and ideas, mind-consciousness and things cognizable by mind-consciousness—then there is a world and the designation 'world'."

   (SN 35:68)

2. " 'All' will I show you, O monks. And what is 'all'? The eye and visible forms, ear and sounds, nose and smells, tongue and flavours, body and tangibles, mind and ideas—this, O monks, is what is called 'all'."

(SN 35:22)

This twelvefold world process is kept going by craving for the six objects and by attachment to the six sense faculties deemed to belong to a "self." Craving itself is kindled by the discrimination between "likes and dislikes," that is, choice and rejection motivated by greed, hatred and delusion.

What "like and dislike" commonly is called,
induced by that, desire comes into being.

(Sn 867)

It is this ego-centred discrimination of "like and dislike" that gives to the world its deceptive colouring—its semblance of reality, meaning and value—which is derived from those subjective emotions. But he who is neither carried away by the unreal nor recoils from the real—and thus neither goes too far nor lags behind—he is able to remove that deceptive colouring (*rāgaratta*: coloured by passion) and to gain dispassion (*virāga*). When the colouring fades away, the bare processes of body and mind will appear in their true nature as being void of a core of permanence, happiness and selfhood. In the sense of that triple voidness, too, this world is unreal.

Look at the world as void,
Mogharāja, ever mindful!
Uprooting the view of self
You may thus be one who overcomes death.

(Sn 1119)

Through freedom from lust and greed (vv.10-11), there is the final fading away of the fictive reality bestowed by attraction.

Through freedom from hatred (v.12), there is the final fading away of the fictive reality bestowed by aversion and aggression.

Through freedom from delusion (v.13), greed and hatred come to an end, and there is the final fading away of all vain hopes and fears concerning the world and of all delusive ideologies about it.

A text in the Itivuttaka (No. 49) of the Pali Canon speaks of the ideological extremes of eternity-belief and belief in annihilation, using figurative expressions similar to those of our Uraga Sutta:

> There are two kinds of view, O monks, and when deities and human beings are obsessed by them, some stick fast and others run too far; only those with eyes see.
>
> And how, O monks, do some stick fast? Deities and human beings for the most part love existence, delight in existence, rejoice in existence. When Dhamma is taught to them for the ceasing of existence, their minds do not take to it, do not accept it, and do not become firm and resolute (about that Dhamma). Thus it is that some stick fast (to their old attachments).
>
> And how do some run too far? Some feel ashamed, humiliated and disgusted by that same existence, and they welcome non-existence in this way: "Sirs, when with the breaking up of the body after death, this self is cut off, annihilated, does not become any more after death—that is peaceful, that is sublime, that is true." Thus it is that some run too far.
>
> And how do those with eyes see? Here a monk sees what has become as become, he has entered upon the way to dispassion for it, to the fading away of greed for it, to its cessation. This is how those with eyes see.

Dormant Tendencies

14. *He who has no dormant tendencies whatever,*
    whose unwholesome roots have been expunged,
    —such a monk gives up the here and the beyond,
    just as a serpent sheds its worn-out skin.

"Dormant tendencies" (*anusaya*) are mental defilements which have become so strong that, from a state of latency, they easily become active in reaction to appropriate stimuli. These dormant tendencies are, as it were, the deepest strata of three levels on which defilements may exist.

At the first level, the most obvious and the coarsest, the defilements become manifest in unwholesome, evil deeds and words. This is called the level of moral transgression (*vītikkama-bhūmi*), which can be temporarily controlled by morality (*sīla*).

The second level is that of a purely mental involvement (*pariyuṭṭhāna-bhūmi*), namely, in defiled thoughts. It can be temporarily suppressed by *jhāna*, meditative absorption.

The third level is that of the dormant tendencies (*anusaya-bhūmi*). These are gradually eliminated by wisdom (*paññā*), arising in the four stages of final emancipation.

At the first stage of emancipation, stream-entry, the tendencies to false views and sceptical doubt are eliminated.

At the second stage, once-returning, the gross forms of the tendencies of sensual desire and ill will are eliminated.

At the third stage, non-returning, the residual tendencies of sensual desire and ill will are eliminated.

At the fourth stage, Arahantship, all remaining unwholesome tendencies have disappeared—those of conceit, desire for any new becoming, and ignorance.

Our clinging to habitual desires and their objects on the one hand, and our emotional rejections and aversions on the other—these are the main feeders of the hidden but powerful tendencies in our minds. The tendencies in turn strengthen our habitual reactions of grasping and repelling, making them almost automatic. Hence they become potent unwholesome roots of evil (*akusala-mūla*), by way of greed or hate, while the unthinking state of mind in which we so react is the third evil root, delusion.

It is mindfulness that can check the unrestricted growth of those unwholesome tendencies. At the beginning mindfulness may not be strong enough to prevent the arising of every instance and degree of mental defilement. But when these defilements in their manifestation are confronted by awareness and resistance, they will no longer bring an increase in the strength of the dormant tendencies.

They are finally silenced, however, only by an Arahant, in whom all "unwholesome roots have been expunged." The Arahant has abandoned "both sides" of the tendencies, those of attraction and repulsion. Being freed of all fetters that bind to existence, he has given up the here and the beyond, the high and the low, of *saṃsāra*.

Anxiety and Attachment

15. *States born of anxiety he harbours none
which may condition his return to earth ...*

16. *States born of attachment he harbours none
which cause his bondage to existence,
—such a monk gives up the here and the beyond,
just as a serpent sheds its worn-out skin.*

"Anxiety" (*daratha*) and "attachment" (*vanatha*), from which similar states of mind are born (*jā*), can be interpreted here as forms of dormant tendencies, as basic moods causing appropriate manifestation.

Anxiety appears as anguish, fear and worry, and as feelings of tension, oppression and depression caused by those emotions. Also inner conflict may be included here, especially as the Pali word *daratha* has the primary meaning of "split."

Hence the range of what we have called "anxiety" may extend to the dark moods resulting from:

> cares and worries, which make the heart heavy, anxieties proper—fears for oneself and for others, fear of death and fear of life; the tension and agitation caused by inner conflict; the feelings of insecurity, helplessness and loneliness; the primordial (or metaphysical) anguish, rooted in those former three and in the fear of the unknown.

All these moods and feelings create a negative emotional background in the character, which may colour one's human relationships and influence decisions of consequence. It may also throw a deep shadow over one's attitude to life in general, and may lead to a shirking of reality, to a recoil from it. When anguish and worry continue to grow in the mind without finding relief, they may become a cause of the anxiety neurosis which is so widespread in times of emotional and social insecurity.

But anguish and anxiety are inherent in human life itself, and their presence in the human mind is not limited to times of particular stress and turbulence. How poignantly the weight of anguish was felt even in ancient India has found a moving expression in words that were once addressed to the Buddha:

The heart is always in a state of fear,
And is always full of anguish drear,
Concerning things that now have taken place
And things that shortly I shall have to face.
If there's a place that's free from ev'ry fear,
That fear-free place will thou to me make clear?

(SN 2:17. Tr. Soma Thera)

Attachment, via "states born of attachment" (*vanathajā*), leads to entanglements in the thicket (*vanatha*) of life. These entanglements through attachment are of many kinds and they throw over man the widespread "catch-net" of craving (Sn 527). Apart from those that are openly seductive, others appear in an innocuous or respectable guise, or are rationalized in more or less convincing ways. Attachments can be pursued actively or enjoyed passively. Of the innumerable forms they may take, only a very few will be mentioned here.

There is the whole scale of five-sense enjoyment, with sex as its strongest; sex in all its varieties, coarse and refined, with all its trappings and subservient arts and enticements.

There is the enchantment of beauty, in nature and art, with man's creative or receptive response.

There is the insatiable craze to get and to grasp, the fierce determination to hold and hoard; thirst for power and domination, in the smallest circle and on a world-wide scale.

On the passive side, there is the felt need and the inner satisfaction to obey and submit; the gregarious instinct, and the wish to creep under the protective shelter of this or that personal or group relationship; the comfortable feeling of following habits and custom; hero worship and leader cult.

And there is also the mystic's loving surrender to his god, which, of course, can have an ennobling effect on the mind, and yet is an "intoxication of the soul," just like the attachment to the bliss of meditation (*jhāna-nikanti*) for its own sake.

"States born of attachment" are at the root of the entire life process, on all its levels. Hence their variety is inexhaustible. Some may show man at his lowest and others at his most refined level. There are attachments that can inspire man to noble virtues, such as loyalty or self-sacrificing love, and to sublime creativity in many fields. But even the most lofty heights reached by refined attachment are no safeguard against a plunge into the lowest depths if one unwarily entrusts oneself to the dangerous gradient of attachment. Therefore, the wise will strive to detach themselves from the high as well as the low, from the *here* of earthly attachments and from the *beyond* of their "divine" and subtle forms. The Master said: "Do you see, my disciples, any fetter, coarse or fine, which I have *not* asked you to discard?"

Anxiety (fear) and attachment (craving) produce each other, but they also set limits to each other. "Craving breeds anxiety; craving breeds fear," says the Dhammapada. And fear and anxiety on their part give rise to an intensified attachment to what is threatened and to a craving for the means to attain security. On the other hand, greed may sometimes be restrained by fear, both in individuals and in nations. But greed may also put shackles on fear: thus, disregarding fear's warnings, a person may set out on a perilous course to satisfy his desires.

Anxiety and attachment—these two well up from an unfathomable past, and again and again become, as our text says, conditions for renewed existence, here and beyond. For "anxiety," our text specifies a rebirth *here* (*oraṃ*), in this human existence. Anxiety, in all the aspects we have mentioned, is so deeply embedded in the human situation that it may sometimes "drag to rebirth" as strongly as craving does. To illustrate that typical human mood of anguish, we have quoted earlier a voice from the Buddha's own days. Closer to our days, it was that great and radical Christian, Soren Kierkegaard, who held that the human predicament demanded from those who seriously desired salvation, an "anxious concern" and even "despair." The Buddha, however, as a teacher of the Middle Way, advocated neither a mood of despair nor of facile appeasement. In his earnest disciples he instilled a "sense of urgency" (*saṃvega*), like that of one "whose turban is on fire." And on the side of "attachment," he urged his disciples to show "keen desire" (*tibba-chanda*) for the task of liberation.

The Arahant, however, has transcended "both sides" even in their beneficial aspects. He is free from "anxious concern" (*asoko*) and free from any clinging (*anupādāno*).

The Five Hindrances

17. *He who has the five hindrances discarded,*
    doubt-free and serene, and free of inner barbs,
    —such a monk gives up the here and the beyond,
    just as a serpent sheds its worn-out skin.

When, in the Arahant, all defiling tendencies have been silenced and become non-existent, they can no longer provide a soil for the growth of the five hindrances, which in *jhāna* and in the worldling's insight are only temporarily suppressed. The pair of opposites in the moral sphere, sense-desire and ill will, can no longer impede, and these painful "inner barbs" can no longer irritate. The extremes in temperament, sloth and agitation, cannot arise and disturb the serenity of one who has reached the perfect equipoise of the faculties of energy and calm; nor can there be any doubtful wavering in one of perfect wisdom.

It is for these reasons that, in this last verse of our text, the Arahant is portrayed as being "doubt-free and serene, and free of inner barbs."

The five hindrances illustrate once more some of the strands that keep the skin—be it fresh or partly worn-out—attached to the body. Unhindered by them and free from all that has been "worn out," the Liberated One serenely goes his way into the Trackless—Nibbāna.

Forest Meditations

The Verses of the Arahant Tālapuṭa Thera

Translated from the Pali with
some reflections by
Bhikkhu Khantipālo

Copyright © Kandy; Buddhist Publication Society, (1977, 1983)

Introduction

On Forest Meditation

On the whole, people have changed little in 2500 years. In those days when the Buddha was alive, there were people living the householder's life with family responsibilities, work to be done and money to be earned to continue life; there were also those who were able to give up their homes and families, to leave all that is valued in the world for the sake of the cultivation of the heart in wisdom and compassion. They were supported by generous householders and in turn they gave their benefactors guidance in the difficulties and troubles of life, guidance which was based on the peace and insight which they had developed.

These two classes of people still exist among Buddhists, the lay people with their many works and burdens, and the bhikkhus (Buddhist monks) and nuns whose only work is the Dhamma, its study and practice. And they still support each other for their mutual benefit.

This book is about the life and experiences of a bhikkhu who reached Arahantship (Enlightenment) in the Buddha's days. It is also about how such a life is still possible now for those who wish to make the effort.

But then someone might say, "What's the use of reading about monks and their lives?" A Buddhist might reply, "In the Buddha's days, as now in Buddhist countries, it was the custom for ordinary people to go and see bhikkhus, those who were cultivating their minds and hearts, to get some refreshment for their minds. Just as when the body is thirsty one drinks, so when one's heart is thirsty it should have the chance to drink the Dhamma's nectar." So let us, as it were, go to visit that monk called Tālaputa and hear what he has to say.

Before we go to 'see' him, though, we should know something about him as a person and why he decided to leave his home and become 'homeless', as a Buddhist monk.

Who was Tālapuṭa?

He lived at the time of the Buddha and had been trained from his youth as an actor. Steadily his fame grew until he became the manager of a travelling theatrical troupe of "five hundred women," a general figure which means a large company. This troupe of actors, dancers and singers became very famous, people coming from far and wide to attend performances.

We do not know how Tālapuṭa first heard of the Buddha but his acquaintance with the Dhamma was, no doubt, a gradual one. As he came to know more and more of the Dhamma, his aspirations to be ordained as a bhikkhu became stronger. In his lay life he must have been a gifted poet and this ability he used to compose the verses of aspiration with which his stanzas begin.

Let us see first, why he wanted to become a bhikkhu.

Why Go Forth to Homelessness?

People become monks and nuns for various reasons, some good, some bad.

Once the King of Kurus mentioned that people left their homes, shaved their heads and put on the yellow robe because of: old age, sickness, loss of relatives and loss of wealth. These are not the best reasons! But there are worse: laziness and desire for an easy life, to get one's belly filled for instance. There were such bhikkhus in the Buddha's days and now they can certainly be found in every Buddhist country.

Tālapuṭa tells why he became a bhikkhu, first naming some of the bad reasons for doing so:

33. Not from lack of luck did I go forth,
    shamelessness, nor caused by mind's inconstancy,
    nor banishment nor caused by livelihood,
    and therefore I agreed with you, O mind.

He did not become a monk because he was a failure in ordinary life: actually he was a great success. He was not driven into monkhood by some king's act of banishment, nor because he had done some wrong and had to flee to escape the consequences. It was not that he had a weak mind and so just did not know what to do. Not like this! He agreed with the wisdom in his own mind and gave up worldly life.

He saw how difficult it is to practise all the Dhamma while leading a household life. The difficulties and problems which the Dhamma solves—the difficulties and troubles all called *dukkha*—have their source in the mind. If he was to disentangle the tangle of mind, time was necessary—for mindful awareness of all actions, for meditation to calm the mind, for developing the penetrating wisdom-mind. The conditions necessary for this work were found in the way the Buddhist Order was organised. So he decided to become a bhikkhu.

The Occasion of his Ordination

One time, when the Buddha was staying in the Bamboo Grove at Rājagaha, Tālapuṭa visited the Buddha and after paying his respects to him, asked this question:

"I have heard, Lord, this ancient traditional saying of the actor's teachers who, when speaking of players, said 'A player who on the stage or in the arena makes people laugh and delights them by counterfeiting the truth, at the dissolution of the body, after death, is reborn in the company of the Laughing Gods.' What does the Exalted One say about this?"

The Buddha did not answer when this question was asked even thrice. The fourth time he agreed to answer it: "In the case of those beings who were not free of lust, aversion and delusion before, but were bound with the bonds of lust, aversion and delusion; in such cases a player who on the stage or in the arena brings about lustful, averse or deluded states of mind so that such beings become still more lustful, averse and deluded; while he himself is heedless and slothful, making others heedless and slothful—such a person on the dissolution of the body, after death, is reborn in the Hell of Laughter. And if his view is as you say: 'that whatever player on the stage... by counterfeiting the truth... is reborn in the company of the Laughing Gods,' then I declare that he is of wrong view. I declare that there will be reappearance in one of two destinations: in hell or birth as an animal."

When he heard these words Tālapuṭa wept, not, as he explained to the Buddha, because of the answer that he had received but because he had been led astray and deceived by his teachers. Then he praised the Buddha and asked for the Going Forth and the Admission to the Sangha as a bhikkhu. After living resolute and secluded, he "in no long time"—a phrase which often means several years, attained the Path and Fruit of the *arahant*.

This is the bare account of how he became a bhikkhu and later achieved arahantship. It should be filled out with his aspirations which he made from time to time while he was still a layman. These are the first sixteen verses among his fifty-five and show the mind of a dedicated layman aspiring to win insight-wisdom (*vipassanā-paññā*). At this point all his verses will be given followed by some sketches and comments.

The Verses of the Arahant Tālapuṭa Thera

I. Thoughts before Going Forth

1. When, O when, shall I live all alone
   in mountain caves, unmated with desire,
   clear seeing as unstable all that comes to be?
   This wish of mine, when indeed will it be?

2. When shall I, wearing the patchwork robes
   of colour dun, be sage, uncraving, never making mine,
   with greed, aversion and delusion slain
   and to the wild woods gone, in bliss abide?

3. When shall I, this body seeing clear —
   unstable nest of dying and disease
   oppressed by age and death, dwell free from fear
   in the woods alone? When indeed will it be?

4. When indeed shall I dwell seizing the sharpened sword
   of wisdom made? When cut the craving creeper —
   breeder of fear, bringer of pain and woe,
   and twining everywhere? When indeed will it be?

5. When lion-like in the victor's stance
   shall I draw quick the sage's sword
   of wisdom forged and fiery might
   quick breaking Māra with his host?
   When indeed will it be?

6. When myself exerting, shall I be seen
   in goodly company of those esteeming Dhamma?

Those with faculties subdued who see things as they are?
Those who are 'Thus'? When indeed will it be?

7. When indeed will weariness not worry me —
hunger, thirst and wind, heat, bugs and creeping things,
while bent on my own good, the Goal,
in Giribbaja's wilds? When indeed will it be?

8. When indeed shall I, self-mindful and composed
win to that wisdom known by Him,
the Greatest Sage, the Four Truths won within,
so very hard to see? When indeed will it be?

9. When shall I, possessed of meditation's calm
with wisdom see the forms innumerable,
sounds, smells and tastes, touches and dhammas too,
as a raging blaze? When will this be for me?

10. When shall I indeed, when with abusive words
addressed, not be displeased because of that,
and then again when praised be neither pleased
because of that? When will this be for me?

11. When shall I indeed weigh as the same:
wood, grass and creepers with these craved-for groups,
both inner and external forms
the dhammas numberless? When will it be for me?

12. When in the season of the black rain-cloud
shall I follow the path within the wood
trodden by those who See; robes moistened
by new falling rain? When indeed will it be?

13. When in a mountain cave having heard the peacock's cry,
that crested twice-born bird down in the wood,
shall I arise and collect together mind
for attaining the undying? When indeed will it be?

14. When shall I, the Ganges and the Yamunā,
the Sarasvati and the awful ocean mouth
of the Balava-abyss, by psychic might
untouching go across? When indeed will it be?

15. When shall I, like charging elephant unbound,
    break up desire for sensual happiness
    and shunning all the marks of loveliness
    strive in concentrated states? When indeed will it be?

16. When, as pauper by his debts distressed,
    by creditors oppressed, a treasure finds,
    shall I be pleased the Teaching to attain
    of the Greatest Sage? When indeed will it be?

II. Self-admonishments after Going Forth

17. Long years have I been begged by you
    'Enough for you of this living in a house.'
    but now I have gone forth to homelessness
    what reason is there, mind, for you not to urge me on?

18. Was I not, O mind, assured by you indeed:
    'The brightly plumaged birds on Giribbaja's peaks
    greeting the thunder, the sound of great Indra,
    will bring to you joy meditating in the wood?'

19. Dear ones and friends and kin within the family,
    playing and loving, sensual pleasures of the world:
    all have I given up and reached at last to this,
    even now, O mind, you are not pleased with me.

20. Mine you are, mind, possessed by none but me;
    why then lament when comes this time to arm?
    Seeing all as unstable this is now renounced:
    longing for, desirous of the Undying State.

21. Said He who speaks the best, Best among mankind,
    man-taming trainer, Physician Great indeed:
    'Unsteady, likened to a monkey is the mind,
    extremely hard to check by one not rid of lust.'

22. For varied, sweet, delightful are desires of sense;
    blind, foolish common men long have lain in them
    seeking after birth again, 'tis they who wish for ill,
    by mind they are led on to perish in hell.

23. 'In the jungle you should dwell, resounding with the cries
    of peacocks and herons, by leopard and tiger hailed:

Abandon longing for the body—do not fail.'
So indeed my mind you used to urge me on.

24. 'Grow in concentrations, the faculties and powers,
    develop wisdom-factors by meditation deep
    and then with Triple Knowledge touch the Buddha-sāsana.'
    So indeed my mind you used to urge me on.

25. 'Grow in the Eightfold Way for gaining the Undying
    leading to Release and cleansing of all stains;
    Plunge to the utter destruction of all ill!'
    So indeed my mind you used to urge me on.

26. 'Thoroughly examine the craved-for groups as ill.
    Abandon that from which arises ill.
    Here and now make you an end of ill.'
    So indeed my mind you used to urge me on.

27. 'Thoroughly see inward the impermanent as ill,
    the void as without self, and misery as bane,
    and so the mind restrain in its mental wanderings.'
    So indeed my mind you used to urge me on.

28. 'Head-shaven and unsightly, go to be reviled,
    among the people beg with skull-like bowl in hand.
    To the Greatest Sage, the Teacher's word devote yourself.'
    So indeed my mind you used to urge at me on.

29. 'Wander well-restrained among the streets and families
    having a mind to sensual pleasures unattached,
    as the full moon shining clear at night.'
    So indeed my mind you used to urge me on.

30. 'You should be a forest-dweller, almsman too,
    a graveyard-dweller and a rag-robe wearer too,
    one never lying down, delighting in austerities.'
    So indeed my mind you used to urge me on.

31. As he who having planted trees about to fruit
    should wish to cut a tree down to the root:
    that simile you made, mind, that do you desire
    when on me you urge the unstable and the frail.

32. Formless one, far-traveller, a wanderer alone,
    no more shall I your bidding do, for sense desires
    are ill, leading to bitter fruit, to brooding fear:
    with mind Nibbāna-turned I shall walk on.

33. Not from lack of luck did I go forth,
    nor shamelessness, nor caused by mind's inconstancy,
    nor banishment nor caused by livelihood,
    and therefore I agreed with you, O mind.

34. 'Having few wishes, disparagement's abandoning,
    with the stilling of all ill is praised by goodly men'
    so indeed, my mind, then you urged at me,
    but now you go back to habits made of old.

35. Craving, unknowing, the liked and the disliked,
    delighting in forms and pleasing feelings too,
    dear pleasures of the senses—all have been vomited:
    never to that vomit can I make myself return.

36. In every life, O mind, your word was done by me,
    in many births I have not sought to anger you.
    That which within oneself produced by you, ingrate,
    long wandered on in ill created by you.

37. Indeed it is you, mind, make us brāhmaṇas,
    you make us noble warriors, kings and seers as well,
    sometimes it is merchants or workers we become,
    or led by you indeed we come to gods' estate.

38. Indeed you are the cause of becoming titans too,
    and you are the root for becoming in the hells;
    sometimes there is going to birth as animals,
    or led by you indeed we come to ghosts' estate.

39. Not now will you injure me ever and again,
    moment by moment as though showing me a play,
    as with one gone mad you play with me —
    but how, O mind, have you been failed by me?

40. Formerly this wandering mind, a wanderer,
    went where it wished, wherever whim or pleasure led,
    today I shall thoroughly restrain it
    as a trainer's hook the elephant in rut.

41. He, the Master made me see this world —
    unstable, unsteady, lacking any essence;
    now in the Conqueror's Teaching, mind make me leap,
    cross me over the great floods so very hard to cross!

42. Now it's not for you, mind, as it was before,
    not likely am I to return to your control —
    in the Greatest Sage's Sāsana I have gone forth
    and those like me are not by ruin wrapped.

43. Mountains, seas, rivers, and this wealthy world,
    four quarters, points between, the nadir and the heavens
    all the Three becomings unstable and oppressed.
    Where, mind, having gone will you happily delight?

44. Firm, firm in my aim! What will you do, my mind?
    No longer in your power, mind, nor your follower.
    None would even handle a double-ended sack,
    let be a thing filled full and flowing with nine streams.

45. Whether peak or slopes or fair open space
    or forest besprinkled with fresh showers in the Rains,
    where frequently are found boar and antelope,
    there will you delight to a grotto-lodging gone.

46. Fair blue-throated and fair-crested, the peacock fair of tail,
    wing-plumes of many hues, the passengers of air,
    greeting the thunder with fair-sounding cries
    will bring to you joy meditating in the wood.

47. When the sky-god rains on the four inch grass
    and on full-flowering cloud-like woods,
    within the mountains like a log I'll lie
    and soft that seat to me as cotton down.

48. Thus will I do even as a master should:
    Let whatever is obtained be enough for me,
    that indeed I'll do to you as energetic man
    by taming makes supple a cat-skin bag.

49. Thus will I do even as a master should
    Let whatever is obtained be enough for me,
    by energy I'll bring you in my power
    as a skilled trainer the elephant in rut.

50. With you well-tamed, no longer turning round,
    like to a trainer with a straight running horse,
    I am able to practise the safe and blissful Path
    ever frequented by them who guard the mind.

51. I'll bind you by strength to the meditation-base
    as elephant to post by a strong rope bound;
    well-guarded by me, well-grown with mindfulness,
    you shall, by all becomings, be without support.

52. With wisdom cutting off wending the wrong path,
    by endeavour restrained, established in the Path,
    having seen the origin of passing, rising too —
    you will be an heir to the Speaker of the Best.

53. You dragged me, mind, as on an ox's round,
    in the power of the Four Perversions set;
    come now, serve the Great Sage, Compassionate,
    He the sure cutter of fetters and bonds.

54. As a deer roams in the very varied woods
    and goes to the pleasant crest garlanded by clouds,
    so there you will delight on that unentangled mount.
    There is no doubt, mind, you'll be established there.

55. Men and women enjoying any happiness
    controlled by thy desires and delighting in life,
    blind fools they are who comply with Māra's power,
    they driven on, O mind, servants are of thee.

Theragāthā Verses
1091–1145

Tālapuṭa's Aspirations

1. Mountain Caves

Best of all for meditation, caves are cool in hot weather, warm in cold weather, and silent. Those in the mountains, high among rocks, are less accessible, places where it is easier to be alone, apart from bats and other local inhabitants. Mountain caves are not for the sociable. You live in them alone. They are quiet and remote, the sort of place that most people would dislike to live in just because of the silence.

Because of craving, people in general want to be mated. They need mate, friend, companion, relatives—and other people generally. Without them, they are uneasy. In Pali language one's 'second' is an idiom for one's wife, but 'being with a second' is also craving. Being without a second is not to have craving. Mountain caves are the sort of place where progress towards being "unmated with desire" can be made.

When you live alone in a solitary place, with few wishes, insight into impermanence becomes easier. How to see impermanence when the mind is distracted by a thousand and one people, possessions, and works? Only when all this entanglement has been given up is there a chance to penetrate to the truth of impermanence.

2. Wild Woods

These are good for meditation too. They have to be far from peoples' noisy houses and machines. A place to reach only on foot, and where animals, more or less wild, also live happily.

A bhikkhu intent on meditation likes such places which are not the favourite dwelling of ordinary people (who only go there for picnics on fine days). The meditative bhikkhu is happy to spend nights and all seasons there wearing his robes made up out of pieces of cloth sewn together—worthless to a thief, and coloured an earthy yellow-brown—unattractive to the layman.

Surrounded by cool green trees what will he "make mine"? The surroundings encourage a cool heart with no craving and a minimum of possessions—just his bowl and robes and a few other things. And it is likely that, given this setting, he will be able to "slay" greed, aversion and delusion, the three Roots of Evil. These three cause all the trouble, (apart from naturally caused disasters: earthquakes, droughts, typhoons and so on—and some diseases) in this world. So when they have been known and seen, through and through, they disappear forever. Why should he not "abide in bliss" then?

3. In the Woods Alone

Tālapuṭa wishes to live in such places "free from fear." Most people, even though they live in the middle of cities where the numbers of people and the seeming regularity of buildings and services bolster their confidence against death, are far from being free of fear. To live in the woods alone where there are no amusements or distractions, nothing to take the mind away from the basic fear—of seeing things as they really are, empty of self—would be intolerable except to the ardent seeker of Dhamma.

Where does he find it? In his own body—an unstable nest of dying and disease. The brood raised in this nest is fear and oppression by ageing and death. But "this body, seeing clear" (with *vipassanā*) breaks up such fear. One fears what one does not understand. This means 'understand' on the deepest levels of insight (*vipassanā*).

So either fear, or understanding of Dhamma, are born of this body, according to the way one looks at it. In places with many people we may feel 'safe' enough but behind that facade of security lurks fear. It is a good test to go to wild and remote places and see how one can live there. With confidence and happiness? Or with longing to get back to familiar people, places and habits? One should echo Tālapuṭa and say "When will it be?"

4. The Craving-Creeper

Creepers in tropical forests are sometimes of immense size. A huge trunk all twisted leans out from the ground towards some overhead support from which its branches twisting here and there drape whole trees with a greenery other than their own. The creeper's branches loop from one tree to the next… out… further…

Craving is like this too. It has the huge and ancient trunk of ignorance (*avijjā*) all twisted round and round with wrong distorted views of reality. The craving-creeper is supported by the forest of sense-impressions. It blankets and strangles true understanding of this world, of this mind and body. And its branches spread out further and further. Even a poor man who cannot 'satisfy' his desires can grow a vast craving-creeper in his heart. Often those in the position to 'satisfy' the unsatisfiable, succeed only in making their craving-creepers grow to monstrous proportions.

Well, this creeper's fruits are not wanted by people generally. Who wants fear or bodily pain or mental distress? Yet everyone grows the craving-creeper! The answer to those poisonous fruits is not the doctor or the psychiatrist, both of whom can only patch things up, but "the sharpened sword of wisdom made."

With this sword the craving-creeper can be cut down—during insight meditation. Nothing else will cut it down.

> Feeding one's wants won't cut it down,
> Hating one's self won't cut it down,
> Averting one's gaze won't cut it down,
> The wisdom-sword *will* cut it down.

5. Like a Lion

Lions are unafraid of other animals. So the Buddha is compared to a lion, quite fearless, and his bold truthfulness to the lion's roar—which still causes consternation among those who grasp at beliefs and views.

The meditator seated upright and alert in some lonely place is like the lion too. Only such a person can draw that wisdom sword quick enough to cut off the defilements. The Buddha is shown routing, with tranquil meditation and penetrative vision, the hosts of Māra at the time of his Enlightenment. The Māras that he routs though pictured as hideous demons are really the more familiar Death, Defilements of the mind, and the processes of making Kamma. It is said that a *deva* (god) called Māra also objects to beings going beyond his realm and tries to hinder this. Most people will consider the first three hindrances enough.

6. Goodly Company of those Esteeming Dhamma

Some get ordination as bhikkhus and with little or no training go off by themselves and live in the wilds. This is foolishness and often points out a person who cannot bear correction, or the sort of person who says quickly "I know" when one tries to show him better ways of doing things. There is no hope that this person can grow in Dhamma. Probably he has and will increase (besides his conceit) only one thing: wrong views.

To have the company of other people sincerely practising the Dhamma is a great support and help, not only those who have reached one's own level of development but those who far surpass it. It is very necessary to live with such Teachers who are worthy of one's respect and devoted service. They alone can give sure advice about difficulties in meditation. When one has no access to them, then the Suttas, the *Visuddhimagga*, and the Commentaries must be one's source of advice. But they are called 'dead' Dhamma, while the words of one's Teacher are 'living' Dhamma.

The further people have gone along the Path of Dhamma the more respectful they are, to the Triple Gem, to their Teachers, to their companions and friends, and to the Dhamma as practised. One way of judging where one has got to on the Path, is to examine whether one esteems Dhamma or not. (Or does one have a carping, sceptical, uncertain mind?) That sort of mind will never see things as they really are.

For that, it is necessary to subdue: eye, ear, nose, tongue, body (touch), and mind—the six faculties. This is a warning to those who think that they can have their worldly pleasures *and* the fruits of Dhamma too. This is just self-deception, another name for delusion. Lead and enjoy a worldly life, or devote mind, speech and body to the Dhamma—a finer enjoyment. In between are various shades of Dhamma-practice hindered by more or less worldly attachment. One should be honest with oneself about where one's at.

"Those who are Thus"—who see things as they really are—they are the *arahants*, the best Teachers, most worthy of respect. But, some people will object, that was all right in the Buddha's days when there were *arahants*. Now there are none. This is not true. Wherever Dhamma is practised intensively it may be expected that the final attainment will be reached. Both Thailand and Burma have great Teachers whose final attainment can be inferred from their Dhamma. In N.E. Thailand for instance, Venerable Ācariya[1] Mun (Bhuridatta Mahāthera) and some of his disciples are believed to have won arahantship in modern times.

---

1. Venerable Teacher (*Tan Acharn* in Thai) a respectful form of address for one's Teacher.

7. Giribbaja's Wilds

When you stand on the top of Mount Vulture Peak (Gijjhakuta) and look down four or five hundred feet to the plain below enclosed by a ring of hills, you see only scrubby jungle and rocks, the site of the ancient city of Giribbaja. Perhaps it looked much the same in Tālaputa's days with some ruins still remaining from the old city.

Like other places we have described it was quiet and secluded. Few human beings went there though there are in any jungle plenty of non-human beings, especially the insects and snakes mentioned by Tālaputa. Living in such a place means having patience with and loving-kindness for all these other beings. Impatient and hot-tempered people cannot live comfortably under rocks or at the foot of trees because they soon come into conflict with other creatures. The cool-hearted person is content with a simple resting place and does not worry about other beings. In fact, when loving-kindness is strong in anyone, he has no fear of tigers and snakes and they do not fear him and so cause him no trouble.

Other discomforts face the jungle-dweller: weariness, hunger, thirst and wind—and heavy rain too if the shelter is not waterproof. All these are a test of his equanimity so that when food, drink and weather are not to his liking he does not get depressed, short-tempered or retreat to more comfortable surroundings.

All these things should be expected by a person bent on his own good. Few will find the Goal of Nibbāna easy to reach; for most the path is sure to be rough and winding (the results of past unwholesome *kamma*), so loving-kindness, patience and equanimity are needed.

8. The Four Truths Won Within

The Four Noble Truths are easy to learn:

> Dukkha (= Suffering of all kinds, physical, mental)
> Causal arising of Dukkha (= Craving)
> Cessation of Dukkha (= Nibbāna)
> Path leading to Cessation of Dukkha (= 8-fold Path).

But they are very hard to see in oneself as the Truth. Why is this? Generally we want to turn away from dukkha, not face it. We turn away to distractions, amusements, anything to avoid looking at the unsatisfactory state of this mind and body and the world it experiences. Why do we not want to look at dukkha? Painful, uncomfortable! Craving turns us away to look at something else and that very craving is the source of dukkha. What is craving then? Craving for sights, sounds, smells, tastes, touches, thoughts—the six kinds of craving for experience of this world. But we crave not only the pleasures of the senses (including mind) but also to exist. I want to go on... on... on. I want to be here and now. I want to exist in some future life. This is craving for existence, for being. But sometimes being becomes too painful because of disease, misfortune or the acts of other people. Then one wishes for non-existence, the craving to end it all, for death and nothingness. Due to the wrong view produced from this craving people commit suicide in many ways, longing not to exist. Their longing, a perverted craving for existence, guarantees that they will exist, though they will have to experience pain and suffering caused by the depressed and self-hating mind which they had when dying. All this craving—for sense-pleasures, existence and non-existence, causes dukkha. This is what is meant by saying: Craving is the condition for the arising of dukkha. When there is no more craving, since the roots of evil—greed, aversion and delusion—have been eradicated by the cultivation of moral conduct, meditation and wisdom, then there is the experience called Nibbāna. While craving is present, Nibbāna cannot be known, but when there is the seeing of this third Noble Truth, it is realized in one's heart which at that time is calm, peaceful and blissful, a peace to which there is no end for there is no source of disturbance in oneself which could end it. This is different from the peace gained through meditation which can be upset later by the arising of defilements. Meditation is the most important aspect of the Noble Eightfold Path, though it cannot succeed unless the practicer's moral conduct is pure. It is based on this and leads to the highest development of wisdom, the seeing of the four Noble Truths in oneself, combined, with the emotionally purified states of renunciation, loving-kindness and compassion. The Noble Eightfold Path, which is the fourth Noble Truth, is composed of factors which form the groups of moral conduct, meditation and wisdom. (See Verse 25.)

These Truths are "very hard to see." Now we may understand why this is so. Intellectually one may know them and occasionally remember them, but "see" here means 'having penetrated with insight' so that one lives with them all the time, so that one's life becomes the Noble Path itself.

9. A Raging Blaze

This world is on fire. With what does it blaze? Greed, aversion and delusion are the fires that burn all beings here. These fires are kindled because of what? Pleasant feeling, painful feeling and neutral feeling. How do they arise? Feeling arises dependent on contact, that is, contacts through forms (sight-objects), sounds, smells, tastes, touches and mental factors (*dhamma*). These six types of contact arise when three factors are present: the appropriate sense organ, its objects, and consciousness by way of that sense. We do not see all this as a raging blaze, blinded as we are by ignorance (of the Four Noble Truths) and led on by craving. So, we have to experience a lot of dukkha because we do not have either "meditation's calm" or "wisdom." We have to get burnt again and again until we are tired of burning, tired of dukkha. Then we are ready to do something about ourselves.

10. Abuse and Praise

The first is taken as painful. It insults 'me', my big ego. The second is welcome because it inflates this ego and makes me feel good. So we fall down between this pair of opposites into rejection and acceptance out of which grow aversion and greed. Worldly ordinary people eagerly grasp gain and honour, praise and happiness, rejecting loss, dishonour, blame, and suffering. These are the eight worldly dhammas, inseparable from existence. The Noble Ones have equanimity towards them all.

11. Wood, Grass and Creepers

When you live in the country these things are all around you, most of them of no particular value. Certainly you do not think "These pieces of wood, blades of grass and strands of creeper are me; they are myself." What one values as oneself is this body, the various kinds of feelings, the process of perception, the thoughts and other mental events and the six sense consciousnesses (including the mind). There is a great difference in one's attitude to that tree dying and this body dying. This shows our ignorance in that we identify a self (or soul), an owner, where there is none.

12. The Season of the Black Raincloud

The Rains in India and South-East Asia last for months. A time of mud, soaking forests and (probably) leeches. Not the time for a pleasant day's picnic in the woods! People stay in their villages and towns, they cultivate rice but do not go much into the forest. So the Rains are when forests are most silent with few visitors. It is then that forest bhikkhus such as those who live with their Teachers in North-East Thailand, make great efforts to practise the Dhamma. Their Teachers, as in the Buddha-time, are those who See.

13. Attaining the Undying

The Undying, the Deathless: this is Nibbāna. These words do not mean an eternal state but point out that which is not born and so does not die. In most people's minds birth and death are continuous as states of mind arise and pass away. The *arahant* when he experiences Nibbāna goes beyond this birth and death. For the attainment of the Undying those mountain caves which we have talked about are ideal. And the peacock's cry close by might seem to say "Come on! Don't be lazy!"

14. The Awful Ocean-Mouth

People then believed in an immense and nearly bottomless pit in the ocean; perhaps a myth originating in sailors' tales about a whirlpool. (About this, the Buddha commented that their belief was foolish but that painful feeling could be called such an abyss.) Tālapuṭa thinks that when he has developed in Dhamma he will be able to cross these stretches of water without even wetting his feet. If when he composed this verse he thought success in such powers necessarily marked an *arahant*, then he was wrong. But he may have known that while some *arahants* have such powers fully developed, others possessed less of them or none at all. Here he aspires to become an *arahant* who does possess them. They are not 'miraculous' but just a natural development of jhāna (deep meditation) and so can be obtained by both ordinary men and Noble Ones, both Buddhists and believers in God or Gods.

15. Charging Elephant Unbound

What is more powerful than this? No machines existed in those days, so the elephant illustrated power and strength. This is what is needed to 'shun the marks of loveliness'—not to be captivated by them, not even to get attached to them. Only when they are shunned (in a cave or forest maybe) by restraint of the senses, is it possible to "break up desire for sensual happiness." Just the thing that we are all trapped in! But unless it is laid aside there is no chance of 'striving in concentrated states', that is, the jhānas. And without them, the mind is weak, too weak to produce insight. The might, strength and power needed to "break up desire for sensual happiness" comes from the jhānas. You might say "Those *arahants* must have been gloomy old sticks seeing only ugliness!" But that is getting it all wrong. Not seeing beauty helps to calm the mind, it is a phase of the training. Mountains, valleys, forest—all are beautiful to an *arahant* but he does not try to seize on them as 'me' and 'mine'. He sees beauty when he wants to and with no attachment.

16. The Pauper

A person is really poor through not making wholesome *kamma*, never doing good. Material poverty may last only for one life but the results of mental-emotional poverty can affect many lives. One is 'poor' when the debts of many evil kammas pile up while the 'creditors' which oppress such a person are the different sorts of resultant dukkha that he or she may perhaps begin to suffer even in the very life when those actions have been done. The 'treasure' that a person finds can be explained in various ways: the Three Jewels (or Treasures)—the Buddha, Dhamma and Sangha in which it is proper to feel confident; or the seven Noble Treasures: faith, moral conduct, shame, fear of evil, learning, generosity and wisdom; or the treasure of Noble attainment as stream-winner and so on, which is meant here. The wealth of this world decays: but 'attainment of the Teaching of the Greatest Sage' is undecaying riches.

* * *

This concludes the stanzas which Tālapuṭa composed while still aspiring for the Going Forth. After these aspirations there are three other verses on Going Forth, followed by others upon The Practices of a Bhikkhu. This section leads on to the main part of the verses which concern The Mind in various ways. A few verses on Delight in the Forest are followed by one which indicates some success in the training. These verses, as they are dealt with in the following pages, are not in the order of the text, but the number of the verse commented on has been indicated.

Going Forth

17. This is one among many verses in which Tālapuṭa holds a conversation with his mind. You could say "But I thought that Buddhists taught that there was no self or soul among the changing patterns of mind and body? But here is Tālapuṭa with two selves, what he calls himself, and his mind! How do you account for this?" The answer is that his 'conversation' is much like what goes on in our own heads when desires are countered by objections to them. Though there are just streams of mind and body processes yet there appear to be two people inside this skull, one saying 'yes' and the other 'no'. In this particular verse the perversity of the untamed mind is well-illustrated. While a layman he aspired to be a bhikkhu but once he had left the household life and gone forth to homelessness, his mind slackened and was no longer enthusiastic. A case of "it's greener on the other side of the fence"—just craving (taṇhā). So he thinks "Come on! Stir yourself, mind! Don't idle!"

19. The same theme. Here is his mind not pleased with bhikkhu-life, though that same mind-stream has brought it about. Mind is full of craving. While it has "dear ones, friends, relatives, playing and loving, sensual pleasures of the world" the mind's craving has something to get involved with, get entangled with. The craving mind is not satisfied with this of course, but its appetite is dulled. It is when Tālapuṭa has given up all this that the mind starts to get agitated. No distractions! No escapes from dukkha! (People living a worldly life sometimes think that monks and nuns are escapists, but the latter, if they really get down to practice, have

no way of escaping dukkha and must face it, while the former have many escape-routes through amusements and sensual variety.) When worldly escape-routes are closed off, then the craving mind is not pleased.

42. Again Tālapuṭa exhorts his mind—"It's not like it used to be, craving mind! You used to be in control but now I am a bhikkhu. The ruination brought on by craving is not for me!" What ruination? The ruins of disease, decay and death, again and again. People are ruined by the defilements in their own hearts, they ruin their own futures and ruin other beings about them. The world is ruined by greed, aversion and delusion, the Roots of Evil. A good bhikkhu is not wrapped up by ruination (lit., not a bearer of destruction); instead, having gone-forth in the Buddha's Sāsana (Teaching, Dispensation), he makes efforts to get beyond craving.

The Practices of a Bhikkhu

28. How does he do this? By leading the kind of life where craving finds little to grab hold of. Take the bhikkhu's alms round as an example. For most people food is very much an object of craving, so they try to get what they like and have as much as they like. A bhikkhu goes out with his black iron bowl and stands silently before people's houses to receive whatever they are pleased to offer him. (He does not 'beg', as he may not, unless sick, ask for anything; nor does he sing or chant but should walk and stand silently.) He accepts food as it comes, the poor with the good, the tasteless with the tasty, the disliked with the liked—which helps to cut down on craving. His head is shaven, too, so the craving and conceit connected with hair does not trouble him. And he wears no ornaments at all, just brownish-yellow robes, so from a worldly point of view he may be "unsightly" but that is just another way of cutting down on craving. In this way he devotes himself to the Buddha's words.

29. In the previous verse, the bhikkhu's exterior appearance was emphasized while this verse deals with his interior attitude while going on his alms round. He is "well-restrained". What is that? As he passes shops he does not gaze in the windows, or at the faces of people who pass by or who give him alms food; he is not attracted by sounds of music nor does he show disgust at any bad

smells that may come his way; his steps are steady, neither showing off pretended calm by slow walking nor exhibiting many desires by rushing along. He just goes steadily "having a mind to sensual pleasures unattached"—content with what he gets. A mind like this he compares to "the full moon shining clear at night"—radiant with loving kindness and free from the clouds of defilements. Finally, in the refrain that runs through many of these verses, he reproaches his mind "You used to tell me to act like this"—meaning that now he does so, the mind plays a different tune.

30. The austere practices which the Buddha allowed bhikkhus to undertake also aim at lessening desires. Tālapuṭa mentions some of them in this verse: *a forest-dweller* (who lives five hundred bowlengths—say half a mile—in the forest); *an almsman* (a bhikkhu who always goes on alms round and does not rely on lay-supporters bringing food); *a graveyard dweller* (he lives at the place where corpses are left exposed or else burnt, so that the impermanence of bodies is obvious); *a rag-robe-wearer* (gathering rags or off-cuts of cloth he patches together his robes, not accepting ready-made ones from lay people); *one never lying down* is a bhikkhu who practises in three postures—walking, standing and sitting—but does not lie down. He sleeps sitting up and in this way manages to restrict his hours of sleep—more time for meditation. These methods and others are practised privately with only the practicer and his Teacher knowing about them. They are never advertised by wise bhikkhus who are not concerned either to get the admiration of others or much support from them. Such austerities as these were an important part of the practice leading to attainment of the *arahants* of old, as today of Venerable Ācariya Mun (Bhuridatta Mahāthera) and his enlightened disciples in N.E. Thailand, who urge the young bhikkhus and novices training under them to use them. Visiting lay people who come to practise meditation are also expected to practise them, such as eating only once a day, another austere practice. (For all these, with explanations, see *The Path of Purification*, Ch. II, and *With Robes and Bowl* Wheel No. 83/84.)

The Mind

The Mind's Inconstancy

30. Practices like these should never be ends in themselves, but aids for controlling the errant mind. We have already come across Tālapuṭa's dispute with his mind and now he is upbraiding it—"You're not a wild elephant going where you like! You're my mind! Now it's time to get ready, so don't grieve! Be joyful!" What should one get ready for? One should be prepared for the great battle against Māra and therefore put on the armour of the Dhamma. Tālapuṭa longs for Nibbāna while seeing that all of this conditioned world (or any other) is impermanent, unstable, liable to arising and passing away and therefore unsatisfactory, or dukkha.

31. But his mind is still attached to "the unstable and the frail." At some other time it made a simile to urge him to give it all up: A man with much labour plants fruit trees, cultivates them for some years until they reach the fruit-bearing stage and then, when they are loaded with fruit about to ripen, cuts them down. Rational? No, but no madder than a person who with great effort has renounced family, money, pleasure and so on only to give way to some impulse which destroys the fruits of his renunciation. There is no safety from the whims of the mind until arahantship is reached, though a certain security is won by the stream-winner.

34. Still his mind goes "back to habits made of old"—while he was a layman, in spite of the fact that when he still lived the household life, his mind urged him to practise Dhamma: to have few wishes, to abandon the disparagement of others, to still all dukkha—these things being praised by wise men. This is opposite to the world's way which is to have many desires and to cultivate them so that they increase. Generally too, disparaging other people is popular in the world—it gives an outlet for our aversion while at the same time boosting our conceit. No wonder it's popular! And people are not concerned with stilling dukkha. When it gets too much to bear then they turn to other things or even take some treatment to reduce it to manageable proportions. They would be lost without dukkha, because their conception of 'selfhood' is dukkha, and where would they be without 'themselves'.

39. Again grumbling at his mind—the mad mind, the mind mad with defilements. There is no sharp dividing line between 'sane' and 'mad', so people are either more sane and less mad or more mad and less sane, according to the development of wisdom (*paññā*) or the strength of defilements (*kilesa*). A madman who plays about senselessly is just the extreme development of ourselves, and all of us, like Tālapuṭa before he attained arahantship, are under the power of craving and defilement. The play that the mad mind shows us is this world, several times distorted through the lenses of permanence, happiness, selfhood and beauty. This is how the mad mind causes us injury again and again through successive births, high and low. His final question to his mind means "What have I *not* done for you?"—and in this Tālapuṭa is the same as everyone else—who follow the urges, wishes and reasons of the mind, whether or not it is defiled, wishing to enjoy the play at all costs.

Desires

21. Here the Buddha is quoted likening the mind to a monkey. Anyone who has watched monkeys will know why. They exhibit unrestrained lust and quarrelsome anger while they can do nothing for more than a few minutes before they get tired of it. They swing from one support to the next, running and jumping and playing. Know anyone with a mind like that? For such a monkey mind *a man-taming trainer* is needed, or else a *great physician* who can tell how it is to be cured. These are both epithets of the Buddha, who is also "He who speaks the best," and "Best among mankind." And what does he say? "It is very difficult to check the mind when one is not rid of lust." Only the person who is prepared to loosen his hold on the pleasures of this world will succeed in taming the monkey-mind. In other words: you can't have it both ways.

22. It's extremely hard for us to check because we as "blind foolish common men long have lain" down in sensual desires which are "varied, sweet, delightful." Someone might object "You can call yourself 'blind, foolish and a common man' if you like, but why should you insult me? I've got two eyes in my head, came tops in school and university and I've a family going back to the Conquest!" In reply a Buddhist might say "You're blind because you don't understand about dukkha and its arising. You're foolish

since you don't restrain yourself and so make bad *kamma* rooted in greed, aversion and delusion which will bring you pain and suffering—more dukkha. And you're called a common man or an ordinary man, like myself, as you have not yet experienced the true nobility of stream-winning, once-returning, non-returning or arahantship. But people who make a certain amount of effort with generosity, moral conduct and meditation are at least called 'beautiful ordinary men' while I fear that you may fall into the class of 'foolish ordinary men'." What any kind of ordinary men get is birth again—that is what they desire but their desire is for what brings dukkha (translated 'ill'), even to the extent that having been led on by sensual desires to make much evil *kamma* they bring themselves "to perish in hell." Here someone is sure to say "Oh come, you Buddhists don't believe in hell, do you?" The answer is easy "We don't believe in it. We understand it!" "What does that mean?" "Hells (or heavens) are not articles of faith but they can be understood by what the mind is capable of. Take two people: one is gentle, compassionate and generally unselfish, always thinking how to help others—a happy smiling person; the other is twisted up by hatred, bursting with anger and resentment, ready to kill and torture. Now the first man is called 'a heavenly man' and dying with that slightly superhuman mind will gain a superhuman birth; while the second even now is 'a hellish man' and when he dies with his evil *kamma* in mind, with that subhuman mind he gains a very subhuman birth. Easy to explain!" But desire for any kind of birth, human, superhuman, or subhuman, is desire for dukkha, because even the heavens, so delightful, are impermanent. And so are the hells.

35. The name for pleasures in this verse may not please some people. "How disgusting to compare sense-pleasure to vomit!" When one knows no better, sense-pleasures are fine (a beautiful girl, a handsome man, sweet music, scent of flowers, fine food, pleasant bodily sensations) but they are *the cords of sense-desire* which tie us down. Having loosened these cords one's mind discovers pleasure far superior to them, heavenly or divine pleasures in the heavens of sensuality and of subtle form. Even these pleasures are nothing to one who has enjoyed the Paramasukha—the Sublime Happiness of Nibbāna free of all attachments. Though one has not got this far yet, if some of the pleasures of meditation have been experienced, then other grosser worldly pleasure will seem to be like vomit. Who will want to eat what has been rejected? So who, having tasted the pleasures of meditation and renunciation will go back to the bondage of the senses?

55. Like the last this is a blunt verse. It tells the worldly person what he does not want to hear while anyone really devoted to Dhamma appreciates such straightforwardness. "Desires," "delighting in life" and "enjoying any happiness" are all *the same as Māra*. What is the power of Māra here? This means the strength of the defilements in one's heart whereby one is driven on to desire, delight and enjoy. And though a person like this speaks of 'my mind' as though he is the owner, truly, as Tālaputa points out, he is only a servant of mind, swept along by the mind's desires. So one knows where one's at! In the Dhamma there is no deceitfulness. Openness and straightforwardness on the other hand are features of Dhamma, and of the people who practise it.

Mind and Dukkha

26. Here is Tālaputa's mind instructing him what he ought to do, instruction which he thought up before his Going Forth, and then found difficult to carry out afterwards. We have met the Four Noble Truths before (see 8) and here three of them are presented as an exhortation. "The craved-for groups" are the five constituents identified as a person: body, feeling, perception, mental formations and consciousness. Since they are impermanent and craved for or grasped at as me and mine, they are the basis for the experience of dukkha. "That from which arises ill" (dukkha) is craving which should be abandoned with the help of insight wisdom. And making an end of ill here and now is another way of saying Nibbāna.

27. Some more instructions about dukkha. Impermanent things, whether 'me', 'mine' or 'not me', 'not mine', are all unstable and so, unreliable. Do not rely for security on what is not reliable. But isn't that what everyone does? So how much security do we have? "I'm secure" says Mr. Moneybags. (He hasn't read the paper yet, so he doesn't know about that bank vault robbery.) "I'm secure" says Mrs. Largeland. (But she isn't aware that the government will nationalize land holdings.) So who's secure? "I'm secure. Don't want your wealth but I'm sure going to live long."

(So says young Bob Cocksure. But how does he know?) Even this body, conventionally called 'mine', is changing all the time and can perish any moment. One has to see the danger in impermanent compounded things, see them as dukkha so that one's grasping can be unwrapped from them. And they are void too. What does 'void' mean? This is not a metaphysical abstraction but a name for what is *void of self*. What is that? Body is void of self and so are feelings, perceptions, mental formations, and consciousness. (Just where we think there is self or soul.) They have to be seen with insight as void, empty, ownerless. And dukkha has to be seen in the same way as really poisonous. As it is now, we are attached to a whole heap of dukkha and think that it is productive of happiness. That illusion has to go—to see dukkha as it really is. None of this can be done while the mind still wanders about, in other words, there is no insight unless a person has developed calm strongly first. When a person has succeeded with jhāna, the fully developed Right Concentration, then insight becomes easy. Without strong calm, the 'insight' that people have is either illusory or else so weak as to vanish quickly.

43. When we feel cornered by dukkha, we can go for a holiday, 'a change of air'. While this may make us feel good, it has not really solved the problem. Some who can afford it, with time and money, are always travelling round—"It'll be better there" they say. And they say it again when they get there, about some other place. These days travel is easy, even in the heavens, so escape appears to be easy too but the end of dukkha is never found just by going elsewhere. Everywhere is the same which means all this world and any other. When they die many people (of many religions) hope to go to a heavenly world and they will do so if they die with a somewhat purified and elated mind. They hope that 'heaven' is perfection where dukkha cannot touch them. "But," asks a Buddhist, "how can a conditioned, dependently arisen state of existence be perfectly free of dukkha? Don't you know that 'conditioned' means also 'impermanent' and that in turn signifies 'dukkha'? Your heavenly life may last long and be very pleasant indeed but it cannot possibly be eternal and so is not secure either. The Sensual Realm of hells, animals, ghosts, human beings and heavens—all are "unstable and oppressed" by dukkha. Then the Realm of Subtle Form—the Brahma-world Heavens gained through the practice of jhāna—even that is all "unstable and oppressed." Further refined are the Heavens of the Formless Realms to which one may attain by practice of the formless concentrations—even such long-enduring states are "unstable and oppressed." These are the three becomings. One may become this or that, here or there, due to one's *kamma*, but one does not get beyond dukkha. So, where are you going, mind, to find happiness? There is only one answer.

53. Round and round treads the ox, hauling water or grinding grain, just like the untrained mind which takes the impermanent to be permanent, that which is dukkha to be happiness, the not-self as self (or soul), and the unattractive as beautiful. These are the four perversions (or distortions) in which the unenlightened mind operates. No wonder there's dukkha! However, if one makes up one's mind to serve the Buddha by practising as much Dhamma as one can, then the fetters and bonds, including these four, can at least be loosened in this life, and possibly cut off completely. Why be a slave to this ox-like perverted mind?

32. What else is it like? Mind is formless, without any kind of body or material, just a collection of processes. And it is a far-traveller, how far and how quickly it goes in an instant! Supersonic jets are just creaking old oxcarts by comparison with the mind's speed. And mind is "a wanderer alone" since its various processes arise in a conditioned way upon the basis of what has gone before. And when one sees all the troubles that come of mind constantly drawn to the senses, how troubled it is, how lacking in peace and security, then one is prepared to aspire to Nibbāna.

36. Notice the contrast between past lives when the mind's wishes and desires had been followed (leading to further rebirth therefore) and Tālapuṭa's present life in which he is not content to drift with the stream of sense-desires but makes an effort to cut across the current. The sensual mind does not like this and becomes discontented and angry. Tālapuṭa accuses his mind of ingratitude since he had so long pandered to its desires and thus was forced to live in the dukkha caused by them. Minds (or mental states) are many and various and what appeals to one kind of mind experienced at one point in time may not be at all attractive to another type of mind occurring later. The only way out of such inner conflict is the cultivation of *sati-*

paññā, mindfulness-and-wisdom, and the best results are attained when one is guided in this by an experienced Teacher. The more confidence one has in that Teacher the greater will be the efforts that one makes to practise his teachings. This is the best way beyond the ocean of rebirths.

Mind as the Source of Rebirths

37. In these next two verses, Tālapuṭa speaks of the mind as the source of whatever rebirths one has to experience. We make *kamma* all the time, every day, by every decision, choice or volition. All those kammas have appropriate results inherent in them—and how many of them will it be possible to experience in this life? Combined with our craving for continuity or existence onwards from the moment of death, these kammas can provide the bases for innumerable future lives. We may then become priests (brahmins) or aristocrats, and from among the latter we may achieve rulership as king or president. Lives as merchants or workers are also brought on by an individual's past *kamma*. Someone is going to say at this point "Oh, you are proposing that rigid old caste structure just as the Bhagavad Gītā does. I thought Buddhists were free of such ideas?" Reply: "In the Buddha's days, brahmins were already imposing their four-caste structure on society as part of a 'divine plan'. The Buddha did not agree with their ideas and made his Sangha of bhikkhus and bhikkhunīs open to anyone of any caste. But he knew the truth that past *kamma* does determine where one is born. It shapes one's inclinations, one's aptitudes and weaknesses. But that one should be completely controlled by past *kamma* as some believed, is a fatalistic view, making impossible new present *kamma*. Everyone has the chance to make good *kamma* now, whatever their birth in this life." They may then gain "gods' estate" in a heavenly rebirth at the end of this life, provided that they have made the right *kamma* for it, that is to say, been generous, truthful and never angry.

38. Titans or demons are the resultant birth for those who love power and ruthlessness. (One would imagine that some politicians and army people get birth among them.) Power is fine when only one or two have it, so the powerful think, but when reborn in this state, everyone has it. Imagine the constant mauling, brawling and wars, much more a feature of demonic life than this human world! And the hells are more overpopulated than this world—by plenty of beings who loved to kill and torture other beings, while they were human. As to animal rebirth, if one wants it then the formula is to take delight only in what delights animals—to make oneself an animal in fact, enjoying only food, drink and sex. Or instead of an animal-man one can be a ghostly man by avaricious hoarding, never giving anything to anyone, and then have to suffer life as a ghost, miserable and beset by unsatisfied cravings. All this is brought about by the mind.

Dhamma to Practise

24. When one knows about this the wise person does something about the wild mind. All the Dhamma taught by the Buddha is for the purpose of taming this mind and Tālapuṭa has mentioned a few useful points in these verses. 'Concentrations' is not really a good translation of *jhāna* for which there is no English equivalent. The formula of the four jhānas had been repeated hundreds of times in the Suttas, while one or more jhānas are also often mentioned. They are the perfection of concentration and the person who possesses ability with the jhānas has a wonderful inner refuge to which he can withdraw for refreshment and peace. When jhāna has been obtained and mastered there is no need to try to meditate, for one has reached the state of perfected meditation. The four jhānas, for a Buddhist, are not ends in themselves but are the basis for the successful practice of mindfulness leading to insight.

The *faculties* and *powers* are different strengths of the same five factors: faith, effort, mindfulness, concentration, wisdom. If one is to grow in the Dhamma in a balanced way then these factors must be balanced, faith with wisdom, effort with concentration, while the fulcrum is mindfulness. The result of imbalance of these faculties can be seen in the holy men of many religions. The seven *wisdom-factors* lead to Enlightenment when fully developed. They are more commonly called 'enlightenment-factors' and have been explained at length elsewhere.[2] It is only through the development of deep meditation that they can be matured. The Buddha's Teaching is only made one's own experience through the *Three Knowledges* of remembrance of past lives with all details and particulars; of

---

2. *The Seven Factors of Enlightenment* (Wheel No. 1).

the workings of *kamma*, seeing for oneself how evil *kamma* will bear painful fruits but good kammas fruit in happiness; and finally, the knowledge of the exhaustion of the taints—the exhaustion of sensual desires, being (existence) and ignorance (of the four Noble Truths). Once it is 'touched' or personally verified in this way, that person is an *arahant*, one who has finished the job with nothing to strive for, but having seen non-self lives compassionately for others' benefit.

25. Some more Dhamma to grow into. The Dhamma does not grow into oneself—it cannot be changed to suit oneself; oneself the practicer must grow into the Dhamma, that is, adapt to the Dhamma, become the Dhamma. That means changing oneself, which is more trouble and less fun than changing the Dhamma. The Eightfold Path is what one should try to grow into since it leads directly to Nibbāna. Under the heading of Wisdom in this Path come Right View and Right Intention. The first understanding of the four Noble Truths is more intellectual to begin with, deepening with experience to include one's understanding of all sides of life, while the second purifies one's emotions so that relinquishment, loving-kindness and compassion dwell in one's heart instead of lust, ill-will and cruelty. Whoever lives his life by these two factors of wisdom is a wise person indeed. Moral Conduct covers the next three factors: Right Speech, Right Action and Right Livelihood. The first is abstaining from falsehood, malicious speech, harsh speech and idle chatter. Do you pass this test? The second means refraining from killing living beings (non-human included), taking what is not given (which is rather more than theft), and wrong conduct in sexual pleasures (and 'wrong' means causing injury in mind or body to someone concerned). Are you pure in these three respects? The third factor covers all sorts of livelihood which involves hurtfulness or breaking any of the Five Precepts. How is your livelihood? The last section of the Path is concerned with developing the mind: Right Effort, Right Mindfulness and Right Concentration, which the Buddha defined in this way: the first is twofold effort: to rid the mind of evil and to cultivate it in goodness.

There are various methods taught for this. The second is mindfulness to be cultivated towards the body, feelings, mental states and mental factors. If no effort is made, no mindfulness will arise. With no mindfulness the last factor of Right Concentration cannot be perfected. This is the four jhānas which have been mentioned earlier. This is a short summary of the Eightfold Path. Only those who are with it in mind, speech and body will make "the utter destruction of all ill."

52. The wrong path then, the one not to follow, is the Ignoble Eightfold Path. How much of your understanding and thought is Wrong View and Wrong Intention? Or how many of your actions of body and speech are Wrong Speech, Wrong Action or Wrong Livelihood? And perhaps you are developing Wrong Effort (for more unwholesomeness), Wrong Mindfulness (to be aware of ways of evil) and Wrong Concentration (upon what leads to sensuality or to destruction)? Using wisdom, one's way is not along this path, but by making effort and becoming restrained from evil, one may be established in the Path, as a stream-winner for instance. This will occur when the causal process of both coming-into-being and passing-out-of-being have been penetrated with insight, at which time one no longer believes in Dhamma but having verified it personally one is actually the Buddha's heir. It is then not the Buddha's Dhamma that one knows but one's own Dhamma, seen for oneself (when 'oneself' has dissolved into the processes of arising and passing away).

Determination

44. "Firm, firm in my aim!" says Tālapuṭa and this is the only way to achieve anything in the Dhamma. Wavering doubts, half-hearted practice, lack of confidence in the Triple Gem, lack of confidence in one's Teacher—all makes for indecisiveness and getting nowhere. People like to see progress in their Dhamma-practice but this will never be seen without determination and firmness of mind which prevents one being deflected on to other matters. When the mind's aim is truly firm then what chance have defiled and egoistic thoughts? Tālapuṭa is no longer in their power and even if they should arise he has enough mindfulness and wisdom not to follow them up, so that they are cut off quickly. Nor can he be misled by feelings and thoughts relating to the body which he compares to something rather dangerous—"a double-ended sack." Or perhaps it is the comedy of relying upon and becoming attached to such a sack which must be constantly

filled at the table and emptied at the latrine, that he speaks of here. He goes further: if a double-ended sack is bad enough, what about "a thing filled full and flowing with nine streams?" Recognise it? It is this body which has nine holes: two eyes, two ears, two nostrils, mouth, anus and urinary duct. And through these holes flow various sorts of dirt: eye-dirt, ear-dirt (wax), nose-dirt (snot), spittle, phlegm and vomit from the mouth, and excrement and urine from the other two. None of them smell, taste or look good, yet they come from the inside of this precious sack which I proudly call 'my body'. How strange it is!

48.   But Tālapuṭa will not be entangled in all this for he is determined to be a master, not a slave, of mind. People wish that their meditation was calm, that their hindrances were subdued, that their defilements were cut off, but their untamed minds are stronger than these wishes and they are slaves to that untamed mind. Tālapuṭa's practice and determination are such that Dhamma is in control, Dhamma is master, while defilements of any sort are slaves which obey orders instantly. That is his inward state. Outwardly he is quite happy with whatever comes—whatever robes, alms food, resting place and medicines (the four supports of a bhikkhu's life), he obtains, he is satisfied with them. He does not always seek for more and different clothes: his three robes are enough. He is content too with the food people give him and is not concerned with flavours, textures, a 'balanced diet' and so on. Resting-places cause him no trouble or expense—a cave, the root of a tree, a hollow among some boulders, or a small hut provided by generous donors. And when he needs medicines he will be offered whatever is necessary to cure the body, and if not, he is not too much concerned. The catskin bag is an illustration of the necessary energy for taming the mind. It seems that catskin required a lot of work to cure it, to make it supple; so does the mind. For the mind to be supple is meant that one can do with it what one likes. "Oh, today I'll stay in third jhāna for a change"—if he can do so, he has a supple, well-tamed mind.

49.   Bull elephants in the mating season can be dangerous. Ordinarily they are very strong, but to this must be added a fiery temper when in rut and it will be a skilful trainer indeed who brings such an elephant under control. A great deal of energy will be necessary—as needed for taming the wild mind too. The wild

elephant is used to going where it likes and when it likes. Nothing can stop it crashing through the forest. In the same way the wild mind goes anywhere, any time and is not restrained at all as it crashes about in the jungle of desires. What has to be done is told in the next verse.

51. "I'll bind you by strength to the meditation base as elephant to post by a strong rope bound." The 'meditation base' is the object of meditation, provided by one's Teacher to fix the mind on, such as Mindfulness of Breathing in and out, Loving-kindness, or Unattractiveness of the body. This like a strong post to which the mind is tied by the rope of mindfulness. Slowly, the wild elephant learns that it cannot get away! But it has to be well-guarded, for successful meditation cannot be mixed with what goes counter to it. If it is well-guarded the mind grows with mindfulness, grows to become aware of many things it had not known before. This growth, through insight-wisdom, goes on until the time of penetrating a Noble Path, perhaps of stream-winning. At that moment there is no leaning on, support or clinging to any of the becomings, not to sensual-desire, nor to subtle form, nor even to the formless realm. If the Noble Path which has been entered is that of arahantship, thereafter there is no support at all, no leaning on any kind of existence.

40. Here is real determination! "Today I shall thoroughly restrain it." Tālapuṭa does not say "I'll restrain it tomorrow, or next year, or when I retire, or when the next Buddha, Ariya Metteyya, comes"—he says *"today."* You might say "It's easy for him, a monk living in the wilds, with no family problems, no money troubles. That's all he has to do!" It is true that some places make the mind's training easier, but life in the forest without the comforts that many take for granted these days, is not so easy. More to the point, wherever one is, one is always in the present. That future time when it will be easier to train one's mind is an illusion. When it comes round to being now, it's just the same old now and things have not changed. So there is only one time to start: NOW. Otherwise of course "this wandering mind, a wanderer," will go on wandering where it wishes—from dukkha to more dukkha.

41. Tālapuṭa tells his mind "Get me across the floods!" But these are not of water; far more powerful are the four floods described by the Buddha. First is the flood of sensual desire. Who

is not swept along by it? Enjoying life here means to be adrift upon this flood of delight in sights, sounds, smells, tastes and touches. This first flood not only sweeps along human beings but also all the subhumans and even laps the devas in the heavens of sensual desire. A mighty flood indeed which is not even recognized by many people who are yet being whirled along in it. The second is the flood of existence (or being), the extent of which is even greater than the first. From the lowest of the hells, through animals, ghosts, humans, gods of sensual desire, and the Brahma gods of subtle form and formlessness, all these beings are borne along by this flood, the desire for existence. A third flood holds all these beings within its bounds too, the flood of views. 'Views' means beliefs, theories, doctrines and dogmas which are proclaimed as 'true' but which cannot be verified through the practice of sīla, samādhi, paññā (moral conduct, meditation, wisdom). Views are a powerful support to the ego ("I believe... "), so that in Thai presentations of Dhamma, one often comes across the combined term *māna-diṭṭhi*—conceit (concepts of oneself) and views. It is not surprising that 'views' are popular! Nor is it surprising that the Buddha's Teaching with its emphasis on taming the self, then seeing self as empty and hollow, is strongly disliked by some! And this flood of views has been the cause of innumerable wars and murders, because, of course, I am right and you must be wrong. Views, though they seem intellectually respectable, can rouse terrible passions.

The last flood of all, the flood encompassing all floods, is that of unknowing (or ignorance—of the four Noble Truths). In the power of this flood beings are tossed about upon the ocean of saṃsāra. If they hold that dukkha is experienced because of no cause (acausally), or from one First Cause, or from the displeasure of numerous divine beings, or merely from material change, then they are lost in the saṃsāric ocean. Even Buddhists who have merely *heard* the Four Noble Truths can only be said to have a distant glimpse of the Further Shore; if they make no effort to practise, certainly they will not get there. Only those Buddhists who are determined to cut down their cravings through Dhamma-practice will approach that shore called Nibbāna. Only when the real causes of dukkha are dealt with will this fourth flood be crossed. Though immense floods to those who do not practise

Dhamma, they can be leapt across by one who does so intensively. The mind purified with wisdom does the leaping—no one leaping to nowhere but attaining liberation having done so. None of this will be accomplished until one has seen "this world—unstable, unsteady, lacking any essence." While one is convinced that this world is stable and steady and very real—to be taken exactly as one's senses perceive it and one's mind thinks about it—it cannot be seen with insight, for one will not have the drive necessary to do anything about oneself. This drive is *saṃvega*—being deeply moved or stirred. The Buddha is the teacher who makes one look at the world (=oneself) as it really is; sometimes he compelled a person to look whether he wanted to see or not. For looking truly at the world means perceiving the necessity of change, and changing oneself can be a painful business.

Delight in the Forest

47. The Rains have just begun after the long dry hot season and the earth which has been bare and brown is now covered by a bright green carpet of new grass. This is the time too when leafless trees burst into flowers of many colours followed by fresh growths of pale green, pink, purple and many other shades.

Tālapuṭa will have been at ease in this season when it becomes cooler, an ease he expresses in the words "like a log I'll lie." Someone might say "Sounds to me as though he is living in solitude just to have a doze, a lazy man avoiding work!" Though a log does rather paint a picture of inactivity, even of decay, that is not the meaning intended here. The Commentary says "being ungrasping like a tree he lies down" perhaps indicating that his ease and pleasure is not like the rest taken by people who do not train themselves. They grasp at the concept (or conceit) 'I am lying down', along with which can go lethargy and drowsiness and other defilements but Tālapuṭa, having made great efforts, does not grasp in this way. Most people do not find a secluded spot in the mountains "Soft as cotton down," even if it is covered with "four-inch grass." But for a meditator who can easily attain jhāna, small discomforts of the body are easily overcome. He is not worried if his meditation seat is hard rock nor delighted if it is a soft cushion. Wherever he is, that is a good place to meditate and since solitude is seldom accompanied by "all mod. cons.," he is content with things as they come. This is not the mark of an idle person, for while the dull-witted may be able to blot out discomfort by much sleep, the way of the meditator is to become more aware. Aware of what? Aware of the dukkha instead of escaping from it.

18. The mind of Tālaputa, like our own minds, is up to its tricks again. "When you get into those cool quiet woods with the rain streaming down and the thunder resounding (believed to be made by the great god Indra or Sakka according to the beliefs of those days, but here rather a poetic embellishment) and an occasional bird's cry, how joyful your meditation will be." But it does not always work out like that. Having got to a remote place perhaps one feels bored and wants to return to where there is more sense stimulation. Or perhaps one feels afraid, as though that aloneness was a threat to one's self (which relies very much upon the support which others give this concept). Again, the woods are attractive when the sun shines and the weather is warm but if one proposes to live there for a long time in all weathers then there may be some hardships to face. And the usual reaction to hardship is to seek enjoyment elsewhere but where will this be found in the wet woods? Maybe the sounds of "the brightly plumaged birds on Giribbaja's peaks" will not be sufficient entertainment for such a dissatisfied mind? But Tālaputa must have overcome this kind of mind eventually so that wherever he was in the wilds and whatever the condition, he always had equanimity, if not happiness. One good result of meditation is that it makes one able to endure all sorts of conditions which, without the development that meditation brings, one could not bear. A point to check up on oneself! This means that at least one's temper is even when things do not go as one wishes; or better than this, one is joyful come what may, a result of what one has experienced in meditation. Depression, boredom and lethargy, which might be the reactions of some, are all born from the evil root of delusion, while dissatisfaction, anger and grumbling arise from the evil root of aversion. The good meditator is at least as joyful as the birds—and he has much a greater cause for joy than them.

46. The peacock is a very beautiful bird and even his strange cries amidst rocks and cliffs would be arresting. But one must admit that the peacock's beauty costs him something. All that magnificent plumage is a burden even to walk around in, what to speak of flying! It appears too, that peacocks are only too aware of their splendour and 'as vain as a peacock' is as true of the bird as of some people. He struts about and shows off his tail from some prominent perch as though saying to human beings "Poor featherless creatures, do you not envy my plumes?" But when he comes to fly his journey is just a hop from tree to tree. The peacock is contrasted by the Buddha with the swan, plain in colour and lacking any ornaments, but how well and how far he flies! This illustrates how (usually) householders are burdened with their wealth and possessions, so that their spiritual flights go not very far, not very long, while bhikkhus through lack of ownership are able, if they make the effort, to fly far and strongly. At this point maybe someone says, "What about the Lady Visākhā or the merchant Anāthapiṇḍika? They were householders of greater possessions and wealth than most people have, yet they became stream-winners. Nor did they renounce all and enter the Sangha. And besides, there are other examples: Yasa's father and mother, and Upāli who at first followed the Jains—they were all rich people." "Ah, but you must not generalize from a few special cases. These people were not ordinary householders for we are told that they had developed their special qualities in previous lives so that when they met the Buddha they quickly penetrated his words." "But there might be some of them around now so that entering the Sangha is not necessary for them. "I might be one! How do I know?" "There could be such people now, certainly. But how you can tell whether you are one or not, probably depends on whether you have been able to meet an *arahant* and penetrate the truth of his words! And one should not assume that one has such great merits! But in any case, the life of a bhikkhu or a nun is not for everyone. If your karma fixes you in a lay person's life with the responsibilities and burdens that it brings, then you have to be content to make short hops from tree to tree." But those 'short hops' can carry one far, by regular practice every day. 'One should not expect arahantship in this life unless conditions, internal and external, are complete for gaining it—this is one extreme view. On the other hand neither should one think 'I cannot get anywhere'—the other extreme. Just keep on with regular meditation practice, every day for an hour or however long one can spare, with concentrated courses from time to time. A great deal can be done in this way and one will find that the peacock plumes drop off as one goes along.

43. Here are some good places for meditation: the peaks of mountains or their slopes, open spaces, forests or caves. All of them to be suited to meditation, should be unfrequented by human beings. Other beings, boar and antelope are mentioned, may be found there but their presence is not so disturbing as human beings. Animals make small noises and only from time to time, while humans, these days especially, are much noisier with their songs, shouts and transistor radios. Some places which should be quiet, such as caves, can be noisy enough if converted into a shrine for instance. Tālaputa tells himself that it will be fine when he gets to silent places. What his mind actually did is related elsewhere.

51. More mountains and forests where Tālaputa hopes to find peace. There are some who would say, "Well, he's quite wrong to take off for those forests because if he could not find peace where he was, then how would he find it elsewhere?" A Buddhist might answer: "Can you find peace in every place, as much in one as another, or are some places more favourable for meditation?" Most people have to answer that some places are conducive to meditation, others not. The Buddha taught three kinds of solitude of which the first, physical aloneness, is conducive to the second, the oneness of mind in jhāna when the hindrances have been suppressed. This 'solitude' in turn is helpful for the final aloneness of the mind which has no more assets (upadhi), another way of speaking about arahantship. So if the second is to be attained the first is very useful, as Tālaputa found and has emphasized in his verses. Those who do not find that these three sorts of solitude follow one upon another are either people who have developed the first sort of solitude in past lives, or those who are just playing about and pretending at meditation ("Daily life is Zen, you know!" as was once told by a very noisy unmindful person). So there is some reason why one meditates best in quiet and lonely places. In the last line of the verse there is something of a puzzle. Tālaputa addressing his mind (the deluded and defiled mind) says "Doubtless, mind, you will perish," but the Commentary explains "by the destruction of saṃsāra, you will be established." It is the defiled mind that gives rise to saṃsāra and the latter ceases through the destruction of ignorance and the

exhaustion of craving. The purified mind is established since there is nothing that can shake it.

23. Not the place where people on the whole like to dwell—unless on some well-protected tour. Leopards and tigers are thrilling through binoculars or even outside the closed windows of one's car or coach but people are not so happy at their close approach if they have no weapons. Fear is in their hearts and from fear is born hatred and the desire to destroy. But what can a bhikkhu do? He never even touches weapons and would not use one even if it was to hand. Yet in Tālapuṭa's days (down to our own as we find in the lives of Venerable Ācariya Mun Bhuridatta Mahāthera and his disciples), bhikkhus often lived in remote areas where large animals abounded. Often bhikkhus did not even have the protection of a hut as they lived at the foot of trees or in caves. What protection then did they have? Their best protection was meditation, for in proportion to their success in purifying the mind, fear becomes less. When fear and anxiety no longer control the mind then a bhikkhu can live happily in a cave where there are snakes, in a forest where tigers and leopards are commonly seen, or near to the haunts of wild elephants. No bhikkhu comes to grief in such places if he cultivates two things: mindfulness and loving-kindness. His mindfulness will prevent him from carelessly treading on snakes (for instance), while his loving-kindness will break up fear of other beings. And if he feels the first stirrings of fear in his heart he can always recite one of the discourses suitable for such an occasion. There is the Discourse on the Supreme Banner for "one who has gone to the forest, to the foot of a tree, to an empty hut," in which the cure for fear, trembling and horripilation is the Recollections of the Buddha, Dhamma and Sangha. Then there is the well-known Discourse on Loving-kindness which by awakening that quality in one's heart banishes fear. Animals know and fear a man who has fear while they are aware of the peaceful vibrations of the fearless meditator. If one is fearful still of wild animals and knows a great Teacher who stays in such a place, it is a good test of oneself to ask permission to stay there with him. No harm will come to such meditators, as is told in Venerable Ācariya Mun's life story, while they will learn how to deal with unfaced fears. Some people, from urban surroundings are unable even to keep their calm over large hairy

spiders, so what will they do if 'hailed' by leopard or tiger? And if one cannot get over these fears, how far can one's meditation go? In the kinds of situation which we have been talking about, 'abandoning longing for the body' becomes rather easier. There are just not the facilities for pampering the body in such remote places. Whatever comforts are found they are simple, more necessities than luxuries. While longing for the body is strong, again how far can one get with meditation? One is just tied down to this bag of bones by all one's concerns for it. And how much dukkha comes from this! While if one can let go of grasping at it through meditation while still keeping it going through food and medicines, much peaceful happiness can be experienced. Perhaps one will not fail to do this given an inspiring Teacher and aspiring fellow-practicers. Certainly one should not fail to achieve some Dhamma in this life for all the fearful conditions of this world, though leopards and tigers may not be among them, are ranged against the continuance of our lives individually and against the Buddha-sāsana collectively.

Success

50. The taming of a wild elephant has been mentioned already, but here the untamed mind is compared to a horse which has not been broken in. An animal like this does not agree to go any direction except the one it chooses. Even if it endures a rider on its back it persists in going to the right and left instead of straight ahead, making it necessary to pull on the reins frequently. The untamed mind also does not want to go straight along the Dhamma-path. It is pulled to this object and that arising through the six bases and then prances and bucks about, controlled by subsequently arisen defilements. It has no straightforwardness, no steadiness. Faced with attending to just one subject of concentration, or even just to one event at a time, it is not happy and turns this way and that to find a way out. A tiresome mind! The trainer of this untamed bronco is mindfulness, the mindfulness of the mindful mind. As practice goes on, the wild unmindful mind loses strength and occurs less frequently, while the mindful mind increases in strength, its occurrence becoming normal. The training of one's own mind must precede the effective training of others. Lord

Buddha would never have been known as "the incomparable Trainer of tameable men"—one who could tame such powerful or wayward characters as the ascetic Uruvela Kassapa, the parricide king Ajātasattu, or the bandit Aṅgulimāla, even an animal such as the maddened elephant Nālāgiri—if first he had not tamed his own mind. Having perfectly tamed that, he was in a position to tame others. The same applies to his *arahant* disciples down to the present day: having tamed themselves they are able to help beings. Or in the words of another simile used by the Buddha, a person stuck in the mud can never pull out another in the same plight. But one who stands upon a firm, dry bank can do so. Tālapuṭa after striving with mindfulness compares his mind to a well-regulated horse which is headed straight towards Nibbāna down the path sīla-samādhi-paññā. This path is "safe and blissful" he says. Is this true? What brings danger and dukkha in this world? Isn't it the Roots of Evil, greed, aversion and delusion, which make life dangerous and cause sufferings of mind and body? Then you may say "But surely a person on a spiritual path is sure to encounter dukkha as a result of his striving?" This is true but such dukkha is not associated with defilements and danger; moreover, it will pass when the need for striving has gone. No dangers arise from the good practice of moral conduct, nor from well-guided meditation, and the same applies to insight-wisdom. Trouble and tension arise from the lack of these path-factors in one's life, or from the wrong practice of them. This "safe and blissful Path" cannot be won by those who do not guard the mind. If one wants to experience it, then half an hour of meditation in the morning (or attempted meditation), followed by many hours of unmindfulness during the day, will not lead to the desired result. Only if one's regular meditation practice is backed up by a steady effort at mindfulness during the day will there be success. One may be mindful of sense objects: "Careful! That sight (sound, etc.) leads to trouble!" Or else check up on thoughts: "Mindfulness! These thoughts lead to defacements and dukkha!" Or look into feelings: "These pleasant feelings may lead to lust and greed!" "Watch out! Painful feelings are the basis for anger and hatred!" "Have care! From neutral feelings arise delusion!" Keep on checking up in this way, at work, at leisure, at home; with friends or relations... This is the way to succeed with guarding the mind. As success comes through this effort, so one's feet are planted firmly on "the safe and blissful Path."

* * *

Conclusion

Our 'visit' to the venerable Tālapuṭa Thera is now finished. We would have heard his verses and perhaps we would have listened to explanations along the same lines as those presented here. One difference would have been in the directness, clarity and compelling truth of his words, as he was an *arahant* and had seen Dhamma for himself. Even though he explained points of the Dhamma which we knew about already, his explanations would be fresh and new, as in our own days when one listens to the disciples of Venerable Ācariya Mun Bhuridatta Mahāthera. For instance, though one had often heard the four Noble Truths, yet Enlightened Teachers explain them in words which make one think "Yes, of course! But why did I never think of that?" They are able to phrase their explanations afresh since they have found the pure source of Dhamma, but we are unable to do this as we are bound and limited by words and by concepts about Dhamma.

Another advantage of listening to this 'live' Dhamma is that it can be uniquely fitted to the character of the hearer. Had we been listening to venerable Tālapuṭa instead of reading this book, he might have so taught the Dhamma that we were able to see it as he talked. As he taught, so the Dhamma-truth might have been penetrated until there was attainment of Path and Fruit. He perhaps could have helped us in this way (if we had already helped ourselves by laying down the foundation for such attainment). He would have known what abilities and troubles people had in their hearts, hidden from those who do not have the knowledge of others' minds. Fortunately, this knowledge and this way of teaching (and perhaps attainment while listening too) have come down to the present day among the great Teachers of North-East Thailand. The Dhamma of attainment, as those Teachers say, is still possible, and the Noble Sangha is not yet extinct.

Their way of practice adheres to the ancient tradition from Lord Buddha's days. They and their disciples, and no doubt others in Burma, still hold aloft the light of the Dhamma by which men and women can find the way out of the darkness of saṃsāra—if they are able to and if they wish to. While this Dhamma-light is still bright one can say with real hope for now and the future:

Ciraṃ tiṭṭhatu lokasmiṃ
Samma-sambuddha Sāsanaṃ

Long in the world may it remain,
the Law of the Perfect Awakened One.

The Noble Eightfold Path and its Factors Explained

(Maggaṅga Dīpanī)

The Venerable Ledi Sayādaw

Translated into English by
U Saw Tun Teik

Revised edition by
Bhikkhu Khantipālo

Copyright © Kandy; Buddhist Publication Society, (1977, 1998)

Introduction

If a Buddhist is asked, "What did the Buddha teach?" he would rightly reply, "The Four Noble Truths and the Noble Eightfold Path." If he is then questioned further as to what they consisted of, he should be able to define them accurately, without uncertainty, ambiguity, or recourse to his own ideas.

This is very important—that the supremely clear words of the Buddha are not distorted, either through ignorance or because of one's own speculations. The Buddha has often praised deep learning, just as he has pointed out the dangers in holding opinions and views which are the result only of one's personal feelings and preferences, or of misinterpreted experience. There is little to excuse such things since the Buddha himself has carefully defined what is meant by the truth of *dukkha* (suffering), or what constitutes right view, just to take two examples.

The Buddha's definitions are unconfusing while convincing since they arise from his Unsurpassed Perfect Awakening. But one's own ideas, or the speculations of those who depart from his words, cannot be so without some bias towards what is more comforting to believe, what, in other words, one's undisciplined emotions draw one to believe (see note 41). Such "tangles of views" are endless in this world and produce much conflict as well. No good comes of holding views.

Those who do so usually do not like to practise the Dhamma; they prefer to think about it and talk about it. But one does not become a Buddhist by mere thinking and talking, only by *practice*, and this Noble Eightfold Path containing within it the Four Noble Truths is the preeminent path of practice—of wisdom, moral conduct, and meditation.

So here is a booklet where the Buddha's own definitions of the Four Noble Truths and the Path are quoted and explained by the venerable author who, as a senior member of the Sangha (Order) in Burma, was both deeply learned and well practised in meditation. This handbook of the Noble Eightfold Path contains all the path-factors clearly described according to the most ancient Buddhist tradition, which has come down to us from the enlightened disciples of the Buddha to the great teachers of the present day in the Buddhist countries of Southeast Asia.

Now it only remains to thoroughly learn the definitions of the path-factors and, of course, to practise them. Then one will be competent to answer questions convincingly since one's own conduct does not depart from Dhamma.

This work was written by the Venerable Mahāthera Ledi Sayādaw in Burmese and was later translated into English by U Saw Tun Teik, an advocate in Rangoon. The Union Buddha Sāsana Council issued this book after revision by their English Editorial Board in 1961, but due to later events in Burma it has long been hard to find.

In making it available once again this opportunity has been taken to rewrite it in a form more easily read by Western people, omitting most of the Pāli words which are found in the first edition. Venerable Nyānaponika Mahāthera encouraged me to take up this work, gave every helpful advice, and sent me his copy of the first edition to work on. Also, some sections from the venerable author's *Sammādiṭṭhi-dīpanī* (*The Manual of Right View*) have been included in the revised edition. In places where the venerable author's explanations are too brief some expansions of his statements have been added by the editor. The footnotes are also mine unless stated otherwise.

Finally, if any error has been made by me during revision, may the translators pardon me, and the venerable author show me his compassion.

May the Dhamma of the Exalted One lighten the darkness of the world!

Bhikkhu Khantipālo
Forest Hermitage
Vassāna BE 2520/CE 1976

Preface

In compliance with the requests of the Englishmen who have entered the Buddhist Order of Monks for elucidation of the Noble Eightfold Path, the Venerable Ledi Sayādaw made use of his relative respite while journeying by rail or steamer from town to town, to write this treatise.[1]

---

1. This Preface was translated from Burmese and sent to the reviser by Myanuang U Tin, who has also supplied valuable information on some difficult points from his own knowledge and from replies elicited from Venerable Mahasi Sayadaw.

The Noble Eightfold Path and its Factors Explained

Namo tassa Bhagavato Arahato Sammā-sambuddhassa

Homage to the Exalted One, the Holy One,
the Perfectly Enlightened One

This is the Noble Eightfold Path:

1. Right view — Sammā-diṭṭhi
2. Right thought — Sammā-saṅkappa
3. Right speech — Sammā-vācā
4. Right action — Sammā-kammanta
5. Right livelihood — Sammā-ājīva
6. Right effort — Sammā-vāyāma
7. Right mindfulness — Sammā-sati
8. Right concentration — Sammā-samādhi.

I. Right View

Three kinds of right view have been distinguished:

(A) That one is the owner of the kamma[2] one makes.
(B) That one has right view in respect of ten subjects concerned with kamma, its fruits, this world, other worlds, and the superknowledge revealing them.
(C) That one has right view regarding the Four Noble Truths.

First we shall examine:

---

2. Kamma (or in Sanskrit, *karma*) means intentional actions by body, speech, or mind, having an inherent tendency to bear fruit in accordance with the kind of action done.

A. Right View on the Ownership of One's Kamma

About this the Buddha has said:

> "All beings are the owners of their kamma, heirs to their kamma, born of their kamma, related to their kamma, abide supported by their kamma; whatever kamma they shall do, whether good or evil, of that they will be the heirs."

Now to take this passage section by section for a fuller understanding.

1. All beings are the owners of their kamma

This is the correct understanding that only two things, the wholesome and the unwholesome deeds done by beings, really belong to them and always accompany them on their wanderings in the wheel of birth and death.

Though people call gold, silver, wealth, and jewels their own since they have acquired them lawfully or otherwise, really they are owners only for the brief span of this life and sometimes not for as long as that. For the things that are "owned" by us must be shared with other forces and beings such as water, fire, rulers, thieves, and enemies which, if sentient, may also regard those things as their own.[3] So such things are as though borrowed for this life, just for use now but to be given up at death. And however little or much one may own of things here, all have to be relinquished at the time of death and cannot be taken with one. When this is taken into account, we may understand how we hardly own such things at all, while by contrast the good and evil done by us is truly owned and such kamma may accompany us through a continuity of lives extending through hundreds of thousands of world-cycles in the future. Kamma cannot be taken from the doer or destroyed in any way, for it is imprinted on

---

3. Venerable Buddhaghosa in his *Path of Purification*, emphasises that even our own body must be shared with beings, i.e. with such parasites as worms or bacteria, which regard it as their own. "Ownership" of any material thing is very tenuous and insecure.

our minds and will bear fruit when conditions permit. Hence the Buddha has said, "*All beings are the owners of their* kamma."

One should therefore love and esteem *good conduct* more than one's own life and preserve it well, while one should dread evil conduct more than the danger of death and so refrain from evil deeds.

The kamma which is one's own consists in the mental, verbal, and physical intentional actions that one has done. Kamma by way of the body means intentional movements of such parts of the body as hands or legs. Verbal kamma includes expressions made with the mouth, tongue, and throat. Mental kamma covers all intentional functions of the mind. In the Buddha's teaching these three are called kamma.[4]

All beings make these three kinds of kamma while they are awake, and whatever work they do, of great significance or little, is all done in these three ways. But when a person is asleep these three kinds of kamma are not made, for at that time states of mind are not volitional. In the case of one who is dead none of the three kinds of kamma are made by that body.

These three may be analysed as to whether they are: (1) good or wholesome, or (2) evil and unwholesome; further as to whether (1) they have results ripening in this life, or (2) have them ripening in a future life.

Kamma is determined to be good or evil according to whether it leads to the cultivation and growth of one's own mind and the benefit of others, or to the deterioration and defilement of one's own mind and the harm of others. Thus by doing the following ten types of deeds one makes evil or unwholesome kamma which will bear the fruits of suffering, but by abstaining from these ten and cultivating their opposites one makes good kamma which will bear the fruits of happiness. These ten are as follows:

(1) Injuring and killing living beings[5]
(2) Stealing
(3) Wrong conduct in sexual pleasures

---

4. Note that kamma means action, *not* the fruit of action as when people say, "It's my kamma." This reduces the teaching of kamma to mere fatalism.
5. These will be explained under right action.

(4) False speech
(5) Tale-bearing
(6) Harsh talk
(7) Useless chatter[6]
(8) Covetousness
(9) Ill will
(10) Wrong view

All kinds of actions done through the "three doors" of body, speech, and mind, that are free of these ten ways of making unwholesome kamma, whether in connection with livelihood, the acquisition of wealth, or the search for knowledge, are good kamma made in the present existence and coming to fruition now. But those actions by way of the three doors which are involved with the above ten, in whatsoever connection they are done, are evil kamma which bears its fruit in the present life.

In a similar way kammas made in this life and due to ripen in the future will also be of two kinds, either wholesome or unwholesome. Whether the wholesome kamma is made by the body, speech, or mind in connection with such actions as almsgiving, Uposatha-day observance, moral conduct (of the Five Precepts), practising meditation, going for refuge to and paying respects to the Triple Gem, etc., they will ripen in the future, giving rise to a favourable birth.[7]

Unwholesome kammas made in this life but ripening in the future will result in birth in the lower planes of existence (as ghost, animal, or hell-wraith).

In this way one should differentiate between good and evil kamma as well as contemplate the three kinds of kamma which are made everywhere—on land, in water, and in the sky. When we have seen with our own eyes how all beings, wherever they are, have been making the three kinds of kamma in all their past existences through endless world-cycles, we can comprehend that they will make them in the future too. And just as in this world

---

6. These will be explained under right speech.
7. The Uposatha day, which falls on the days of the full moon and the new moon, is the Buddhist observance day. The Triple Gem is the Buddha, the Dhamma, and the Sangha.

system, so there are in all directions an infinite number of other world systems where such beings, living on land, in water, and in the sky, also make the three kinds of kamma.

When one has thought about this, it becomes clear that all these beings are living by the three kinds of kamma which they make individually for themselves. By making wholesome kamma in these ways they enjoy the fruits of happiness, while by making evil kamma in these three ways they encounter various kinds of misery and suffering.

So the three kinds of kamma made by body, speech, and mind are truly the property owned by beings, for kamma can never be destroyed by fire, water, thieves, and so on. Though a person may own nothing, not even a single coin, yet he can achieve happiness if he has made mental kamma connected with knowledge and wisdom.

Hence the Buddha declared: "*All beings are the owners of their kamma.*"

Now let us take an example which illustrates the results of kamma made in the present life. People who wish for worldly gain, such as wealth, government position, or honour in this life, can fulfil their desires if they make an effort to acquire education and knowledge. If such wishes were merely a matter of worship of some God without any effort being needed, then there would be no need for the worshippers of God to engage in trading, farming, or learning arts or sciences. It would be enough just to worship God. But in fact that is not the case, for like Buddhists, Christians and Muslims also make the three kinds of kamma and caused by it they acquire worldly gain. It is not God but the three kinds of kamma which have given them these things.

Similarly, we can understand how past kamma bears fruit in the present life. For while worldly gains in this life are kamma-produced and not due to any supernatural favour, so the benefits of being reborn in a wealthy family or in a heavenly world are not God-given either, but depend on the power of kamma, such as almsgiving and purity of the moral precepts practised in former lives. One who is reborn into a wealthy family becomes the owner of the riches there, so that all his possessions are due to his past kamma.

Here there is an analogy with vegetative growth. It is usually said that the growth and form of plants depends on the seed. But according to the Abhidhamma, the element of kinetic energy (*tejo*), classified as material change (*utu*), is the cause. The seed is just this element, and it is this which can be called the real seed. In the same way all beings have kamma as their seeds of becoming (or existence): wholesome kamma such as almsgiving, moral conduct, and the like, and unwholesome kamma such as destroying living beings, and so on.

The process of becoming variously men or animals is due to the kamma made in past existences. Having made wholesome kamma, beings are reborn as men or as gods (*deva*), while it is because of making unwholesome kamma that they obtain birth in the four lower worlds: hell (*niraya*), animals, ghosts (*peta*), and titans (*asura*).

From the seeds produced by old plants, a new generation of plants grows so that seeds from a tree and trees from seeds appear successively: a cycle of seeds and trees. Similarly, beings have planted kamma-seeds in their past existences and from these seeds new existences spring up. Thus beings make kamma which in turn gives rise successively to new states of existence.

But here we have to notice a difference between the example in this simile and the case of living beings. A tree is only a stream of material events (without a mental stream or consciousness)[8] and from one tree many fruits may be produced, from which in turn many trees may grow. In the case of beings, however, there are both mental and material streams of events of which the mental ones are chief. Though during life (as with trees) many progeny may be produced, one body giving rise to many others, the stream of mental factors continues with one mental factor giving rise to one other.

Thus at death the last moment of consciousness gives rise to the rebirth-linking consciousness of the next life. Therefore, although a being has planted many seeds of both wholesome and

---

8. Trees and plants have only the life faculty (*jīvitindriya*), which is material. They have no consciousness and so are not part of the cycle of rebirth. Some recent books (*The Secret Life of Plants*, for example) propound theories and offer evidence that plants can sense. In some cases this could be accounted for by the presence of a tree-spirit (*rukkha-deva*) or dryad.

unwholesome kamma in one existence, one moment of volition (*cetanā* = kamma) alone produces one other resultant moment in the next existence.[9] As there is only the production of one mental factor (the first moment of consciousness at conception or spontaneous birth) so at the time of death the continuity or stream of the past material body gives rise to only one new body-stream, not more than this.

Just as earth, water, sun, moon, and stars, come into existence from the seeds of kinetic energy included in material change and were not created by a God, so such beings as men and animals come to successive existences because of the seeds of their past kamma made in previous lives, even in previous world cycles. A view such as this is known as right view (*sammā-diṭṭhi*).

But to hold that a God creates beings is a wrong view, and it is the wrong view of those who, not knowing fully the operative power of kamma and material change, imagine that they were created by a God. Hence the Buddha, whose purpose was to make people abandon wrong view and to rely instead upon kamma, knowledge, and wisdom, said: "*All beings are the owners of their kamma.*"

Further as exposition of "ownership of kamma" the following objection and reply is appropriate.[10]

Question: "Well, friend, if it is true that the Supreme Buddha had properly refuted the view 'all that is experienced is rooted in past kamma,'[11] why and for what reason did he declare the following in the Subha Sutta (or Cūḷakammavibhaṅga Sutta, Majjhima Nikāya No. 135): 'Beings are the owners of their kamma, young man, heirs to their kamma, born of their kamma, related to their

---

9. It might be objected here that a little time spent making wholesome kamma (as in the cases of Anāthapiṇḍika and Visākhā) is still producing centuries of good results, or a short while producing unwholesome kamma (as with Devadatta) brings centuries of pain, but the author is pointing out the strict sequence of events at the time of death, when one kamma at the end of life produces only one resultant moment, the rebirth-linking consciousness.
10. This passage up to the end of this section is taken from *Samma-diṭṭhi-dīpanī, The Manual of Right View.*
11. For this view, see *Aṅguttara Nikāya Anthology*, Part I (BPS Wheel No. 155/158), pp. 43–44.

kamma, abide supported by their kamma. Beings are divided by kamma, that is to say, among low or excellent existences'?"

Reply: This may be answered in three ways.

(1) Those who hold the view "all that is experienced is rooted in past kamma" (*pubbekatahetu-diṭṭhi*) maintain that all pleasures and sufferings experienced by beings in the present life are conditioned and caused only by the volitional actions (kamma) done by them in their past existences. They reject all present causes such as energy and wisdom. As this view rejects all present causes it is known as the "one-sided base opinion" (*ekapakkhahīna-vāda*), "one-sided" because it ignores present kamma.

(2) Those who hold the "creation rooted in God view" (*issaranimmāna-hetu-diṭṭhi*) maintain that all pleasures and sufferings experienced by beings in the present life are created by a Supreme Brahma or God. They reject all past and present kamma made by beings; so their view is called the "both-sided base opinion" (*ubhayapakkhahīnavāda*), "both-sided" because it ignores both past and present kamma.

(3) Those who hold the "no cause no condition view" (*ahetu-appaccaya-diṭṭhi*) maintain that all pleasures and sufferings experienced by beings in the present life come into existence by themselves, without causes and conditions. As this view rejects all causality it is known as the "completely base opinion" (*sabbahīna-vāda*).

But the Buddha, on this occasion speaking to a young brahmin, desired to refute the creation rooted in God view and the no cause no condition view; so he declared, "Beings are the owners of their kamma, young man, the heirs to their kammas...."

He declared this in a general way. He did *not* say: "Beings are the owners of their *past* kamma, the heirs to their *past* kamma." In a passage addressed to the young brahmin, Subha, the words "owners of their kamma" and "heirs to their kamma" refer to both past life and present-life kamma. So one should understand this passage in this way: "Beings are the owners of their past and present kammas."

2. The heirs to their kamma

Only the wholesome and unwholesome deeds done by all beings are their inherited properties that always accompany them wherever they may wander in many lives and world cycles. Those who inherit from their parents are called their heirs, but they are not so in the true sense of this word. Why is this? Because things like gold, silver, jewels, and wealth only last temporarily, and those who inherit such temporary things cannot be called true and real heirs. Such legacies are our property only until death and when we die we have to leave it all behind. Certainly it does not accompany us into the future life. Also, legacies like this are subject to destruction by fire, water, thieves, and so on, before our death takes place, or they may be used up by us during our lives.

When we consider the three kinds of kamma, however, they belong to the beings who made them, even through future lives. They can never be destroyed by other persons or exterior forces, and for this reason kamma is said to be the only property inherited by beings. Beings are sure to reap the results of their own kamma in succeeding existences. Even feeding animals such as pigs, dogs, and birds can result in many births full of happiness, while the wholesome kamma made by offering food to virtuous bhikkhus (monks) can give rise to countless numbers of happy lives as man or *deva*. From the gift of almsfood worth half a crown in this life may come beneficial results worth thousands of pounds in future existences.[12] And if a person kills an animal, such as a fish, fowl, or pig, he may in turn have to suffer being killed in more than a thousand future lives.

This may be illustrated by the banyan tree, for if one of its tiny seeds is planted, a great tree will grow out of it, bearing innumerable fruits during a thousand years or more. The same will be true of mango or jak seeds from which will grow large trees yielding thousands of fruits in the course of many, many years.

Just as a small seed is able to yield thousands of fruits, leaves, branches, and twigs, so a seed of wholesome kamma such as a almsgiving, moral conduct, and meditation can bear in future lives good results many thousands of times over. Likewise, an unwholesome kamma-seed, such as destroying a living being, can yield evil and painful results in numerous future existences.

From just one kamma made by some person the results will follow him in many lives as pleasure or pain, when conditions

---

12. The text is worded in terms of Burmese currency.

are opportune. He can never be rid of that past kamma (until its force is exhausted, its fruits ripened completely), but has to enjoy or suffer its results. For this reason the Buddha has declared: "*All beings are the heirs to their kammas.*"

Look at it another way.[13] A being has two groups (*khandhas*)—the body-group and the mind-group (*rūpakkhandha, nāmakkhandha*). The first means the body with head, hands, legs, and so on, while the mind-group refers to thoughts and consciousness.

Of these two, the body-group comes to dissolution once in each existence, in each life having different shape and colour (according to kamma, parental appearance, etc.). But the mind has no break in its continuity, and mental states arise and pass away successively through innumerable existences. Wholesome kamma, such as giving and moral conduct, causes the subsequent arising in happy existences. And wherever the mind-group arises there a new and appropriate body-group is formed. In the same way, unwholesome kamma brings about the arising of mind in the lower states of existence, such as among dogs, pigs, fowl, and birds, where a body will be formed according to that arising. So a person is also "heir to kamma" with regard to these two groups.

3. Born of their kamma

Only the wholesome and unwholesome deeds done by beings are the origin of their wanderings in so many life cycles. To illustrate this, let us take the example of the banyan tree again. For its growth there are several causes: the banyan seed is the primary cause; the earth and water are secondary causes.

Wholesome past deeds such as almsgiving, moral conduct, etc., which cause one to be reborn as a human being, and the past unwholesome deeds such as destroying life, etc., causing one to be reborn as an animal, are the primary causes, comparable to the banyan seed. One's parents are the secondary causes, just as earth and water are secondary causes for the growth of the banyan tree.

To take another example: working as a labourer for wages, the present kamma is the primary cause, while the place of work, spade, basket, and the employers who pay the wages

---

13. This passage forms an Appendix in the English booklet, but has been added here.

are the secondary cause. In the same way, one's own kamma made in the present existence with wisdom or without it is the primary cause; present results, pleasant and painful, are the wages for these actions.

So we can see that both past kamma and the kamma made in this life are primary causes of the results experienced, and one's parents are not primary causes. Nor has it anything to do with a God. And so the Buddha declares: *"All beings are born of their kamma."*

4. Related to their kamma

Only the wholesome and unwholesome kammas made by beings are their relatives and true friends (or false friends in the case of unwholesome kammas!), always accompanying them wherever they may wander through many lives and world cycles.

By way of explanation we can say that although there are parents, brothers, children, relatives, teachers, and friends whom we love and rely upon, we can only do this for a short time—until our death. But one's own physical, verbal, and mental deeds are constant companions who accompany one and give happiness and prosperity (or misery) in one's future lives. So wholesome deeds alone are one's true relatives and friends who should be esteemed and relied upon. Therefore the Buddha declares: *"All beings are related to their kamma."*

5. Abide supported by their kamma[14]

Only the wholesome and unwholesome deeds done by beings are their real support wherever they may wander through many lives and world cycles.

To explain this: the word "support" means what can be relied upon, or what one can take shelter in, what can save or give protection against troubles and dangers. Those who wish to enjoy

---

14. This phrase is kamma-*paṭisaraṇa* in Pāli. *Saraṇa* has the meaning of refuge, as in the Three Refuges (*tisaraṇa*), but to use this as the original translator has done is awkward since it makes no sense to talk of past unwholesome kamma as a refuge, though it can be one's support. There is some ambivalence of explanation of this factor.

long life in the world have to rely upon food and drink as the protection against the danger of starvation. Similarly, doctors and medicine are needed for protection against bodily troubles and diseases, while weapons are protection against enemies. (And all kinds of support or refuge in the world may be considered in the same way.) So this word '*saraṇa*' does not refer only to the Going for Refuge at a shrine or in the presence of a bhikkhu, it means also reliance upon and taking shelter, as was explained already.

Now how is kamma one's support? In this life an ordinary man with no possessions soon comes to distress. Fearing to experience this we are supported by the work (or kamma) which we do and so acquire money and possessions.

Again, as a lack of wholesome kamma leads to rebirth in the lower worlds where there is grievous suffering, so fearful of this, some people make wholesome kamma leading them to rebirth as human beings or as devas.

Just as the present kamma made by work using knowledge and wisdom can protect us from dangers in this life, in the same way wholesome kamma such as almsgiving and moral conduct protects us from the dangers of future lives in the lower worlds. As we must rely on our work in this life, so we must also rely on wholesome kamma for the future. It is for this reason that the Buddha declares: "*All beings are supported by their kamma.*"

This subject of support or refuge should be analysed as follows.

In the Buddhist religion there are four refuges for the future: (1) the Buddha, (2) the Dhamma, (3) the Sangha, and (4) one's own wholesome kamma.

This can be compared to the four kinds of refuge or support for sick people. First is the chief physician, second the suitable medicine, third the assistant doctors, and fourth, the actions of the patient following their directions confidently. In this simile, the chief physician and the assistant doctors are accounted as supports (or refuges) for the patient because they are capable of prescribing suitable medicines for this particular ailment, while the medicine is his support in that it can actually cure him. The sensible actions of the patient in following the doctor's directions are also his support, for without such actions on his part the other three supports would be ineffective and he could not be cured. All four can be clearly seen to be real supports or refuges for sick people.

Now persons who make evil kamma and indulge in sensual pleasures are like those sick people. The Buddha is like the chief physician, an expert in curing afflictions. The assistant doctors represent the Order of Bhikkhus, while the Dhamma is pictured as the medicine. The bodily, verbal, and mental wholesome deeds are like those sensible actions of the ailing man in which he follows the doctor's instructions.

In this way we can reckon that there are four refuges (or supports) in the Buddha's Teaching, and of these four, three—the Buddha, Dhamma, and Sangha—are not found outside (in other teachings). The fourth refuge or support, making wholesome kamma, exists both within and outside Buddhism. While we are commoners (*puthujjana*) we shall never be free of making kamma and experiencing results of kamma—for kamma and its fruits are in operation for all beings in the world system—so it is wise to make only wholesome kamma.

So we see that the subject of "All beings are owners of their kamma" applies to all beings in all world systems, whether Buddhism exists there or not. It is for this reason that the support (or refuge) in kamma has been dealt with here but not the Three Refuges of Buddhists. Together these form four refuges or supports that can be relied upon both for good and wise conduct in this life and for rebirth in the happy existences.

We have noted already that *saraṇa*, usually translated "refuge," means that which can save, give support or protection, so that food and drink are the *support* for long life, medicines and diet are the *support* for the sick, kings and rulers are *protection* against bandits and thieves, buildings are *protection* against the elements and for comfortable living, boats are a *support* for those who travel on water. Similarly, the earth is a *support*, and so are water, fire, and air for their respective purposes. So there are numerous supports or refuges in this existence. This concludes the exposition about the different kinds of refuges in Buddhism.

Refuge in other religions

Religions apart from Buddhism have only one refuge—that is, refuge in God. Whatever comes into existence and whatever is destroyed is therefore attributed to God.

I shall clarify this point. In religions such as Christianity and Islam[15] the bare meaning of refuge—in making good kamma—is not understood so that followers regard God as their only refuge. They assume that the appearance and disappearance of the world and of the beings on it is due to the power of God. So they believe that God saves those who have faith in him by means of his supernormal power. And by means of this power he can wash away all the sins and evils done by beings, giving them eternal happiness and eternal life after death. Thus the good and bad things experienced by beings depend on the will of God.

People like this disbelieve in kamma and do not think that it can be the cause of results. It is really very surprising that people who are making kamma all the time, in this way disregard their own actions.[16] Kamma, as we have already said, means all intentional physical, verbal, and mental actions. Now all of these actions are done by people, whether Buddhist or otherwise, and some will be done by non-Buddhists in the worship of their religions, whatever forms it takes. So they make kamma by practising and undertaking such things as baptism, worship of God with body, speech and mind, obedience to his commandments, prostrations and offerings; all these things, as they are intentional, are kamma. Though these outsiders believe that God saves those who have faith in him and perform such actions (and does not save those who do not know of him or believe in him and who therefore do not do these things), really there is just the kamma made by those people who in time will receive its fruits, from their own hearts, not from God.

In these God-worshipping religions, as in Buddhism, one can also discern four refuges (supports), even though only one is usually spoken of. They are:

---

15. The venerable author's treatment of this point applies to Hinduism only in part since there is here generally a belief in kamma and in one or more gods who have some or all of the attributes of the Biblical God as Creator, Judge, Compassionate Father, etc. When kamma and such god-belief are brought together there is confusion, as it is not clear whether what one experiences is to be attributed to one's kamma or to God.

16. For if one understands clearly the law of kamma and its fruits there is no room for the God-idea.

(1) God;
(2) the commandments and teachings of God;
(3) prophets such as Mohammed or saviours such as Christ, and the saints and priesthood; and
(4) the kamma made in the performance of religious rites and duties.

The priests and missionaries of those religions do not realise that even in their own teachings there are several kinds of refuge. They do not analyse but treat God as their only refuge, disregarding kamma. Thus they believe in something which is in some senses "outside" and different from themselves, rather than kamma which is "inside" (one's own mind, speech, and body) and certainly part of oneself. Consequently they believe that the good and evil, prosperity and poverty, happiness and suffering of all beings, are created only by God and not due to other causes. They do not know that there are various and different causes for these events.

Is it simply by worship, by praying to God, that poor people who deserve wealth can obtain it? Would they not get it rather by their present kamma while diligently working as a labourer, farmer, or trader? (Note that "kamma" can mean labour or work as well as morally productive action.)

The answer to these questions which accords with cause and effect is that wealth is not usually obtained by prayer to God, whereas acquisition of property is clearly evident as a result of present kamma. As such is the case, it is believable that wealth in this life is got by making kamma now, and has nothing to do with God.

God has no power to give things to people, but present kamma can do so.[17] If God had such power then his followers would have no need to work (= to make present kamma), for they would all enjoy riches given by him. Also those who do

---

17. Many of the "prayers answered by God" and "miracle cures" are due to present kamma. Example: devotee enters a church, mosque, or temple and prays. The mind becomes calm—peace and happiness results—an answer is born in the calm mind which could not arise because of grief in the agitated mind. The prayer is "answered" or the "cure" effected by the intense faith of the sufferer. No God is needed.

not believe in him would not get anything even though they worked (= made kamma) diligently. But this is not so. Devout followers of a God have to work and make kamma in order to obtain wealth, while those who are not his followers can also become rich by making the appropriate kamma. We do not find only wealthy God-believers; on the contrary there are many poor people among them. Therefore, consideration of these reasons shows that acquisition of wealth in this life is the result of present kamma. It is not a gift of God.

In the same way, if one desires education and knowledge, it can be obtained by the present kamma of studying and learning. But it cannot be got by the worship of God.

Again, if one wishes to become a government officer, it is necessary to study the requirements for particular posts. Government jobs cannot be obtained by praying to God.

So we can see for ourselves that all worldly gains are obtainable only by the power of present kamma, not by the supposed power of God.

Let us examine another side to this matter. God-believers have faith that by humbly worshipping God they are freed from their sins and evils, including sickness. However, generally the sick are not cured only by taking the refuge and support of God; for a cure most of them must treat their bodies with medicines and diets. It is the present kamma made by regulating the body in this way that is the cause of their cure. Everyone has seen this for themselves, for Buddhists who are not believers in God and the God-believers all can be cured if the right conditions are present.

How surprising it is that God-believers think that they can be freed in the next life from the results of their sins in this one just by worshipping God sincerely, when even a disease such as ringworm in this life cannot be cured in this way!

It is surprising, too, that as even trifling wealth cannot be got in this life by praying to God, they believe the wealth of everlasting life and happiness in heaven can be acquired in this way!

Now since we have seen for ourselves that wealth and happiness not yet attained in this life are got by virtue of the different ways of making good kamma, not by the favour of God, we can fully believe that there is no other refuge apart from present kamma to get these things.

In the same way, we can believe that attainments of some higher plane of existence, a heaven world (*devaloka*), after death, is also due to present kamma. This has nothing to do with God, for a person who has made no wholesome kamma cannot be reborn in a higher plane by the fiat of God, while those who do not believe in him or worship him but have made wholesome kamma can certainly attain to higher states of existence.[18]

As to what is called "eternal salvation," those who believe in God, take refuge in him, and revere him throughout their lives believe that only such persons as themselves, believing as they do, can be saved by him when they die, while non-believers will not be saved. But it is quite clear that such believers are not saved by God at all but by their own kamma of "believing in God," "taking refuge in God," and "revering God." God is thus a concept, a conditioned phenomenon, in the minds of such believers.

The various beneficial results in a future life of present wholesome kamma cover such possibilities as rebirth into a ruling family or one that is prosperous, and rebirth in the *deva*-worlds or the Brahma-worlds as a *deva* or Brahmā.[19]

Knowing the power of kamma the Buddha has declared: "*All beings abide supported by their* kammas."

6. Whatever kamma they shall do, whether good or evil, of that they will be the heirs

When bodily, verbal, and mental kammas have been made, whether wholesome or unwholesome, the beings who have individually made them will receive their fruits even after many lives or aeons.

(The first five phrases of the quotation which have been used as headings above refer to past kamma which bears fruit in the

---

18. This paragraph is from the *Sammādiṭṭhi-dīpanī*.
19. A *deva* is a being with a subtle body and superlative sense pleasures. He may be, at lowest, a local spirit of a tree, river, rock and so on, or at highest an inhabitant of the plane of "deities wielding power over others' creations" (*paranimmita-vasavatti deva*). For such birth some purification of mind is needed but no great success in meditation. But for birth in the Brahma-worlds it is necessary to attain *jhāna*, intense inward concentration, as a result of which there is a partial purification of mind. The Brahma-worlds are more tranquil and less sensual than the *deva*-worlds.

present life, but this sixth phrase concerns present kamma which will bear fruit in the future.)

The explanation of the right view on the ownership of one's kamma is finished.

* * *

B. Right View regarding the Ten Subjects

This means having right view of the following ten matters. The Buddha has said:

"There is (moral significance in) giving alms. There is (moral significance in) large offerings. There is (moral significance in) small gifts. There is the result and fruit of good and bad deeds. There is (moral significance in what is done to) one's mother. There is (moral significance in what is done to) one's father. There are beings of instantaneous rebirth. There is this world, there is another world. There are in the world ascetics and brahmins of right attainment, of right practice who, having realised by their own super-knowledge (the truth regarding) this world and other worlds, make it known to others."

By way of explanation we can say:

1. There is (moral significance in) almsgiving[20]

This is the right view that almsgiving—such as giving food to animals, to lay people, to bhikkhus, and so on—if done with benevolence, leads to beneficial results, that kamma in a previous existence sometimes bears fruit in subsequent existences.

2. There is (moral significance in) large offerings

The right view that generosity, performed with faith and respect for the virtuous qualities of the recipient, yields beneficial results in the future.

---

20. The Pāli has only the rather terse "There is almsgiving" but the Buddha's intention in making such a statement was to refute those non-Buddhist teachers in his time who taught that neither good kamma nor bad kamma bear any results. See Makkhali Gosāla in *Dictionary of Pāli Proper Names*.

3. There is (moral significance in) small gifts

The right view that gifts, even those given on a small scale, if given with loving kindness, bring benefit to the doer in the future.

4. There is the result and fruit of good and bad deeds

The right view that cruel actions done in previous lives yield painful results in future lives, while refraining from such evil deeds and cultivating wholesome deeds subsequently bears the fruit of happiness.

5-6. There is (moral significance in what is done to) one's mother and to one's father[21]

The right view that good and evil deeds done towards one's mother or father bear pleasant and painful fruits respectively, possibly in future lives.

7. There are beings of instantaneous rebirth

The right view that there really are beings born instantaneously who are (generally) invisible to human eyes. Instantaneous rebirth refers to those beings who do not take conception in a womb. Due to the force of their previous kamma they are born complete with limbs and other organs of the body which need no development further but remain as they are.

Mahābrahmā, the being of greatest power in this world system, has his abode in the three lowest planes of the Brahma-world. He is regarded as God in other religions in which the existence of still higher planes is usually unknown.[22]

Even when men are close to such beings, they are generally unable to see them with human eyes. Only when those beings

---

21. Mother and father, especially in their old age, should be treated well by their children—out of gratitude and love for what they have done for oneself. The fruits of maltreatment of parents will be long and painful. Their hard work for their children can only be repaid by teaching them the Dhamma. (see *Anguttara Nikāya* I, pp. 11-12).

22. For this see the Discourse on the Invitation of Brahmā (*Majjhima Nikāya* 49), *Middle Length Sayings* I, pp. 388 ff. See also *Buddhism and the God-Idea*, Wheel No. 47.

cause their forms to become visible can they be seen by people here. Normally they are invisible to human beings[23] just like God, the angels, and devils of other religions.

The understanding that there really are such beings born instantaneously is also called right view.

8. There is this world

The right view of this world as the human world (one of several planes in the level of sensuality and lowest among the planes of good rebirth).

9. There is another world[24]

The right view that "another world" (= states of existence differing from this one) consisting of the four planes of lower birth—hells, animals, ghosts, and titans, collectively known as the planes of deprivation—together with the *deva* and the Brahma-planes, really do exist.

In other religions, apart from the human and animal planes, these worlds are not known properly. (The heaven-worlds of the devas and the hell-worlds may be thought of as permanent when they are really impermanent states of long existence; the ghosts and titans may be ignored except in exorcism rites, while even the animals are not understood properly as beings also in the round of birth and death.)[25]

Another explanation is possible of the last two phrases: that this world system with its human world, the four lower worlds, the heavenly *deva* and Brahma-worlds, are termed "this world," while in all directions from this world system there are an infinite number of other world systems which are called "the other

---

23. Human eyes can perceive only a small range of the light radiations, similarly with human ears. A large range of waves cannot be perceived through human senses so that much of the world system remains unknown unless explored by way of the mind.
24. Those people who say "I am a Buddhist but I don't believe in other states of rebirth"—please note!
25. See *The Wheel of Birth and Death*, Wheel No. 147/149.

world(s)." These world systems are generally not recognised in other religions.[26]

10. There are in the world ascetics and brahmins of right attainment, of right practice, who having realised by their own super-knowledge (the truth regarding) this world and other worlds, make it known to others

There are such possibilities for spiritual development as the super-knowledges (*abhiññā*),[27] and the all-knowing knowledge (*sabbaññuta-ñāṇa*).[28] Ascetics and brahmins who exert themselves diligently in performing the perfections (*pāramī*) and practising the meditations through calm and insight in this very world can attain such knowledges. Such people are born into this world from time to time who, because of their efforts and practice in past lives, are possessed of these knowledges.

But some people, due to their limited *pāramī* or perfections, are only able to gain the super-knowledges, and then they can see the four lower worlds, the six *deva*-worlds and some of the Brahma-worlds, just as if they looked at them with their usual human eyes. Other people are capable of both the super-knowledges and the all-knowledge so that they see clearly all the countless beings, the infinite worlds and world systems. People who have both these knowledges are called "Buddhas."

---

26. Note in this respect recent Christian concern as to whether Christ's message will save beings on other planets. Buddhism has always known of an infinity of inhabited worlds where the Four Noble Truths must always be true.
27. Super-knowledges are five or six in number as generally listed: the magical powers, the divine eye (clairvoyance—the venerable author refers to this super-knowledge below), the divine ear (clairaudience), knowledge of past lives, knowledge of kamma and its results. These five can be experienced by non-Buddhists also, but the sixth, the destruction of the pollutions (*āsavakkhaya*), is only won by those who develop path and fruit wisdom (*magga-phala-ñāṇa*), difficult to find outside Buddhism.
28. Note that the Buddha disclaimed that he was omniscient in the sense that he knew everything at the same time. But he said it was possible for him to know everything about a particular subject if he turned his mind to it.

These two kinds of people appear in the human world from time to time and impart their knowledge of this world and other worlds to others who often become their followers. But it is only a Buddha who can explain the round of rebirth in terms of cause and effect and clarify the arising and passing away even of the world systems.

In regard to this there are three kinds of understanding: (1) that beings with super-knowledges and the all-knowing knowledge do appear in this world from time to time; (2) that their teaching if based on the six super-knowledges is thoroughly reliable, and if on five of them at least partly so; (3) that other worlds do exist. All this constitutes right view.

Those who have this right view do not doubt that a Buddha arises only in the human world, not in the heavenly worlds. But in religions where such right view is not understood they imagine that the all-knowers and all-seers, those having the all-knowing knowledge, appear only in the highest heavens and not in the human world. Only in the human world can one strive towards the all-knowing knowledge. Why is this so? The devas and Brahmās are too comfortable—they see no suffering, their lives are too long so they do not see impermanence. But the beings in the planes of deprivation have so much suffering that they cannot practise Dhamma. Only human beings have rather short lives and so are pricked by impermanence, only they have a mixture of pleasure and pain. Diligent effort is needed if one would attain the all-knowing knowledge and those who are able to make this effort are human beings. And it is the rare human being who attains Buddhahood here in this human world. This is the marvel and the wonder of a Buddha, that he is a human being, not a *deva* or Brahmā. If he were such a heavenly inhabitant then there would be nothing very remarkable about his knowledge and wisdom. But as he is born normally of human parents and has a body essentially the same as that of all other people, he is wonderful and marvellous for showing what a human being can attain to if he makes the effort.

It is only in the Buddha's Dhamma that profound, sublime, and wonderful teachings are found, for they are revealed by the Buddha's all-knowing knowledge. They all belong to the sphere of super-knowledge, hard to find outside Buddhism.

One should know that there are two spheres of power: the power of knowledge and the power of kamma. In the latter, the most effective is the power of *jhāna* (intense concentration) which is a "heavy" kamma. It can cause one to arise in the form or formless planes as a Brahmā with an immensely long span of life. But the power of kamma cannot cause one to become a Perfectly Enlightened One. Even though one has made the merits to be reborn as Mahābrahmā himself, still one has no super-knowledge to know and see all.

To strive in this life to become a wealthy person is one path, while to strive for insight knowledge and so become a teacher for other beings is another. Striving to become a Mahābrahmā is similar to the effort to attain wealth, while to strive as a bhikkhu or lay hermit for insight knowledge is actually the way of the Buddha and the *arahants*.

Here is another example. Birds such as parrots, crows, and vultures have wings with which to fly but they do not possess knowledge and wisdom like men. Human beings have varying degrees of knowledge and wisdom but having no wings they are unable by themselves to fly.

The wholesome kammas which the Mahābrahmās have made by developing *jhāna*, and the wholesome kammas of the devas residing both here on earth and in the various *deva*-worlds, resemble the wings of birds. But the super-knowledges and the all-knowing knowledge of lay hermits and bhikkhus are like the wisdom of the man in the above example.

It is due to the power of their wholesome kamma made by developing *jhāna* that the Mahābrahmās live in the higher planes of existence, long-lived and powerful. But they do not possess the two kinds of super-knowledge and so do not penetrate the deep truths of impermanence, suffering, non-self, and voidness. Their knowledge is confined to just what they experience personally.

To summarise some important points of this section, we can note that the knowledge which makes clear: (1) that a Buddha has the all-knowing knowledge and arises only in the human plane, not in the higher planes of existence; (2) that only ascetics of the human race complete in the super-knowledges and in the all-knowing knowledge can clearly teach the conditioned nature of aeons and world systems, how beings wander in the round of birth and death and how wholesome and unwholesome kamma operates; and (3) that the teachings of the monks compiled as the Sutta (Discourses), Vinaya (Discipline), and Abhidhamma are true, is called the *right-view knowledge that there are (enlightened) ascetics and brahmins in the world*.

On the other hand, wrong views should be rejected, such as the view that an Enlightened One with the all-knowing knowledge does not appear in the human plane but only in the highest heavenly abode. Also that the gods are not many but only one God, as well as the idea that this one God, being highest and noblest, must be eternal and free from decay, disease, and death.

The Buddha has rejected all such tangles of views.

C. Right View of the Four Noble Truths

This right view means:

(1) Knowledge of real suffering.
(2) Knowledge of the true causal arising of suffering.
(3) Knowledge of the cessation of suffering.
(4) Knowledge of that right path leading to the cessation of suffering.[29]

1. Right View of the Truth of Suffering

Attachment to sensuality and the troubles caused thereby

Because of this attachment, human beings, devas, and Brahmās are subject to great pains and sufferings which have existed in the past, continue in the present, and will be experienced, while attachment remains, in the future. The eye, ear, nose, tongue, body (touch), and mind are the six internal sense-spheres which operate, in the unenlightened person, in conjunction with defilements of greed, aversion, and delusion whenever they are stimulated by an external sense object. These six sense faculties

---

29. The following explanation of the Four Noble Truths is brief. For a detailed explanation see the author's *Explanation of the Four Truths* (*Catusaccadīpanī*) translated in *The Light of the Dhamma*, Vol. V, No. 4 and Vol. VI, No. 1, 1958–59).

are the suffering which, though not apparent to many people, is real, constant, and oppressive.

How does attachment to the senses oppress? It may be explained by this group of factors: kamma-formations, instability, and suffering. In another way there is oppression through kamma-formations, burning, and instability. Or it can be explained through birth, decay, and death. Again, there is oppression by way of stoking up the fires of greed, aversion, and delusion, conceit, wrong view, the mental defilements (*kilesa*) and the pollutions (*āsava*), by stimulating evil conduct such as destroying living creatures and so on, or by fuelling the fires of birth, decay, sorrow, lamentation, pain, grief, and despair.

Now I shall explain some of these points.

Oppression by kamma-formations (saṅkhārā)

Possession of the sense faculties of a human being, *deva*, or Brahmā means that good kamma has been made in a past life, for if good kamma had not been made the senses of a hell-being, animal, ghost, or titan would have come into existence. So the senses of a higher being are oppressive to him because of the good kamma-formations which must be made continually to ensure the continuation of those faculties. And those same kamma-formations oppress him in the next existence also because he has still to protect and sustain his conduct so that he will not lose those sense faculties in the future. So there comes about a constant oppression. As the eye and other senses do not arise independently of the kamma-formations, it is said that kamma-formations always "oppress" the "owner" of those senses throughout the beginningless round of birth and death.

Oppression by instability (vipariṇāma)

This means "oppression by liability to immediate destruction, whenever cause exists for destruction." From the time of conception onwards there is not a single moment, even for the winking of an eye or a flash of lightning, when there is no liability to destruction. Moreover, there is always the anxiety caused by impending destruction. And when destruction comes, then many sorts of suffering have to be experienced. This is what is meant by saying that the senses are oppressive because of their instability.

Oppression by the painfulness of suffering

This means both physical and mental suffering. The suffering experienced while the sense bases grow (in the womb) and the experience by way of them during birth needs no comment. The painfulness of suffering is also evident when the senses come into contact with an unpleasant object. Also, whenever one inflicts bodily pain upon others out of the unpleasant feelings which arise when seeing or hearing them—then this oppression is experienced. And when the eye or another sense organ contracts some disease, or whenever there is physical and mental trouble in the preservation and protection of the eye, etc., then oppression by suffering occurs. In this way all the senses beginning with the eye oppress beings with the suffering associated with them.

Oppression by burning (santāpa)

The senses are the source of so much suffering by means of the defilements which they awaken in the hearts of people. These defilements are like great fires which are continually refuelled and burn without dying down from the beginningless past to the endless future in the round of birth and death. These great fires are three in number: the fires of greed, aversion, and delusion, and when they are refuelled through the eye, ear, nose, tongue, body, and mind, they ensure that one's future in saṃsāra will be long and miserable.

It is right-view knowledge that gives one understanding of the immense sea of sufferings born of attachment to sense pleasures, whether in the sensuality sphere, the fine-form sphere, or the formless sphere.

2. Right View of the Causal Arising of Suffering

In the round of birth and death, so long as there is attachment to the senses as "mine" or "myself," so long continues oppressiveness and suffering. So it is craving, desire, and greed connected with the senses that is the true cause for the arising of suffering.[30]

---

30. One should not understand craving as the one and only cause. Where craving (taṇhā) is found, there will be ignorance (of the Four Noble Truths) as well as other factors of dependent origination.

It is right-view knowledge that gives one understanding of the causal arising of suffering by way of craving.

3. Right View of the Cessation of Suffering

In whatever life the craving and greed connected with the senses finally cease, the suffering and oppression finally cease as well. The senses do not arise again after the death of the person who has extinguished craving.

It is right-view knowledge that gives one understanding of the cessation of craving.

4. Right View of the Path Leading to the Cessation of Suffering

When, as a result of practising Dhamma in general and developing the mind in meditation in particular, the true nature of the senses is seen and understood, craving connected with them ceases in this very life. It does not arise again and so sense oppression likewise does not arise.

It is right-view knowledge that gives one understanding of the true path leading to the cessation of craving. Among all the parts of the Noble Eightfold Path, this right view of the Four Noble Truths is most essential.

This concludes the brief exposition of right view of the Four Truths.

II. Right Thought[31]

This is explained under three headings:
1. Thoughts of renunciation (= generosity).
2. Thoughts of non-harming (= loving kindness).
3. Thoughts of non-violence (= compassion).[32]

---

31. *Saṅkappa*, a word not easy to translate. The translation "thought" does not convey the emotional connotation of the three kinds of *saṅkappa*. "Intention" is sometimes used.
32. These three terms seem to have been chosen by the Buddha for their wide range of possible meanings. The negative terms for positive mental states (common usage in Pāli) makes for a range of possible meanings which a positive term would not be able to express.

1. Thoughts of Renunciation

The mental state where there is absence of greed, which therefore makes it possible to renounce the five sense pleasures, that is pleasant sights, sounds, smells, tastes, and touches. Or it is ability to renounce attachment to the five groups (*khandha*), or to mind and body. Thought arising out of such absence of greed is this mode of right thought.[33]

2. Thoughts of Non-Harming

Loving kindness (*mettā*) for all beings, visible such as men and animals, or invisible such as devas and ghosts; the mind or heart which wishes their good and welfare.[34]

---

33. Here is a place where giving comes into the path; we have already seen it mentioned under right view. "Renunciation" does not necessarily imply cutting off one's hair and leading a homeless life; here the emphasis is on interior renunciation. If one is able, to start with, to loosen one's greed and attachment to things, it is possible then to become generous in giving to others. This is the first step, in one sense, along any spiritual path. For if material possessions cannot be given up for the benefit of other living beings, what hope is there of progressing further along that path where greater renunciation, as explained by the author, must be made? The renunciation spoken of here is not something forced, though one should make efforts to be more generous. It comes quite naturally with the practise of the other path factors. When right concentration is practised and some success in it attained then the things of this world become less interesting and can be given away or given up quite naturally and easily. Generous giving and giving up must be cultivated for successful practise of the Buddha's Dhamma. Without it, though one may have much knowledge, all one's Dhamma stays in the head, or comes out of the mouth—it is never expressed through the hands. No one can be a successful cultivator of the path unless they support liberally the Buddha, Dhamma, and Sangha, and are generous to other people in general.
34. This is a very short notice of a most important subject! A person can claim to be a Buddhist and certainly have right view as defined in the previous section but still have enmity towards others or speak slander about them. All one's book learning will not change harmfulness into loving kindness; only Dhamma practice, particularly the development of *mettā* through meditation, can do this. This means hard work on oneself which may be painful emotionally but then the result of accomplishing just a little here is

3. Thoughts of Non-Violence

Compassion and sympathy for all beings, all of whom are subject to some suffering while most beings have much suffering to bear. Thoughts which, to use the Pāli idiom, "tremble with" the sufferings of others are the practice of this aspect of right thought.[35]

This finishes the explanation of right thought.

III. Right Speech

There are four types of right speech:

1. Restraint from false speech.
2. Restraint from tale-bearing.
3. Restraint from harsh talk.
4. Restraint from useless chatter.

The first of these means abstinence from both speaking untruth in such a way that it appears to be truth and speaking truth as though it were untruth.[36]

The second is found where a person abstains from bearing tales which would cause two friends to lose confidence and regard for each other, and so create dissension and trouble.

The third abstinence is from words uttered in anger which are rough, harsh, and abusive, such as insinuations regarding race, family, personality, and occupation.

And the fourth, abstinence from useless chatter, refers to such plays and novels[37] as contain no worthy goals (*attha*), no rightful

---

that one becomes a "solid" Buddhist, not just one with a Buddhist facade. And, of course, one gains many good friends.

35. The meditative aspect of loving kindness and compassion has been emphasised in these two sections as they constitute right thought. This is implied by the practice of the first precept (see right action) and by the Buddha's constant exhortation to gentleness in dealing with others. One is not truly a Buddhist unless one's actions conform to Dhamma.

36. The first is common lying while the second refers to cunning ways of corrupting what is true so that it appears to be false.

37. "As *Enaung* and *Ngwedaung*" in the first English edition. Myanaung U Tin writes: "*Enaung* is a work of fiction written about 100 years ago during the reign of King Mindon. It is hardly known to the present generation. *Ngwedaung* is a legend relating to Kayah State on the borders of Thailand. It is still well known

means thereto (*dhamma*), and no reference to good conduct (*vinaya*). Such matters do not inspire those who read or listen to them though they may have transient entertainment value.

Words which relate to goals (*attha*) describe such things as long life, health, and rightly acquired wealth enjoyed in this life, while in a future life they are such good results as being born a human being or a *deva*.

Words relating to the means (*dhamma*) make clear the ways in which the above goals can be realised.

Those words which deal with the rules of conduct (*vinaya*) for both laity and religious (the five, eight, ten, or 227 precepts) are the basis for the destruction of greed and aversion.

Now words about such goals, means, and good conduct are not found in the type of books and dramas referred to here, so narrating and acting works like this amounts to useless chatter.

Also included under this heading are the thirty-two types of vulgar talk[38] which are spiritually unbeneficial [and obstruct the noble fruits of stream-winning, etc., and also rebirth in the higher planes. They are as follows: talk about rulers, criminals, ministers of state, armies, dangers, battles, food, drink, clothing, dwellings, adornments, perfumes, relatives, vehicles, villages, towns, cities, provinces, women (or men), heroes, streets, baths, relations who have died, this and that, the origin of the world, the origin of the ocean, eternity views, annihilation views, worldly loss, worldly gain, self-indulgence, self-mortification].[39]

Anyone who wants to develop wisdom regarding goals, means, and good conduct should not waste time indulging in these thirty-two kinds of talk. Further, a person who is developing the meditation practices leading to calm (*samatha*) or to insight

---

and often staged. Quite naturally, fiction, legend, and fairy tales are considered to be *samphappalāpa*." The reference is obviously to literature and drama which is liable to lead to deterioration, not to growth in Dhamma.

38. "Vulgar (lit. animal-like) talk" is so called either because it is worthy only of animals—and if one sees the list of what is contained in it, most of it is what journalists call "news" (!)—or it is "animal talk" because it goes on all fours like animals and not in an upright way like human beings.

39. These brackets contain the material found in Appendix I in the first edition.

(*vipassanā*) should know the limits even of speech dealing with goals, means, and good conduct.

This ends the description of the four types of right speech.

IV. Right Action

This is threefold:

1. Restraint from killing living creatures.
2. Restraint from taking what is not given.
3. Restraint from wrong conduct in (sexual)[40] pleasures.

The first of these means the intentional killing or destroying of beings either by physical action or by verbal incitement ranging from killing the eggs of lice and bugs, or causing abortion, to the slaughter of living creatures including human beings.[41]

Restraint from taking what is not given means abstaining from taking, with intention to steal, living beings or non-living articles which have an owner, removing or appropriating them without the owner's consent either by physical effort or by inciting another to do so.

Restraint from wrong conduct in sexual pleasures means abstention from sex which will cause pain and suffering to others. Examples will be adultery (for this causes the disruption of marriage), rape, intercourse with minors protected by parents, etc., and the perversion of others. Included here also are abstention from the five kinds of intoxicants and gambling with cards, dice, and so on.[42]

This ends the explanation of three sorts of right action.

---

40. The pleasures (*kāma*) mentioned under the third of the Five Precepts all relate to sex but here, as we shall see, other pleasures are included.
41. The kamma made in all these actions is unwholesome, but of course not all of the same strength. In dealing with the world wisdom has to be used to decide what should and should not be done.
42. These three headings are the equivalent of the first three of the Five Precepts, each of which is prefaced by the phrases: "I undertake the rule of training to refrain from ..." Into the last of these three is incorporated the fifth precept on intoxicants, while the fourth has been explained already under right speech. Although the explanation of these precepts is brief, their importance cannot be too greatly emphasised. Unless they are practised

V. Right Livelihood

1. Restraint from livelihood based on wrong conduct.
2. Restraint from livelihood based on improper means.
3. Restraint from livelihood based on deception of others.
4. Restraint from livelihood based on low worldly knowledges.

Wrong conduct means either the threefold unwholesome bodily action beginning with killing living creatures described under right action, or the fourfold unwholesome verbal action such as lying, described under right speech—any livelihood gained in this way will be wrong. So will be a living made by the sale of the five kinds of merchandise[43] which should not be sold. When one abstains from such wrong conduct in livelihood, right livelihood is practised.

The second heading, improper means, refers to ways of wrong livelihood not to be practised by the bhikkhus (Buddhist monks) and lay hermits (*isi*, the Pāli form of the Sanskrit word *rishi*, represented by a class of lay followers in Burma). These wrong ways of getting a livelihood involve such matters as a bhikkhu giving flowers and fruit to families, or medical preparations, or flattering them in some way, or acting as their messenger. In such wrong ways, a bhikkhu may hope to increase his gains though actually he earns only contempt.

Under the third heading above, livelihood is gained by deceiving others and while much of this section applies to bhikkhus, it does have application to householders as well. Five sorts of deception are given, as follows. The first is all sorts of trickery so that people understand that one can work wonders or attain deep states of meditation or the noble paths and fruits, or feigning deportment so that they think one is an ariya (noble one), or again causing people to have a high opinion of oneself

---

diligently there is no hope of developing the mind in meditation, or of gaining insight or wisdom.

43. "Weapons, living beings, meat, intoxicants and poisons—these five kinds of merchandise should not be traded in" (*Aṅguttara Nikāya*, The Fives). This note is from the first edition. The words quoted are the Buddha's.

by pretending that one does not wish to receive alms and accepts only for the sake of the donors. The second is talk which pleases donors so that they make a gift, while the third is making all sorts of hints and gestures so that offerings are made. Fourth comes harassing a donor with words so that he is obliged to give in order to get rid of oneself, and fifth comes giving a small gift so as to get a bigger one. All this is trickery and deception.

The fourth heading, wrong livelihood based on low worldly knowledges, means that one gets a living by prognostication, by palmistry and interpreting other bodily marks, or by astrology and other such low arts which run contrary to the bhikkhu's practice of Dhamma. When bhikkhus and lay hermits refrain from such things their livelihood is pure in this respect.

This brings to an end the exposition of right livelihood.

VI. Right Effort

This path-factor is analysed into four components. The first two deal with unwholesome volitional actions (kamma), divided into unwholesome mental states which have arisen and those which have not yet arisen. These two constantly cause anxiety, corruption, and debasement for living beings. The second two deal with wholesome kamma, either with those states which have arisen or those which have not. They always bring peace, purity, nobility, and progress for beings. Now to define these four in greater detail.

The ten paths of unwholesome kamma have already been mentioned. Now, whatever of those kammas have already arisen in the past or arise in the present, they are all called "arisen unwholesomeness." But if such kammas have not yet been made though one may be liable to make them in future, then this is called "unarisen unwholesomeness."

To illustrate wholesome kamma, arisen and unarisen, let us take the seven stages of purity:

Purity of moral conduct (attained by keeping precepts)
Purity of mind (attained by meditation)
Purity of view
Purity by overcoming doubt

Purity by knowledge and vision of what is and what is not the path

Purity by knowledge and vision of the practice-path

Purity by knowledge and vision (the last five attained by wisdom)

Now whatever purity has arisen in oneself in the past, or in the present, that is called "arisen wholesomeness." But the purities which one has not experienced, though one may do so in the future (provided that the necessary effort is made), are called "unarisen wholesomeness."

If the Noble Eightfold Path is practised and developed in this life, then by virtue of its power the bad conduct already arisen will never arise again until one attains Nibbāna without remainder of grasping (when there is no possibility of its doing so). Also, by virtue of the Noble Eightfold Path the bad conduct which has not arisen in oneself during this life, but which could arise in future, will have no chance to arise at any time until Nibbāna without remainder of grasping is attained.

In the same way, when this path is practised and developed here and now, due to its power any one of the purities which has already arisen for oneself becomes indestructible and constant until the attainment of Nibbāna without remainder of grasping. Likewise, the purities which so far have not arisen in oneself, which have not been attained or reached, by virtue of the Noble Eightfold Path are reached and attained in this life.

(In explaining the terms "arisen" and "unarisen" people can easily understand unwholesomeness by way of the ten evil paths of making kamma while wholesomeness can best be illustrated by the seven kinds of purification.)

Bhikkhus and lay people who have encountered the Buddha's teaching, being confident and faithful, should be convinced by these reasons that only right effort in the practice and development of the Noble Eightfold Path leads to their real welfare and prosperity. The things of this world should be carried out only in essential matters such as are unavoidable.

This is indeed the way of elucidating right effort which is a fundamental factor for Buddhist practice. The summary of this most important subject in relation to the Eightfold Path is as follows:

1. Regarding what is unwholesome

To practise the Eightfold Path with the intention to prevent bad conduct from arising at all in this life and the following existences, is the first kind of right effort.

2. Regarding what is unwholesome

To practise the Eightfold Path with the intention to prevent bad conduct which has not yet arisen for oneself in this life, but which is liable to arise in the future, from arising at all until one attains Nibbāna without remainder of grasping, is the second kind of right effort.

3. Regarding what is wholesome

To make effort in practising the Eightfold Path in such a way as to attain without fail the higher purities (*visuddhi*) which have not yet been attained in this life, is the third kind of right effort.

4. Regarding what is wholesome

To make effort in such a way as to keep unbroken one's purity of moral conduct—the five precepts and the precepts with livelihood as the eighth (*ājīvaṭṭhamaka-sīla*, for this see below) which one observes in this life until one attains Nibbāna when they become permanent—this is the fourth kind of right effort.

These four are the right efforts which have been explained in this way for easy understanding. They are four in number only with reference to their four functions (namely: avoiding, overcoming, developing, maintaining). But really there is only one factor here—effort or *viriya*—for the reason that when one tries to attain to any of the purities, the effort so exercised covers these four functions automatically.

Here ends the exposition of the four kinds of right effort.

VII. Right Mindfulness

The minds of most beings are never steady but fly about here and there. They have no control over their minds and so cannot fix them steadily on a subject of meditation. As they cannot control their minds they resemble mad or mentally deranged persons and

for such people society has no regard. So people who begin to
meditate find that their uncontrolled minds resemble those of
persons who are deranged. To eliminate the unsteady and flighty
mind and to fix it continuously on the meditation subject one has
to practise the four applications of mindfulness. They are:

1. The application of mindfulness to contemplate the body
(*kāyānupassanā-satipaṭṭhāna*)

This means that one's mind is firmly bound to the body-group by
the rope of right mindfulness. What is meant here is that the mind
is constantly looking at or concentrating upon bodily phenomena,
such as breathing in and out and the other exercises listed in the
discourse on the application of mindfulness.[44] When such practice
has been continued for three or four months, the unsteadiness of
the mind disappears and it is possible all the time to concentrate
the mind upon the body group. This requires steady practice
from day to day which may be from just an hour, or up to six
hours daily, upon mindfulness of breathing in and out or one of
the other subjects listed in the above discourse. At this point the
meditator has control of his mind so that it can be fixed on any
meditation subject.

2. The application of mindfulness to contemplate feeling
(*vedanānupassanā-satipaṭṭhāna*)

This means that one's mind is firmly bound by the rope of right
mindfulness to the feeling group (= pleasant feeling, painful
feeling, neither painful nor pleasant feeling), which occur all the
time in the body varying according to conditions. Repeatedly
fixing the mind on these feelings will put an end to restlessness of
mind, and when this occurs then one has mental control so that
the mind will be concentrated on any subject of meditation.

---

44. See translations in *The Heart of Buddhist Meditation*, Nyanaponika
Thera (Kandy, BPS); *The Way of Mindfulness*, Soma Thera (Kandy, BPS); *The
Foundations of Mindfulness*, Nyanasatta Thera (BPS Wheel No. 19); *Middle
Length Sayings*; Vol. I, Discourse 10, I.B. Horner (PTS London).

3. The application of mindfulness to contemplate mind (*cittānupassanā-satipaṭṭhāna*)

Here the meaning is that the mindful mind is firmly bound with the mindfulness-rope to the contemplation of the mind when it is associated with greed and aversion, which have been present in one's mental continuum from time to time according to conditions. When this is often practised the restless mind disappears and the mind becomes workable so that it can be fixed on any meditation subject.

4. The application of mindfulness to contemplate dhammas (*dhammānupassanā-satipaṭṭhāna*)[45]

The rope of right mindfulness here binds the mind to the contemplation of such mental objects as sensual desire, ill will, mental and physical sloth, distraction and worry, and uncertainty (= the five hindrances) and other subjects given in the discourse which arise conditionally in one's mind-continuum. When this has been repeated many times restlessness disappears and with this mind-control the mind can be directed to any subject of meditation.

So the applications of mindfulness really mean the meditative work of getting rid of the mad, deranged, hot and burning states of mind that have always formed part of one's mental continuity from successive past lives, by binding the mind with the mindfulness-rope to four of the five groups comprising oneself. Thus body-contemplation is applied to the *body*, feeling-contemplation to the *feelings*, mind-contemplation to *consciousness*, and dhamma-contemplation to *mental formations*. This should be done diligently and regularly in daily practice so that the mind does not stray to external objects but is centred upon the four groups mentioned above.

---

45. Here this means subjects which are discovered through close scrutiny of the mind. Such subjects as the five hindrances to meditation, the five groups or aggregates which compose what is called "self," the six internal and external sense spheres (with mind and mind-objects as the sixth), the seven factors of enlightenment, and the Four Noble Truths. See the discourse for details.

VIII. Right Concentration

In the world, when one is learning how to read one has to begin with the letters of the alphabet and it is only when these have been mastered that higher education can be acquired. The same principle applies to the process of mental development where mindfulness must be practised first, for only when it is strong will the mad, deranged mind be got rid of and only then can the higher stages of meditation be practised with steadfastness.

So when the work of the applications of mindfulness is in order and one is able to concentrate the mind without disturbance for one or two hours or more daily upon one of the exercises in the contemplations of the body, feeling, etc., one should turn to the development of the pure mind (*cittavisuddhi-bhāvanā*), known also as the four levels of collectedness acquired by the practice of calm (*samatha-jhāna-samādhi*). This can be compared to the higher Buddhist studies on the Discourse on Blessings, the passages for paying respect (to the Triple Gem and to one's teachers), the protection discourses, Pāli grammar, and the Manual on the Meaning of Abhidhamma,[46] which are mastered after having learnt the alphabet first.

Among these four levels of collectedness, the first is called the first *jhāna* and is attained by intense practice of one of the meditation subjects listed below, after having passed through three successive stages of development (*bhāvanā*): the preparatory work on development (*pari*kamma-*bhāvanā*), the access development (*upacāra-bhāvanā*), and the attainment development (*appanā-bhāvanā*). The twenty-five meditation subjects (kammaṭṭhāna) for attaining the first *jhāna* are:

10 kinds of *kasiṇa* devices (4 colours, 4 elements, space, light)
10 kinds of unattractiveness (decaying corpses)
1 exercise on the 32 parts of the body
1 exercise on mindful breathing in and out
3 kinds of divine abidings =
    loving kindness (*mettā*)
    compassion (*karuṇā*)

---

46. The Pāli in the first edition runs: Maṅgala Sutta, Namakkāra, Paritta, (Grammar and), Abhidhammattha-saṅgaha.

joy-with-others (*muditā*).⁴⁷

When a person takes up meditation and makes an effort with the exercise of mindfully breathing in and out, this "preparatory work on development," which is just to get rid of the mad and deranged mind, is included in the first *jhāna*.

It should be noted that the practice of applying mindfulness to breathing in and out serves both purposes: the establishing of mindfulness and the attainment of the first *jhāna*. For a full explanation of the four jhānas *The Path of Purification* should be consulted.

Here ends the section on the four kinds of right concentration.

This concludes the full explanation of the Noble Eightfold Path.

---

47. For all these subjects of meditation described in detail see *The Path of Purification* (*Visuddhimagga*), trans. Ñāṇamoli Thera (BPS).

Practising the Path

The Three Rounds and the Four Kinds of Wandering-On

In the present time, while the Buddhasāsana still exists, if people practise and develop the Noble Eightfold Path they can free themselves from the suffering of the rounds (*vaṭṭa*). I shall explain them to you.

There are three kinds of *suffering* produced by the rounds, and these are:
(1) the round of defilement (*kilesa-vaṭṭa*);
(2) the round of intentional action (kamma-*vaṭṭa*);
(3) the round of resultants (*vipāka-vaṭṭa*).

They are also classified in this way:
(a) the three rounds connected with the wandering-on in states of deprivation;
(b) the three rounds connected with the wandering-on in the good bourns of the sensual realm;
(c) the three rounds connected with the wandering-on in the realms of subtle form;
(d) the three rounds connected with the wandering-on in the realms of formlessness.

(a) In the case of the three rounds connected with the wandering-on in states of deprivation:
(1) the round of defilements refers to personality view and uncertainty;
(2) the round of intentional action refers to the ten evil paths of kamma;
(3) the round of resultants refer to the five resultant kamma-produced groups (*khandha*) of hell-beings, animals, ghosts, and demons.

(b) In the case of the three rounds connected with the wandering-on in the good bourns of the sensual realm:
(1) the round of defilements refers to desire for sensual pleasures, such as pleasant sights, sounds, smells, tastes, and touches;

(2) the round of intentional action refers to the three ways of making merit (good kamma), that is, by giving, moral conduct, and meditation;
(3) the round of resultants refers to the five resultant kamma-produced groups (*khandha*) of human beings and of devas in the six *deva*-planes.

(c) & (d) In the case of the three rounds connected with the wandering-on in subtle form, or those of formlessness:
(1) the round of defilements refers to attachment to subtle form or formlessness in the realm of subtle form, or the realm of formlessness, respectively;
(2) the round of intentional action refers to wholesome kamma leading to and practised in the form and formless realms;
(3) the round of resultants refers to the five resultant kamma-produced groups (*khandha*) of the Brahma-gods in the form realm, and to the four resultant mental groups of the Brahma-gods in the formless realm.

So one should understand that there are these three rounds in both form realm and formless realm.

This is the end of the exposition of the three rounds with the four divisions of each of them.

Path-Factors and Rounds

The Eightfold Path may also be divided as it pertains to the experience of stream-winners, once-returners, non-returners, and *arahants*.

The Eightfold Path, as it is experienced by a person who becomes a stream-winner (at the time when the mind turns away from continuance in the wandering-on towards Nibbāna), completely terminates the three rounds connected with rebirth in the states of deprivation (*apāya*). As regards the rounds connected with wandering-on in the sensual good bourns, it completely terminates all the three rounds that would otherwise arise after seven more existences.[48]

---

48. A stream-winner may undergo a maximum of seven more lives, none of them below human level.

The once-returner's Eightfold Path completely terminates two of the three rounds, the defilements-round and the resultants-round, connected with the realm of sensuality which would otherwise arise in the last five of the seven existences (spoken of above). In other words, the once-returner completely terminates all the three rounds connected with good birth in the sensual realm in two more lives.[49]

The non-returner's Eightfold Path completely terminates the rounds connected with fortunate birth in the sensual realm and goes beyond the two existences of a once-returner, leaving only the rounds for existence in the form realm and the formless realm.

The path, as it is experienced by a person who attains arahantship, completely terminates the three rounds connected with wandering-on in the form and formless realms. All defilements are forever extinguished.

This concludes the explanation of the interrelation between path-factors and rounds.

The First, Second, and Third Levels of Views

The three rounds connected with the states of deprivation, among all the four kinds of wandering-on each with its three rounds, are of great urgency for Buddhists today. As Lord Buddha has said, it is a matter of the greatest urgency when one's head is on fire to extinguish it immediately. No delay is possible even for a minute. Well, it is *more* urgent for followers of Buddhism to terminate completely the three rounds connected with the deprived states than for that man to put out the fire on his head. For this reason I have dealt with the Noble Eightfold Path as it is able to terminate those three rounds.[50] How does it do so?

---

49. The once-returner will be reborn once again as a human being or a *deva* and in that life attain Nibbāna.
50. Venerable Nyanaponika Mahāthera writes: "The Noble Eightfold Path intended here seems to be noble (*ariya*) in the strict sense of the noble path of stream-winner, etc. And when on the latter, *apāya-saṃsāra* is actually cut off because *sīla* (moral conduct) is unbroken and unbreakable. I feel that it is just the absence of *personality view* and *uncertainty* (*sakkāya-diṭṭhi, vicikicchā*) that makes *sīla* finally unbreakable, not just normal restraint. The unwholesome kamma-paths are extreme forms of unwholesomeness,

Of these two defilements (cut off by the stream-winner)—personality view and uncertainty—personality view is the most important. When this view is no more, naturally there is no more uncertainty and the ten unwholesome paths of kamma can no longer be created so that the wandering-on in deprived states is extinguished.

Personality view is just another name for self view (*atta-diṭṭhi*) in which the eye, ear, nose, tongue, body, and mind are regarded as "I" and "mine." This view is held tenaciously by all ordinary people (*puthujjana*). When we say that the sense organs are tenaciously viewed as "I" and "mine," this means that whenever a visible object is seen, people firmly and tenaciously believe "I see it, I see it." The same is true of the other senses and their objects (with mind as the sixth). This is how personality view is established on the foundation of the six internal bases.

Let us take the example of a being who in past lives has made many stupid mistakes so that in his successive lives all these old evil kammas born of personality view are attached to and always accompany his life continuity. Proceeding in such a way, this being will in future existences also make foolish mistakes, thus making new evil kamma arising from personality view. So when personality view is extinguished, the results of past evil kamma leading to subhuman birth cannot arise, nor can more evil kamma be made. For this reason there is no longer any possibility of wandering-on in the deprived states; for such a person there are no more rebirths in the hells, the animal world, the ghost realm,

---

covetousness (*abhijjhā*), which is the greedy thought leading to robbery, or ill will (*byāpāda*), the hateful thought of killing or harming—which are absent in the stream-winner, though he has still the milder forms called sensual desire (*kāmacchanda*) and aversion (*paṭigha*) among the ten fetters. As he still has the fetters of sensual desire, attachment to subtle form and formlessness (*rūparāga, arūparāga*), rebirth in the good bourns (*sugati*) has not ceased for him. He, being on the path of seeing (*dassana-magga*), has abolished only the *view-root* of self-view (= personality view); its other two roots, craving and conceit, are abolished only on the three noble paths called the path of development (*bhāvanā-magga*). The complete cutting off of personality view is not however a purely intellectual process; it must be based on perfect *sīla* and the *vipassanā* experience."

or the demons—these are all extinguished. A person like this attains to his first experience of Nibbāna, called Nibbāna-with-the-grasped-at-groups-remaining (*sa-upādisesa nibbāna*), meaning that for him the three rounds connected with the wandering-on in the states of deprivation are utterly extinct. He then becomes a noble one (*ariya*) in the noble supermundane plane, one to be reborn in successively higher planes of existence.[51]

Now we come to consider the three levels of views whereby personality view is established.

The first is called the *latency level* (*anusaya-bhūmi*), that is, the view of personality which always accompanies the life-continuity of a being in the beginningless round of rebirths and resides in the whole person[52] as the seed or potential for the three kinds of kamma, i.e. of body, speech, and mind, before they are made. When objects which can cause the doing of evil deeds come into contact with any of the six doors, such as the eye-door, unwholesome kamma stimulated by that latent view is made in the mind. This is the second level called *obsessive level* (*pariyuṭṭhāna-bhūmi*), represented among the ten unwholesome paths of kamma by the threefold mental kamma (covetousness, ill-will, and wrong view). Thus the stage of mental kamma has been reached. If no steps are taken for the control of the mind, then unwholesomeness spreads from the obsessive level to the third level called the *transgressive level* (*vītikkama-bhūmi*), the stage where unwholesome verbal or bodily kamma is made. These are, respectively, the fourfold verbal action (false speech, tale-bearing, harsh talk, and useless chatter), and the threefold bodily action (killing living creatures, taking what is not given, wrong conduct in sexual pleasures).

Suppose we take the example of a match. When the matchbox with its nitrous surface is available then the potential for fire lying

---

51. See the extensive notes on this subject in *The Requisites of Enlightenment*, Wheel No. 171/174, pp. 47–48.

52. Myanaung U Tin writes: "Actually *anusaya* (potentiality) does not reside in any part of the person. It arises only with the necessary conditions. For want of a better word 'reside' has been used. Potentiality is there in the whole personality, that is all." The seven latent tendencies or proclivities (*anusaya*) are: sensual desire, aversion, views, uncertainty, conceit, desire for existence, and ignorance.

in the match head can be activated. Flames result and with such a lighted match a heap of rubbish can be set alight. The matchbox's striking surface represents the six sense objects—sights, sounds, smells, tastes, touches, and thoughts—and the potential for fire in the match head may be compared to the latency level. When these objects present themselves to the mind, like the striking of the match, then heat and fire result—the obsessive level. From that small fire a great one can be lighted, burning and scorching other beings with the bodily and verbal kamma of the transgressive level.

This concludes the explanation of the first, second, and third levels of views.

Forming the Path into Three Groups

The Noble Eightfold Path falls naturally into the following groups:

(1) Morality group: right speech, right action, and right livelihood.
(2) Concentration group: right effort, right mindfulness, and right concentration.
(3) Wisdom group: right view and right thought.

If the three constituents of the morality group are considered in detail then they become the set of precepts with livelihood as the eighth, in this way:

I shall refrain from killing living creatures.
I shall refrain from taking what is not given.
I shall refrain from wrong conduct in sexual pleasures and from intoxicants—these three comprise *right action*.
I shall refrain from false speech.
I shall refrain from tale-bearing.
I shall refrain from harsh talk.
I shall refrain from useless chatter—these four comprise *right speech*.
I undertake *right livelihood*, refraining from dishonesty, violence, and killing.

Permanent precepts, that is, those which are taken to be kept all the time, such as the lay person's Five Precepts, the Ten Precepts observed by hermits and wanderers (perhaps non-Buddhist), and the Ten Precepts practised by Buddhist novices (*sāmaṇeras*), together with the bhikkhu's 227 precepts contained in the Pātimokkha, are generally contained within the group of precepts with livelihood as the eighth. In the same way, the Eight Precepts are improvements on the Five Precepts and the above group of precepts with livelihood as the eighth.

Right speech, action, and livelihood, which are the constituents of the morality group, are the factors to use for the destruction of the third level of personality view, the transgressive level, when evil unwholesome kamma, fourfold of speech and threefold of bodily action, is committed.

Right effort, mindfulness, and concentration, the factors of the concentration group, are the factors to use for the destruction of the second level of personality view, the obsessive level, when the threefold evil unwholesome kamma of the mind is made.

Right view and right intention, comprising the wisdom group, are the factors to use for the destruction of the first level of personality view, the latency level, which has always existed in the life-continuities of beings in the beginningless round of rebirths.

Here ends the formation of the Eightfold Path into three groups.

How to Establish the Morality Group

To rid oneself of the three unwholesome verbal deeds born of personality view, the three constituents of the morality group must be established in oneself, which is another way of saying that the set of precepts with livelihood as eighth should be accepted and practised.

One cannot guard against the three unwholesome mental deeds born of personality view in this way, so when one no longer wishes to make them, the three factors of the concentration group in the Noble Eightfold Path should be practised and established. Such firmness of mind only results when exercises such as mindfulness of in-and-out breathing, or the meditation on the unattractiveness of such things as bones, or the meditations on colours, elements, etc., called *kasiṇas*, are practised *for at least one hour a day*.

The method whereby one may rid oneself of the transgressive level of personality view is by establishing oneself in purification of virtue as represented by the set of precepts with livelihood as the eighth, as mentioned above. One may either first recite the precepts, as given below, and then practise them, or just decide to observe them so that from this day forth, throughout one's life, one does not kill living creatures, etc. It is not necessary to request these precepts from a bhikkhu; one has only to practise them accordingly. One may then either recite or determine, as follows:

(1) From today throughout my life, I shall refrain from killing any living creatures.
(2) From today throughout my life, I shall refrain from taking what is not given.
(3) From today throughout my life, I shall refrain from wrong conduct in sexual pleasures and from intoxicants.
(4) From today throughout my life, I shall refrain from false speech.
(5) From today throughout my life, I shall refrain from setting one person against another.
(6) From today throughout my life, I shall refrain from harsh and abusive words regarding any person's status in society and beliefs.
(7) From today throughout my life, I shall refrain from speaking in ways not conducive to the welfare of beings in this present life, or of those in the wandering-on, or of those in the supermundane plane.[53]
(8) From today throughout my life, I shall refrain from wrong livelihood.

When this set of precepts has been taken, it remains in force until it is broken. Then only the precept which has been broken should be undertaken once again, though of course there is no harm in taking again those precepts which have not been broken. This is really unnecessary, but if an unbroken precept is taken again it will be strengthened in this way.

It is better, therefore, to undertake these precepts everyday. But these precepts are permanent, that is, they apply every day, like the Five Precepts. They are not like the Eight Precepts observed only on the Uposatha days. Bhikkhus who have 227 precepts and sāmaṇeras who observe ten precepts, as well as hermits and wanderers, need not take these precepts.

---

53. Such as *arahants* living now.

Now the constituent factors which are required for the breaking of the first seven of these precepts should be examined.

The five conditions for killing living creatures

(1) The being must be alive.
(2) There must be the knowledge that it is a living being.
(3) There must be an intention to cause its death.
(4) Action must be taken to cause its death.
(5) Death must result from such action.

If all these five conditions are fulfilled then the first precept has been broken and should be taken again.

The five conditions for taking what is not given

(1) The property must be the possession of another person.
(2) It must be known to oneself that it is the possession of another person.
(3) There must be an intention to steal.
(4) Action must be taken to steal.
(5) By that action the property must be taken.

If all these five conditions are fulfilled then the second precept has been broken and should be taken again.

The four conditions for wrong conduct in sexual pleasures

(1) There must be a man or a woman with whom it is improper to have sexual intercourse.[54]
(2) There must be intention to have sexual intercourse with such a person.
(3) Action must be taken to have such intercourse.
(4) There must be enjoyment from the contact of the sexual organs.

If all these four conditions are fulfilled then the third precept has been broken and should be taken again.

---

54. Bhikkhus, bhikkhunīs, and other religious observing the holy life, or persons protected by marriage or by parents.

The four conditions for false speech

(1) The statement must be untrue.
(2) There must be an intention to deceive.
(3) There must be an effort made as a result of this intention.
(4) The other person must know the meaning of what has been said.

If all these four conditions are fulfilled then the fourth precept has been broken and should be taken again.

The four conditions for tale-bearing

(1) There must be persons to be disunited.
(2) There must be the intention to disunite these persons.
(3) There must be an effort made as a result of this intention.
(4) The other person(s) must know the meaning of what has been said.

If all these four conditions are fulfilled then the fifth precept has been broken and should be taken again.

The three conditions for harsh talk

(1) There must be a person to be abused.
(2) There must be anger.
(3) Harsh language must be directed towards that person.

If all these three conditions are fulfilled then the sixth precept has been broken and should be taken again.

The two conditions for useless chatter

(1) There must be intention to say things which bring forth no wholesome benefits.
(2) Such things must be said.

If these conditions are fulfilled then the seventh precept has been broken and should be taken again.

As regards "things which bring forth no wholesome benefits," this means plays and novels which do not lead to the growth of good qualities. Nowadays we have numerous plays and novels which satisfy all the conditions of useless chatter.

Fulfilment of the conditions given above for the first three precepts and for harsh speech, the sixth one, are sufficient not only to break these but also to make kamma which will be a "path of kamma" leading to rebirth in the states of deprivation. But in the case of the precepts dealing with false speech, tale-bearing, and useless chatter, the following have to be added if these actions are to be paths of kamma:

(1) In the case of false speech, another person suffers loss or damage.
(2) In the case of tale-bearing, disunion must be brought about.
(3) And in the case of useless chatter, others must think that the plays and novels are true accounts.

These are the conditions relating to the seven kinds of wrongdoing which should be known by those who daily keep the precepts with livelihood as the eighth.

And this concludes the brief explanation of the way to establish in oneself the three constituents of the path's morality group.

How to Establish the Concentration Group

As we have explained already, the good practice of the three constituents of the morality group leads to the establishment in the purity of moral conduct, while wrong livelihood and the seven kinds of bad conduct, three with the body and four with speech—which are all born of personality view—are completely cut off.

Then, in order destroy the second level of wrong view supported by the three mental evil kammas, the factors of the concentration group in the Eightfold Path—right effort, right mindfulness, and right concentration—must be established in oneself.

By this is meant practice of one of the forty subjects of meditation. Here the way of practice for "mindfulness of breathing in and out" will be described briefly. If Buddhist householders have no time during the day to do this practice, they should do it everyday without fail in the early morning after rising, say for an hour, and in the evening too, for one or two hours before going to bed.

The method to follow in this practice is as follows. According to the Buddha-word: *"Mindfully he breathes in, mindfully he breathes out."* So during the whole period during which one has determined to sit, the mind is concentrated just on the breathing and is not allowed to stray here and there. To accomplish this one needs bodily effort and mental effort. Here, bodily effort means the effort made to practise for a fixed period each day, never letting a day go by without practice. Mental effort is the extreme care that one takes when breathing in and out that the mind may not stray elsewhere, as well as the intense application of the mind to the meditation subject so that sleepiness and sloth do not creep in.

As the breath touches the nostrils during exhalation one should be mindful just of the breathing out. Similarly, when inhaling be mindful just of the touch of air passing in. The mind should be fixed continuously upon the region of the nostrils. So right effort here means these two kinds of effort, bodily and mental, as mentioned above.

When one applies the mind in this way for a fortnight, a month, or even two months, one's mindfulness becomes fixed upon breathing in and out. Such mindfulness is indeed called right mindfulness.

And once the three factors of the morality group in this path have been established, mental restlessness decreases day by day.

It is apparent to everyone who begins meditation practice that they have no control over the mind as far as meditation subjects are concerned. Now in this world madmen who have no control over their minds are useless in worldly affairs. In like manner it can be said of people thought sane by this world that, as regards the practice of meditation, they are really mad, for they have no control over the meditation subject. Such people are useless when judged by the standard needed for successful meditation practice. When viewed in this way, we can see the necessity for the establishment of the three factors of the concentration group so that restlessness of mind is cured.[55]

Even though the two aspects of concentration called access concentration and attainment concentration (*upacāra-* and *appanā-*

---

55. For more detailed information about right concentration see *The Requisites of Enlightenment* (Wheel No. 171/174) and *Ānāpānadīpanī*.

samādhi) have not yet been attained, if the mind can be fixed on the meditation subject for a period of an hour or two every day then it will become easy to concentrate the mind whenever one wishes and on whatever meditation subject one takes up.

For a person who has attained purity of mind after being successful in establishing the three factors of the concentration group in the Noble Eightfold Path, the three unwholesome mental kammas of covetousness, ill-will, and wrong view born of personality view become extinct. And the second level (obsessive) of views represented by the above three mental kammas is also extinguished. Again, the mental restlessness caused by the five hindrances also disappears.

This concludes the explanation of how to establish the three factors of the concentration group of the Eightfold Path.

From the time when the factors of the morality group become established in a person, so long as he does not violate them he is said to be complete in the purity of moral conduct. On the very day when the precepts are perfectly established, the concentration group—right effort, right mindfulness, and right concentration—should be practised. Now people who are reasonably diligent should not take more than five or ten days to rid themselves of mental restlessness. Having done so and attained a steadfast concentration of mind on breathing in and out, the three factors of the concentration group are established. From that day one is said to have established oneself in purity of mind. One should then go on to establish the wisdom group of the Eightfold Path in oneself.

How to Establish the Wisdom Group

Right View

Whoever has been successful in establishing purity of moral conduct and purity of mind should then try to establish the wisdom group of right view and right intention so as to destroy the latency level of personality view. To have established these two path factors means the establishment in due order of the five purities of wisdom, which are: purity of view, purity of overcoming doubt, purity by knowledge and vision of what is and what is not the path, purity by knowledge and vision of the practice-path, purity by supermundane knowledge and vision.

To bring this about, we should consider the four great primaries which are, literally, earth, water, fire, and air. Let us look at them in relation to the body. Hardness and softness make up the earth (extension) element; cohesion and liquidity comprise the water element; heat and cold compose the fire (kinetic energy) element; while support and motion are the characteristics of the air element. In the case of the head there are only these four elements present and the same applies to the rest of the body—legs, arms, head-hair, body-hair, nails, teeth, skin, flesh, sinews, bones, marrow, kidneys, heart, lymph, fat, lungs, intestines, stomach, excrement, and brains. All are just collections of the four elements.

If we look at them we can see:

(1) hardness is the strong form of *earth*, softness the weak;
(2) cohesion is the weak form of *water*, liquidity the strong;
(3) heat is the strong form of *fire*, cold the weak;
(4) stillness is the weak form of *air*, motion the strong.

Now to consider these in pairs.

Let us take the example of sealing wax, in which the various changes can be observed. In its usual state, hardness, the strong form of earth, is conspicuous. But when it comes into contact with fire, the hard earth element disappears and soft earth is manifest. But when the fire is removed then the softness naturally disappears and hardness reappears.

In the case of cohesion or liquidity, in its usual state sealing wax shows a weak form of water so that cohesion is present. But with contact of fire the cohesive water element disappears and liquid water is manifest. Again, if the fire is taken away then liquidity disappears while cohesiveness becomes manifest again.

As regards heat and cold, in its usual state sealing wax has weak fire element while coldness is conspicuous. When there is contact with fire the cold fire element vanishes and is replaced by hot fire, but by its removal the process is naturally reversed.

Lastly, considering stillness and motion, sealing wax in its usual state shows a weak form of air, that is, stillness. But when it is heated a strong form of the air element is manifest: motion. With the removal of the fire, however, the strong form naturally disappears and the weak form returns.

This example has been given so that people are able to understand the meaning of arising and passing away (*udayabbaya*) in insight or *vipassanā*. The word '*udaya*' means arising, increase, or appearance, while '*vaya*' has the meaning of passing away, decrease, or disappearance. '*Udayabbaya*' is the compound of the two words. These elements are evident in the sealing wax. Now we shall turn to their practical application.

Head, body, legs, and hands can all be analysed in the same way as the sealing wax so that the elements become clear. For instance, heat and cold, the two aspects of the fire element, arise and pass away alternately. Heat increases little by little in the body from sunrise until two in the afternoon, after which the body begins to cool, meaning that heat decreases and cold increases. This is everyone's experience. We easily understand that the same is true of other bodily processes as well.

The increase in the body heat in the head and so forth is like the sealing wax coming into contact with the fire, while as coolness increases in the body it resembles the sealing wax from which the fire has been removed. This increase and decrease of the fire element in the body is the arising and passing away spoken of above.

So too with the other three elements; their pairs of modes also arise and pass away like the fire element. Earth element with its modes of softness and hardness, water element seen as liquidity and cohesion, and air element in its forms of motion and stillness—they increase or decrease in the same way.

These four elements in the body resemble the innumerable tiny bubbles quickly appearing and disappearing on the surface of a big pot of boiling water. The whole body, in fact, resembles a lump of foam. Vapour appears in each small bubble and it bursts to disappear as all the rest disappear.

It is the same with seeing, hearing, smell, taste, touch, and knowing. All these mental phenomena depend on the four elements and vanish when the elements vanish. So the six consciousnesses—of eye, ear, nose, tongue, body, and mind—together with the four elements are impermanent, transitory, and unstable. They are all *anicca* (impermanent) and therefore *dukkha* (unsatisfactory), too, since they are associated with unceasing arising and passing away; and such transient and unsatisfactory phenomena are therefore also *anattā* (not self or not soul) because they are without essence or substance.

Taking the head as an example, let us see how personality view arises on the basis of the four elements and how it should really be seen with right view. People who cannot discriminate the four elements in the head do not understand that the head's solidity is only the earth element. They understand that it is head, and so on; they perceive a "head," they conceive "my head," they view it as "my permanent head," taking it as an unchanging entity.

Understanding that it is head is a delusion of mind (*citta*).
Perceiving "a head" is delusion of perception (*saññā*).
Conceiving "my head" is delusion of conceit (*māna*).
Holding a view of it as "my permanent head" is a delusion of view (*diṭṭhi*).[56]

Understanding, perceiving, conceiving, and holding a view of the head, instead of directly seeing it as four elements, is viewing it as permanent and as *attā* or self. Thus to consider the four elements as the head is a fallacy based on taking what is impermanent as permanent, and what is not self as self.

These four elements, which naturally arise and pass away extremely rapidly, are truly impermanent and not self, thus illustrating the Buddha's words: "*Khayaṭṭhena aniccaṃ asārakaṭṭhena anattā*," meaning, "Because it is destroyed it is impermanent, because it is essenceless it is not self." The head of a man does not normally break up during his life, nor does it disintegrate when he dies; it remains looking much the same until the body reaches the burning ground. For these reasons it is regarded as permanent and taken to be self. When the four elements are not penetrated with insight, then the misconception "head" arises, taking what is changing as unchanging and what is not self as self.

Understanding, perceiving, conceiving, and viewing hair, teeth, skin, flesh, muscles, bones, brain, as the composite parts of the head, rather than penetrating them with insight as the four elements alone, is taking what is impermanent as permanent, not self as self. It is just personality view to see the elements,

---

56. The first, second, and third items are the three perversions or distortions (*vipallāsa*), on which see *The Manual of Insight* (BPS Wheel No. 31/32, 2nd ed. 1975), p. 5.

such as hardness, as head, hair, and so on. Such a view displays ignorance (*avijjā*).

Right view (acquired by insight) sees that hardness is the earth element, not a part of "my body" such as bones. In the same way cohesion is the water element, heat and cold the fire element, and stillness and motion the air element. They are not to be seen as my hair, my teeth, my flesh, my brain. In the ultimate analysis (made in deep meditation, not by intellectual effort), there is no such thing as the head or its parts. Such penetration is called right view. It is not necessary to emphasize that what has been said here about the head—the personality view which depends on wrong view, and the right view which arises when the view of a "person" is abandoned—applies to all the other parts of the body, too.

Right Thought

To consider ways and means for understanding these four elements is right thought. While right view may be compared to an arrow, right thought is the strength in the hand that aims the arrow at the target. In brief this is how right view and right thought, the two factors of the wisdom group in the Noble Eightfold Path, should be established in oneself. For detailed explanations, see the *Vijjāmagga-dīpanī* and the *Bhāvanā-dīpanī* written by me.

The Need for Effort

These two factors of the wisdom group are established by continual contemplation and deep meditation upon arising and passing away (*udayabbaya*). This means the incessant arisings and passings of the four elements in their combinations throughout the body in all its parts, beginning with head hair, and so forth. It applies also to the six kinds of sense consciousness—of the eye, ear, nose, tongue, body, and mind—where arising and passing away continue without any break. All this can be compared to the small bubbles in a pot of boiling water. Now when this insight has been established in oneself and when some insight has thereby been gained into the characteristics of impermanence and not self, one must make an effort to continue in the direction of complete penetration throughout one's life, so that stage by stage the paths and fruits are won.

To take an example of how this may be done: farmers in the course of their cultivation should practise contemplation on the arising and the passing of the psychophysical elements in all parts of the body.

So by repeated and persistent practice of this meditation, there is born the (insight) knowledge of right view regarding the arising and passing of all physical and psychological phenomena. Such knowledge permeates the whole body, and at this time the first level of personality view regarding the body as "mine" disappears. In this way the latency level view of the body as a person, which has accompanied one's life-continuity throughout the beginningless round of rebirths, is extinguished without remainder. The whole body is then transformed into the sphere of right view. The potential for making the ten unwholesome kammas is totally destroyed while the ten wholesome ways of making kamma are firmly established. The round of rebirth in the states of deprivation is destroyed for such a person and there remain for him only rebirths in the good bourns, such as among human beings, devas and Brahmās. The person has attained the level of a noble one, a stream-winner.[57]

So this brings to a close the exposition of personality view as illustrated by the head and concludes as well the full explanation of the practice of the Noble Eightfold Path with its three factors of the morality group, three in the concentration group, and two in the wisdom group.

How to Establish the Noble Eightfold Path

Complete and careful observance of the set of precepts with livelihood as the eighth is the practice of the morality group comprising right speech, right action, and right livelihood. The practice of the mindful breathing in and out is the concentration group of right effort, right, mindfulness, and right concentration put into action. Contemplation of arising and passing of the four elements as illustrated by the head, and of the six sense consciousnesses, makes up the wisdom group comprising right view and right thought.

---

57. The original has a "*bon-sin-san* noble one." See *The Requisites of Enlightenment*, p. 47.

According to the method followed by the dry-visioned person (*sukkha-vipassaka puggala*), the way of calm (*samatha*) through such exercises as mindfully breathing in and out is not practised separately. Such a person, having established in himself the three factors of the morality group in the Eightfold Path, then undertakes the practice of the wisdom group. In this practice the three constituents of the concentration group accompany the two wisdom factors and are together known as the path with five factors (*pañcaṅgika-magga*). These five, in such practice, form one group and with the three remaining factors, the morality group, make up the Noble Eightfold Path. But insight-only as practiced by these dry-visioned people can succeed only if one has great penetrative wisdom and makes strenuous effort.[58] Mental restlessness will then disappear as it does with the practice of calm.

After the knowledge of right view has become clear (through meditation) in respect of the whole body, whether such direct knowledge is attained in this life or the next, then whenever one contemplates within, there are no such entities as a person, individual, woman, man, oneself, another person, head, leg, or hair. When such knowledge arises, the personality view which takes hardness and so on to be the head (etc.) disappears forever. Whenever this contemplation is done, there arises the right view of the truth that "head" does not exist apart from a collection of elements. This principle applies to the other parts of the body.

When right view and right thought, the wisdom factors of the path, have been established in one's personality, then the three rounds connected with wandering-on in the states of deprivation disappear forever. Whoever experiences this is from that moment on completely freed for all time from the suffering arising from these rounds, that is, from the pain and misery of being born in the four lower worlds. He or she has reached and is established in the first experience of Nibbāna with the grasped-at groups remaining and is a stream-winner.[59]

---

58. This warning is needed! It is possible to find teachers who stress that *vipassanā* (insight) only is required and that calm is not necessary. Their pupils, not possessing either great wisdom or strenuous effort, arrive only at weak and easily lost "insight," if they attain anything at all. Such one-sided views produce no good results.

59. See the extensive note in *The Requisites of Enlightenment*, pp. 47–48.

However, as such a person has yet to acquire the knowledge associated with the mark of unsatisfactoriness (*dukkha-lakkhaṇa*)[60] there still remain in him craving (*taṇhā*) and conceit (*māna*) which cause him to delight in the pleasures of men, devas, and Brahmās. So he continues to enjoy these three kinds of pleasures while being reborn in successively higher planes.[61]

Here ends the brief explanation of the way to establish the Eightfold Path in oneself. It is also the conclusion of *The Manual of the Path-Factors* (*Maggaṅga-dīpanī*).

---

60. See note 49.
61. See *The Requisites of Enlightenment*, pp. 47–48 note.

ABOUT PARIYATTI

Pariyatti is dedicated to providing affordable access to authentic teachings of the Buddha about the Dhamma theory (*pariyatti*) and practice (*paṭipatti*) of Vipassana meditation. A 501(c)(3) nonprofit charitable organization since 2002, Pariyatti is sustained by contributions from individuals who appreciate and want to share the incalculable value of the Dhamma teachings. We invite you to visit www.pariyatti.org to learn about our programs, services, and ways to support publishing and other undertakings.

Pariyatti Publishing Imprints

Vipassana Research Publications (focus on Vipassana as taught by S.N. Goenka in the tradition of Sayagyi U Ba Khin)
BPS Pariyatti Editions (selected titles from the Buddhist Publication Society, copublished by Pariyatti)
MPA Pariyatti Editions (selected titles from the Myanmar Pitaka Association, copublished by Pariyatti)
Pariyatti Digital Editions (audio and video titles, including discourses)
Pariyatti Press (classic titles returned to print and inspirational writing by contemporary authors)

Pariyatti enriches the world by
- disseminating the words of the Buddha,
- providing sustenance for the seeker's journey,
- illuminating the meditator's path.

www.ingramcontent.com/pod-product-compliance
Lightning Source LLC
Chambersburg PA
CBHW020348170426
43200CB00005B/96